International Competitiveness
and the Balance of Payments

International Competitiveness and the Balance of Payments

Do Current Account Deficits
and Surpluses Matter?

Barbara Dluhosch, Andreas Freytag and Malte Krüger
Institute for Economic Policy, University of Köln, Germany

Edward Elgar
Cheltenham, UK • Brookfield, US

Published by
Edward Elgar Publishing Limited
8 Lansdown Place
Cheltenham
Glos GL50 2HU
UK

Edward Elgar Publishing Company
Old Post Road
Brookfield
Vermont 05036
US

British Library Cataloguing in Publication Data
Dluhosch, Barbara
    International competitiveness and the balance of payments:
    do current account deficits and surpluses matter?
    1. Competitiveness, International 2. Balance of payments
    3. Balance of trade
    I. Title II. Freytag, Andreas III. Kruger, Malte
    337

Library of Congress Cataloguing in Publication Data
Dluhosch, Barbara.
    International competitiveness and the balance of payments : do
    current account deficits and surpluses matter? / Barbara Dluhosch,
    Andreas Freytag, and Malte Krüger.
    Includes bibliographical references and index.
    1. Balance of payments. 2. Competition, International.
    3. Balance of payments—Case studies. I. Freytag, Andreas.
    II. Krüger, Malte. III. Title.
    HG3882.D58   1996
    382'.17—dc20   95–40197
                                                                   CIP

ISBN 1 85898 210 3
Printed and bound in Great Britain by
Hartnolls Limited, Bodmin, Cornwall

Contents

Figures

vi

Tables

Preface

In 1991, the German Ministry of Economic Affairs asked the Institute for Economic Policy at Cologne University to prepare a report on international competitiveness and trade flows. The problem that triggered the report was the German balance on current account which took a rather sharp swing after having shown huge surpluses over many years. Four years later, the discussion about international competitiveness and the balance of payments is more intense than ever thanks to the trade conflict between the United States and Japan. Therefore, the subject is still on the agenda.

Although the contributions to the subject of international competitiveness have mushroomed in the last years, our impression is very much that a unified analysis of trade and capital balances is still lacking. Therefore, we decided to present a translated and revised version of our 1991 report. What emerged in the course of our working on the most recent discussion became a whole new book which we hope sheds more light into the debate.

We are grateful to the German Ministry of Economic Affairs for giving its consent to make the main results of our work now accessible to an even wider audience than the original German report. In working on the issue, we are heavily indebted to Juergen B. Donges, Christian Watrin, Hans Willgerodt and Jürgen Wieners with whom we had numerous lively discussions on the subject. Their careful reading of the original report supplied us with many helpful comments and improved both our understanding of the matter and the presentation of our ideas. For us, it was always a pleasure to work with them. While preparing the new book we benefited from suggestions by Carl Christian von Weizsäcker, valuable comments by José Viñals, Renate Ohr, Peter Blies and Stephan Boll and remarks of an anonymous referee which we very much appreciated. We would also like to express our gratitude to Herbert Giersch for the encouragement in the production of the book. Thanks are due to Christian Pietsch for providing us with technical assistance. All of them contributed significantly to the efficiency and pleasantness of the work. And last but not least, we would like to acknowledge the help of the friendly staff of Edward Elgar which lent us support in all questions concerning publishing and which made everything so smoothly running through the different stages of production. However, all errors in or shortcomings of this book remain solely ours. The opinions expressed are our own and do not relate to any of the institutions mentioned.

Cologne
Barbara Dluhosch
Andreas Freytag
Malte Krüger

1. The Problem

International trade and capital flows have increased since world war two at a rate much higher than the average rate of world output. This development was fostered by trade liberalization which began with the first GATT round in 1949. However, until 1973, imbalances, if recorded at all, were relatively small. This changed decisively during the 1970s and 1980s when capital movements were liberalized. Both of gross and net flows increased and current account deficits and surpluses widened. At the same time, large swings in nominal and real exchange rates took place.

Often, these large capital flows have been interpreted as a reflection of an improved international allocation of capital. If there are no restrictions, capital can look for the highest return on investment under a given risk or for the lowest risk under a given return. It does not have to be invested in the very country where the savings take place. Consequently, countries which simply turned out to be more attractive for either foreign direct investments or portfolio investment experienced net capital imports. Other countries have taken over the position of an international supplier of capital, exhibiting a deficit on capital account.

Although the proposition that the liberalization of capital flows improves the international allocation of capital is usually accepted in principle, one of its implications – larger balances on current account – is more controversial. First, these imbalances are often interpreted as a sign of international disequilibria which call for action. Second, especially trade deficits have received additional attention because they are interpreted as an indicator of low competitiveness or as a proof that the trading partners use 'unfair' protective measures. This interpretation is not only applied to overall balances on current account, but also to bilateral or sectoral imbalances in trade flows. The trade conflict between the United States and Japan provides a case in point. The high American trade deficit in bilateral trade with Japan has motivated the US administration to use trade barriers against Japanese products, in particular high-tech products.

Hence, either implicitly or explicitly, imbalances are interpreted as a sign of a disequilibrium in international relations. The world-wide allocation on markets for commodities and capital is said to be distorted. Are imbalances on current account and capital account on that high a scale really an indicator for the existence of international disequilibria? In an accounting sense, the balance of payments as a whole never is in a disequilibrium. As the current account is only part of the balance of payment it has to be argued very carefully why the term disequilibrium is applied on an imbalanced current account. Just to argue, as many do, that large imbalances indicate a disequilibrium in international relations and are therefore 'bad' is not convincing (Machlup 1964). It may well be argued

1

that the opposite is true. Feldstein and Horioka (1980) and Feldstein (1994) have argued that balances on capital account (and hence on current account) should be even higher if capital was truly mobile.

A proper evaluation of current account balances has to be based on a theoretical analysis of its determinants. From a theoretical point of view, two competing approaches concerning the determinants and interpretation of current account balances can be distinguished, the competitiveness approach and the intertemporal approach. According to the former, trade surpluses indicate a relatively high competitiveness of a country as a whole. Deficits on current account are interpreted as a sign of low competitiveness. Competitiveness in this sense is defined as ability to sell. Following the intertemporal approach, the current account is determined by capital flows. Thus, the interpretation of balances is not that easy and unambiguous as the competitiveness approach suggests although, under certain conditions, net capital inflows (and therefore current account deficits) can be regarded as a sign for high competitiveness in the sense of 'locational quality'.

In order to answer the question to what extent surpluses and deficits on current account signal high and low competitiveness, we discuss the theoretical merits and weaknesses of both the competitiveness and the intertemporal approach. In the following chapter the theoretical foundations of both approaches are analysed. As competitiveness is somewhat of a 'weaselword', the chapters three and four are dedicated to a variety of indicators of competitiveness in both theoretical systems. The practical value of commonly used indicators is examined. The fifth chapter shows the relevance of the theoretical reasoning in four case studies, namely the United States, Japan, Germany and Spain. Although embedded in different regimes (trade policy regime, currency regime etc.) and exposed to different situations, all of these countries showed huge and persistent balances in their current accounts in the near past. In the last chapter, we summarize the results of our analysis and discuss some lessons for economic policy.

2. Determinants of the Current Account

I. The competitiveness approach: emphasizing 'ability to sell'

A. Competitiveness as Ability to Sell

The general discussion about competitiveness focuses mainly on the balance on current account (or the trade balance). Large surpluses are interpreted as an indicator of high competitiveness and deficits as an indicator for economic weakness. If local goods are cheaper and/or better than foreign goods, foreigners will be – so the argument goes – importing more goods than they are exporting. Consequently, the high competitiveness of local goods will show up in a current account surplus. This argument is also applied to sub-balances of the current account. Germany's bilateral surpluses in trade with the US have been interpreted as an indicator of superior competitiveness, and the deficits in bilateral trade with Japan as inferior competitiveness. The diagnosis of 'high' or 'low' competitiveness is frequently combined with the call for economic policy measures. This approach which can be labelled the 'competitiveness approach' focuses only on trade transactions as registered in the balance of payments.

Although often rather vague, the interpretation of the current account as an indicator of competitiveness seems to be frequently based on the following notions:

– The competitiveness of a whole economy (or nation) can be interpreted as the ability of local enterprises to sell their goods in world markets. Therefore, competitiveness is interpreted as 'ability to sell' (Balassa 1964, p. 26).

– A rise in the overall competitiveness leads *ceteris paribus* directly to a surplus on current account because of local goods attracting a larger share of world demand. This suggests a quite robust relationship between competitiveness and the current account.

In addition, two different types of competitiveness are distinguished: price and non-price competitiveness (Orlowski 1982, van Suntum 1986). Price competitiveness is determined by the prices of local and foreign goods and by the exchange rate. Thus, for a given exchange rate price competitiveness increases when the local inflation rate for tradeable goods is lower than the corresponding inflation rate in foreign countries, and for given prices competitiveness increases when the local currency depreciates. Non-price competitiveness consists of the quality of products, service, timely delivery, etc. If local firms adapt faster to changing consumer

3

wishes, if they are more reliable and offer better service, then they are said to gain in non-price competitiveness. However, both concepts are not independent of each other. Since it is difficult to measure changes in non-price competitiveness, measures for price competitiveness are difficult to interpret. For example, a rise in prices of local goods or an appreciating exchange rate can also be due to an increase in non-price competitiveness. Therefore, instead of trying to measure price and non-price competitiveness directly, the balance on current account is often used as an indicator of the overall competitiveness of local firms.

However, both this definition of competitiveness and the postulated relationship between competitiveness and the balance on current account are open to criticism. First, 'ability to sell' is not well suited as an indicator of competitiveness, even at the level of the firm. After all, a firm can always lower its prices in order to sell its products. What counts is 'ability to sell' at prices which make it at least possible for the enterprise to pay the factors used. If an enterprise is not able to pay the factor incomes demanded in the market, mobile factors will move to other enterprises. Therefore, simply to be able to sell products is not a sufficient condition for survival.

Second, the 'competitiveness approach' is based on an analogy between the competitiveness of an economy and the competitiveness of a single enterprise. But the usefulness of this analogy is doubtful. Competitiveness is a relatively unproblematic attribute when applied on a microeconomic scale. For a single enterprise is competing with other local and foreign firms. Its costs and prices, the variety of its products and their quality, its service, timely delivery, etc., determine its market share. However, the competitiveness approach goes one step further: it stipulates that the competitiveness of a nation can be derived by simply aggregating the 'ability to sell' of single firms and sectors. Consequently, the balance on current account is derived from bilateral or sectoral balances which are simply added up. For sure, in an accounting sense everthing has to add up. But it is not that simple. Just adding up everything would imply that the competitiveness of one sector or firm is independent of the competitiveness of other local sectors or firms. Yet, this is not true. The reason is that enterprises do not only compete in product markets, but also in factor markets. If one enterprise improves its competitiveness and therefore wants to expand its production, it will pay at least marginally higher factor prices in order to attract more factors. Other enterprises will either have to pay higher factor prices as well, or they will lose factors and will have to reduce production. In fact, there are two different layers of competition (see Figure 2.1), competition for customers (in goods markets) and competition for factors (mainly labour and capital). Hence, if factors are mobile between firms, the competitiveness of one firm or one sector does depend on the competitiveness of the other firms and factors.

Figure 2.1:   Different levels of competition

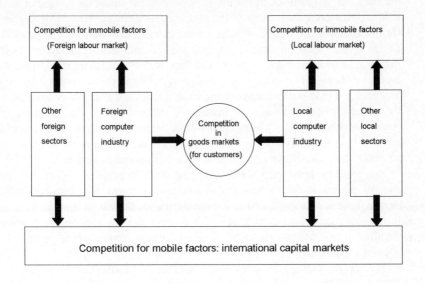

In international economics, it is commonly assumed that capital is internationally mobile, whereas labour is internationally immobile. In this case, international competition for factors is restricted to competition for capital. But on the national (or regional) level, firms compete for labour as well. This implies that the position of a local firm or sector is not only adversely affected when foreign firms offer better or cheaper products. The same is true when other local firms increase their competitiveness and offer higher wages. Since the wage increase is restricted to the home country, foreign competitors are not affected, so that indirectly their competitive position is improved. If, on the other hand, the capital demand of some local firms rises, then all other firms – local as well as foreign – are affected. They all have to pay (marginally) higher interest rates.

The matter becomes more complex, once traded and non-traded goods are introduced. In this case, an increase of capital demand by local firms can affect the competitive position of other local firms *vis-à-vis* their foreign competitors. If a number of local firms import capital, part of the capital will usually be spent on non-traded goods. This corresponds to a rise in the overall demand for local non-tradeables. Consequently, the relative price of non-traded goods is going to rise and producers of non-tradeables can offer higher wages thus attracting labour. The resulting wage increase reduces the competitiveness of firms which produce tradeables.

This shows that the lack of international competitiveness of a part of the local firms can be due to the high competitiveness of other local firms.

Therefore, it is highly problematic when the decline of certain sectors and the rise of foreign competitors is assumed to indicate a decline in international competitiveness of the economy as a whole.[1] The same applies for the analysis of sectoral or bilateral balances. These are not independent of each other. Consequently, an analysis of sub-balances can by itself hardly give any information about the factors which determine the overall balance. These shortcomings of a disaggregated analysis of trade balances are mainly due to the fact that a basic insight from trade theory is neglected: the principle of comparative advantage. According to the theorem of comparative advantage, it is not possible to compete a country out of world markets because it always enjoys a comparative advantage in some sectors – no matter how much more productive the other countries may be.[2]

The analogy between an economy and an enterprise is ill-founded for another reason. A firm which loses its competitiveness goes bankrupt. The labour force will leave the firm and the capital stock will be liquidated. The firm simply ceases to exist. Even if a country experiences strong relative declines in productivity, it cannot go bankrupt since most of the people are not prepared to leave.

Still, if the analogy between a firm and an economy is to be employed, what would be the right definition of competitiveness? For a firm, to be sure, profits are a good indicator of competitiveness. However, profits seem to be too narrow a measure once an economy as a whole is considered. Not only is the measurement of profits a big problem already on the level of the firm, in addition, high profits are not necessarily tied to high factor incomes. Yet an economy which not only generates high profits but also high factor incomes is clearly better off or more competitive than an economy which depends on low factor incomes in order to generate high profits. Therefore, factor incomes should be included as well in a measure of competitiveness. Adding factor incomes to profits yields net value added or aggregate income (social product).[3] So, if we want to know whether an economy is competitive or not we may simply look at the level of per capita

---

[1]   This matter has been thoroughly discussed under the heading 'Deindustrialization' or 'Dutch Disease'. See Corden and Neary 1982.

[2]   It is sometimes stated that under increasing returns to scale, the principle of comparative advantage is not applicable. See for instance Romer 1990. Yet in this case the exogenous comparative advantage due to ex-ante differences in endowments might be less important in shaping trade patterns than endogenous comparative advantages. Anyway, the concept of comparative advantage is still applicable. The range of welfare improving specialization and trade might even increase in comparison to the pure Heckscher–Ohlin case. For a thorough discussion on the consequences of economies of scale for international trade see Baumol 1993, Deardorff 1994 and Markusen et al. 1995.

[3]   This could also be used as a measure of success of a single firm. However, if competitive factor pricing and factor mobility are assumed, factor prices are equal for all firms, so that the question simply is, whether a firm can generate value added above its factor costs, that is profits.

income or – if a more dynamic version is to be preferred – at the growth rate of per capita income.

B. The Balance on Current Account as an Indicator of International Competitiveness?

In the competitiveness approach, it is assumed that an increase in international competitiveness, that is ability to sell, shows up in a surplus on current account. In this framework, increased competitiveness can be due to a depreciation of the local currency (increased price competitiveness) or a quality-improvement of the goods produced (increased non-price competitiveness). Although the competitiveness approach is not a systematically developed theory, it can draw on a number of balance of payments theories which describe the relationship between ability to sell and the current account in a similar fashion. For many balance of payments theories also focus directly on exports and imports when it comes to explaining the balance on current account.[1] They focus primarily on goods markets, not on capital markets. Demand and supply in international goods markets are usually traced back to aggregate demand and relative prices. For example, as Glick (1991) points out, the Japanese current account surpluses have so far mostly been analysed in terms of relative prices and income levels. While relative prices ('price competitiveness') also have an important role to play in the competitiveness approach, aggregate demand is missing therein. However, changes in aggregate demand and changes in non-price competitiveness are often analysed in the same fashion. An increase in foreign demand and an increase in (non-price) competitiveness both lead to higher export demand. The consequences of such a change in export demand are treated similarly. Therefore, both cases have a lot in common. The significance of the exchange rate which is treated in the competitiveness approach as an important factor for price competitiveness, is also emphasized in balance of payments theories, like the elasticity approach and the asset market approach. Just as in the competitiveness approach, the exchange rate is often regarded as a variable which exogenously influences imports and exports of commodities.

a) Emphasizing demand

Keynesian balance of payments models
The relationship between demand and the balance on current account is usually analysed in simple multiplier models (Meade 1951, Alexander

---

[1]   For the sake of simplicity, foreign capital incomes and transfers are usually not included in the analysis.

1952,[1] Kenen 1985). The main focus of attention lies on the impact of fiscal or monetary policy on the balance on current account. The results vary with respect to the underlying assumptions. Of special importance are assumptions concerning the exchange rate regime and the degree of capital mobility. In early models, a system of fixed exchange rates with immobile capital was assumed.[2] Under these assumptions, an increase in domestic demand due to an expansionary fiscal or monetary policy leads to a deficit on current account and a corresponding reduction in foreign reserves. This result seems to form the theoretical basis for the assumed relationship between competitiveness and the current account which can be found in the competitiveness approach.

However, the assumption of immobile capital is no longer appropriate. In the 1950s, when tight capital controls were the rule rather than the exception, it made sense to assume immobile capital. But nowadays, capital is fairly free to move internationally. If the assumption of immobile capital or of fixed exchange rates is dropped, the balance of payments effects of an expansionary policy may be quite different, as has been shown by Mundell (1968). In a system with flexible exchange rates and mobile capital, an expansionary monetary policy does not result in a deficit on current account, but in a surplus.[3] This result is based on the assumption that an increase in money supply leads to lower interest rates and consequently to a capital outflow. The same principle may also be at work in the case of a relative decline in international competitiveness. In such a case, investors may find it more rewarding to lend to foreign firms which are more competitive. Capital flows out and the current account 'improves'.

A general problem with these Keynesian balance of payments models lies in the fact that only short-run phenomena are analysed. Repercussions due to changes in foreign reserves or price changes are usually not included in the analysis. Therefore, they are more suitable for the analysis of short-term business cycle phenomena.

The monetary approach to the balance of payments
The monetary approach focuses on demand changes as well. However, in monetary models changes in demand are primarily due to changes in money demand or supply (Frenkel and Johnson 1976). In contrast to Keynesian balance of payments theories, long-term phenomena are analysed. Although

---

[1]   Alexander 1952 analyses the effect of a devaluation on the current account. So far, he might not seem to belong to this paragraph. However, Alexander does not derive the balance on current account from the relative price effect of exchange rate changes. Rather, he focuses on the effects of a devaluation upon income and absorption.

[2]   See Bordo and Schwartz 1989, p. 240. Meade 1951 allows for capital mobility. However, his assumption of interest pegging by the central bank insures that there is a complete 'sterilization' of net capital movements. Thus, in the 'Meadean' world capital flows are equivalent to money flows and there is no real transfer.

[3]   An expansionary fiscal policy, however, still leads to a deficit on current account.

the adjustment mechanisms in these models are different from those in Keynesian multiplier models, the balance of payments effects are quite similar. Under the assumption of fixed exchange rates and immobile capital, an increase in domestic demand due to an expansionary monetary policy results in a temporary deficit on current account. This deficit is accompanied by a decline in foreign reserves. In the long run, balance of payments equilibrium is restored by changes in reserves and corresponding changes in money supply. Just like in Keynesian models, these results change fundamentally, when capital mobility is introduced. In the case of mobile capital and flexible exchange rates, an increase in the money supply results in a current account surplus.[1]

In simple Keynesian multiplier models as well as in monetary models, lines of arguments can be found which form the theoretical basis of the competitiveness approach. Higher demand, just like lower competitiveness, leads to a current account deficit. However, this is true only in a short-run analysis under the assumption of fixed exchange rates and internationally immobile capital. Especially in early Keynesian models and a certain variant of the monetary approach ('current account monetary models'),[2] private capital flows (sometimes referred to as 'autonomous' capital flows) have been neglected. This can be explained by the fact that capital controls persisted for a long time after the end of the second world war.[3] Similarily, the long period of fixed exchange rates (system of Bretton Woods) has strongly influenced balance of payments theory. However, the progressing liberalization of international capital movements and the change to flexible exchange rates led to further developments of these models. The results derived under the assumption of mobile capital and flexible exchange rates are quite different from the older results. Given these new assumptions, the relationship between demand changes and the balance on current account is no longer definite.

In an evaluation of the competitiveness approach these restrictions have to be kept in mind. In a flexible exchange rate system, changes in export or import demand result in exchange rate changes and do not directly affect the balance on current account. If capital flows are not affected, the balance on current account will remain unchanged.[4] This holds in the case of a change in domestic or foreign demand as well as in the case of a change in

---

[1]   This is, for instance, the result of Dornbusch's well known overshooting model and Frankel's real interest rate differentials model. See Dornbusch 1976 and Frankel 1979.

[2]   Brooks, Cuthbertson and Mayes 1986, pp. 59-82, distinguish between 'current account monetary models' and 'capital account monetarist models'.

[3]   This fact is mirrored in the title of Kenen's description of the post war development of macroeconomics: 'Macroeconomic Theory and Policy: How the Closed Economy was Opened'. See Kenen 1985.

[4]   This does not mean, however, that in a properly functioning system of flexible exchange rates the current account is always balanced.

competitiveness. If capital is internationally mobile, it has to be analysed how changes in competitiveness affect capital flows. If an improved competitiveness induces capital imports, it will result in a deficit on current account – not in a surplus, as predicted by the competitiveness approach.

In a system of fixed exchange rates, adjustment cannot be brought about by exchange rate changes. Therefore, in the short run an improvement of competitiveness can indeed result in a current account surplus and a corresponding increase in foreign reserves. However, if the monetary effects of a change in foreign reserves are taken into account, the current account effect will be reversed in the long run. Furthermore, under the assumption of mobile capital a deficit may arise, even in the short run.

The relationship between international competitiveness and the current account which is postulated by the competitiveness approach holds without restrictions only in a short-run model, under the assumption of fixed exchange rates and immobile capital. If capital is mobile, there is no definite relationship. It is still controversial, however, whether the relationship between competitiveness and the current account is even further relaxed in a system of flexible exchange rates.

b) Does the exchange rate determine competitiveness?

In the competitiveness approach the competitiveness of a nation is defined as ability to sell. The exchange rate is regarded as a mostly exogenous variable which influences the ability to sell of local firms. Exchange rate changes are not traced back to 'fundamentals'.[1] Instead, it is assumed that the exchange rate is determined in international financial markets. Since these markets supposedly are driven by speculation, the volatility of exchange rates is often considered 'excessive'. To support this line of reasoning, it is frequently pointed out that the volume of transactions in the foreign exchange markets is about thirty or forty times larger than the volume of the transactions which are booked in the current account.[2] Interpreted in this way, exchange rates are more or less independent of international trade. Exchange rate changes are due to erratical expectations. Therefore, they cannot serve to facilitate adjustment in the case of fundamental changes. Quite the contrary, exchange rate changes make changes of fundamentals necessary. This is the reason why interventions to reduce exchange rate volatility are often called for. Most prominent is

---

[1]   The term fundamentals is often used but seldom explained. The following factors can be considered to be fundamentals: the structure and the level of demand, the structure and the level of supply, the propensity to save and invest, money supply, money demand, government interventions, public deficits, technical progress, etc. Some of these fundamentals are discussed in Edwards 1988, pp. 7-9.

[2]   See for instance Aliber 1987, pp. 210-2, and Siebert 1991, p. 354. According to a report by the Bank for International Settlements (BIS), daily turnover in the foreign exchange markets amounted to approximately US$ 880 bn (BIS 1993). This is about 50 times more than the volume of international trade in goods and services.

James Tobin's proposal 'to throw some sand in the wheels of our excessively efficient international money markets' (Tobin 1982a, p. 489).[1] Tobin advocates a tax on capital transactions which is supposed to reduce short-term capital movements without much hurting long-term capital movements.[2]

b1) Which exchange rate?
Since there are many different exchange rate concepts (see IMF 1984, ch. 3) the question arises which concept is best suited when it comes to discussing the relationship between competitiveness on the one hand and exchange rate changes on the other. Generally, bilateral and effective as well as nominal and real exchange rates have to be distinguished. Most of these exchange rates are measured on a monthly, quarterly and yearly basis. Some are also measured weekly, daily or for even shorter intervals. Therefore, the problem arises which period (or interval) should be chosen. Is the nominal short-run bilateral exchange rate more important when it comes to analysing the current account and the structure of production or should instead a real long-term effective exchange rate be used?

Nominal versus real exchange rates. Purely nominal exchange rate changes which are due to divergent price level changes in different countries serve to avoid misallocations caused by monetary policy. In principle, such exchange rate changes need not distort competitive positions. Rather, they are symptoms for divergent strategies in monetary policy. As long as nominal exchange rate changes only reflect differences in costs and prices they are beneficial. However, nominal exchange rate changes are frequently larger than price- or cost-differences. In these cases nominal exchange rate changes go hand in hand with real exchange rate changes.[3] On the one hand, real exchange rates changes can be necessary to bring real adjustment processes about which are caused by fundamental changes. On the other hand, it is often feared that real exchange rate 'misalignments' can cause misallocations of resources and severe macroeconomic problems (Williamson 1985). As it is obviously the change in relative prices which matters, an analysis of the relationship between exchange rates and the current account has to focus on real rather than on nominal exchange rates.

---

[1]   Dornbusch 1988a, p. 256, even wants to use 'rocks'. See also Eichengreen, Tobin and Wyplosz 1995.

[2]   Since long-term capital movements as well as international trade are often fully or partly hedged or undertaken on the premise that hedging is cheaply and rapidly possible, such a tax may influence long-term capital movements and international trade in a way unforeseen by Tobin. See Krüger 1995. Furthermore, short-term capital movements may be required to stabilize a flexible exchange rate system. See McKinnon 1986 and Mayer 1985.

[3]   The real exchange rate can be defined in a number of ways. See chapter 2.II.A and chapter 3.II.C.

Bilateral versus effective exchange rates. For a single firm which exports into one currency area only the bilateral exchange rate is of vital importance.[1] But if firms sell their products in a wide array of countries, depreciations and appreciations may partly neutralize each other. Therefore, what matters for these firms is the average appreciation or depreciation of the local currency. Since the various foreign currencies are not all equally significant, they have to be weighted according to their importance. Such weighted averages are labelled 'effective exchange rates'. If we look at an entire economy we usually find a well diversified foreign trade, with a huge number of countries with different currencies. Therefore, from the perspective of an entire economy, the development of bilateral exchange rates is not very important. What matters for aggregate exports and imports are effective exchange rates. The volatility of such effective exchange rates is usually much smaller than the volatility of bilateral exchange rates.

Figure 2.2:   Bilateral and effective exchange rates

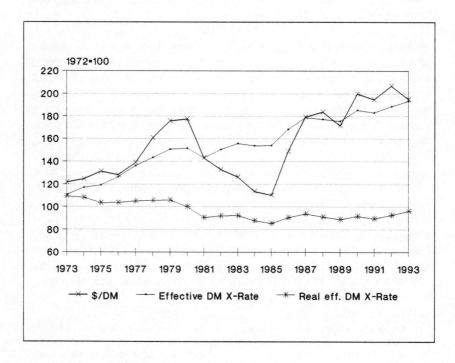

Source: IMF (a), own calculations.

---

[1]   Note, however, that this firm may have competitors in other countries so that it also matters how the exchange rate moves with respect to these countries' currencies.

Hedging and the appropriate unit of time. It is not only necessary to choose an appropriate exchange rate concept. In addition, it has to be analysed which period is relevant for the decision of firms and individuals as to their supply and demand. Many international transactions are stretched out over an extended period of several months or even years. In these cases short-term exchange rate changes, to the extent that they are offsetting, do not directly affect firms, even if these short-term changes are considerable in magnitude. If, however, the time horizon of an economic agent is short she may wish to insure against short-term exchange rate variations.[1] This can be done by using the forward, futures or options markets.[2] For periods up to one year these markets are highly liquid and the costs are very low, especially in the futures and forward market. The IMF estimated the average costs (which are equal to the bid-ask spread) of a 12 months US$/D-Mark forward contract to be under 0.2 percent in the period from 1974 to 1982 (IMF 1984, p. 9).

Even if short-term variability does not affect the parties involved very much, they face the risk of medium- or long-term exchange rate variability.[3] For periods over 12 months, hedging costs are rising fast. Therefore, hedging longer term transactions can become more expensive.

Anyhow, the discussion of the various exchange rate concepts shows that the significance of short-term bilateral exchange rate volatility can easily be overestimated. The effect on international transactions in goods and services seems to be astonishingly small.[4] This judgement contrasts with the huge amount of attention which is given in the public discussion to short-term variations of nominal bilateral exchange rates such as the US$/Yen or US$/D-Mark exchange rate. What matters for the allocation of resources is the long-term development of the real effective exchange rate. The volatility of this exchange rate is generally much lower than the volatility of nominal bilateral exchange rates. But since even the long-term real effective exchange rate has shown considerable variability, the question arises whether this is due to market failure thus distorting competitive positions on commodity markets.

---

[1]   Of course, exchange rate volatility poses only a problem for a firm if invoicing takes place in a foreign currency. However, invoicing in local currency does not eliminate exchange rate risk. It only shifts the risk to the foreign firm.

[2]   A firm with a high standing in international credit markets can also use a money market hedge.

[3]   In the literature, short-term 'variability' and long-term 'misalignments' are distinguished. See Bailey and Tavlas 1988, p. 207. This distinction goes back to Williamson 1985.

[4]   See Côté 1994 for a recent survey. Summing up the findings of recent empirical research, she observes: 'The recent literature suggests that exchange rate volatility, rather than having a direct effect on trade volumes, may well have a greater influence through investment location decisions' (p. 23).

Figure 2.3:   Short-run and long-run volatility

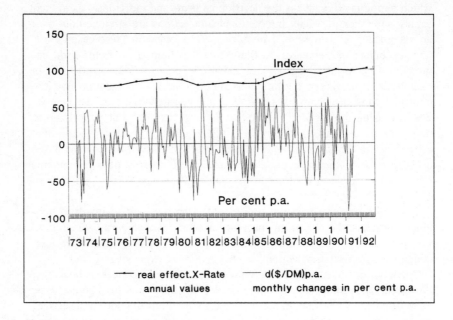

Source: IMF (a), own calculations.

b2) Volatile fundamentals: the world since the end of Bretton Woods
Yet, the simple fact that exchange rates have not been stable since the end of the system of Bretton Woods does not mean that flexible exchange rate systems do not work properly. Volatile exchange rates may also be due to volatile fundamentals. In this case, they reduce distortions rather than increase them.

Often, purchasing power parity is used to delimit necessary from excessive exchange rate changes (McKinnon 1988, Williamson 1987). But the applicability of purchasing power parity (PPP) theory is questionable because it assumes the constancy of the real exchange rate. Based on PPP every change of the real exchange rate would have to be interpreted as a malfunctioning of the exchange rate system. Such an interpretation hardly makes sense. In the medium- or long-run fundamental changes make changes of the real exchange rate necessary.[1]

---

[1]   See Dornbusch 1988b who criticizes McKinnon's attempt to calculate equilibrium exchange rates with the help of purchasing power parity. Machlup 1980 argues that PPP should be used as a rule of the thumb which is most useful when inflation differentials are bigger than a few percentage points.

Looking back at the period since the end of the system of Bretton Woods, it is easy to discern numerous real shocks and long-term developments which all made changes in real exchange rates necessary. To name a few: two oil price shocks in the 1970s and the subsequent decline of oil prices in the 1980s, different approaches in economic policy to deal with the two oil price shocks, radical changes in economic policy (including monetary policy) in various countries, the catching up process of several south east Asian economies (the 'Tigers'), the third world debt crisis, the breakdown of communism and the subsequent opening up of the ex communist economies, the widening and deepening of European integration, NAFTA, several wars, liberalization of international capital movements, the enormous growth of international capital markets, rapid technological change, etc.

Given these disturbances, it is not surprising that exchange rates changed erratically in this period. As far as the observed changes of real exchange rates can be explained by monetary and real shocks, they have to be interpreted as a necessary part of the adjustment process. Moreover, they would have occurred in a fixed rate system as well. Real exchange rate changes are not confined to flexible exchange rate systems (see case study Spain).

In the Bretton Woods system, for example, real exchange rates were not constant either. However, their variability has been lower than in the period of floating (IMF 1984, p. 12 and p. 38). The lower variability of real exchange rates under the Bretton Woods system has to be interpreted with caution though. During the 1950s and 1960s many restrictions on international trade and especially on international capital movements were in existence. Hence, lower exchange rate variability had its price, since these restrictions involve costs for producers, traders and investors which may well exceed the price of exchange rate variability (Johnson 1969). This has to be taken into consideration when the Bretton Woods system and flexible exchange rate systems are to be compared. Moreover, some economists have doubted that a system of fixed exchange rates would have survived the severe shocks of the 1970s and 1980s without capital controls (Obstfeld 1985, Bailey and Tavlas 1988), a belief which has been supported by the recent EMS crisis.

In addition, a comparison with equity and commodity prices shows that exchange rates are by no means more variable than other asset prices (DeGrauwe 1989, pp. 169-74). Quite the contrary, nominal bilateral exchange rates have not only been less volatile than the prices of commodities which are traded in organized markets (Bui and Pippenger 1990) but also less volatile than various national stock indices. This is somewhat surprising because the appropriate comparison would be between a nominal effective exchange rate (which is usually much less volatile than bilateral exchange rates) and a stock index. Therefore, this finding has been interpreted in support of inertia of exchange rates – rather than excess volatility (DeGrauwe 1989).[1]

b3) Inherent instability of flexible exchange rates?

Even if exchange rate variability has been to a large extent due to real and monetary shocks, it cannot be proven that all of the observed variability can be explained in this way. The possibility exists that part of the variability is caused by the inherent instability of flexible exchange rates. This is at least the result of several models which try to explain why there may be excess variability in flexible exchange rate systems.

The elasticity approach and the J-curve effect. The elasticity approach emphasizes the significance of relative prices for international adjustment (Machlup 1939/40, Robinson 1949). It tries to derive the conditions which ensure the 'normal' reaction of the balance on current account in case of exchange rate changes.[2] It is also applied for the analysis of related problems such as the effects of tariffs on the current account balance. Earlier balance of payments theories have made use of this approach. It has to be observed, however, that this approach is based on a partial equilibrium model. Exchange rate changes are not explained, they are simply assumed.[3] Repercussions on other variables than imports and exports are often neglected.[4] Such exogenous exchange rate changes can only be found in fixed exchange rate systems, where the authorities can set nominal exchange rates. In flexible exchange rate systems exchange rate changes have to be traced back to exogenous changes originating elsewhere. Therefore, the elasticities approach is hardly suited to give a general explanation of the interaction between exchange rates and the current account.

The literature about the J-curve effect has much in common with the elasticity approach. However, as Anne O. Krueger observed, 'it is based more on empirical observation than on theory' (Krueger 1983, p. 39). The J-curve effect is based on the proposition that exports and imports which were agreed upon in the past will not be altered by exchange rate changes. Thus, if international trade is mostly invoiced in the currency of the exporter, a trade balance deficit will be increasing in the short-run right

---

[1]   For this reason, Goodhart 1988 has characterized exchange rate behaviour as 'random walk with a dragging anchor'.

[2]   These conditions are the well known Marshall/Lerner condition and the more precise Robinson condition.

[3]   For instance, it is never quite clear why a current account deficit should be existing for a certain period until the exchange rate finally depreciates. After all, if there is a clear cut relationship between the current account and the exchange rate, one should expect that the exchange rate depreciates as soon as the current account falls into deficit, thus keeping the balance close to zero. If this does not happen, it has to be explained economically.

[4]   More general variants of the elasticity approach are discussed in Krueger 1983, pp. 31-9.

after a depreciation. Only in the longer run, as exports and imports adjust, will the deficit be reduced. This would imply that unless there are stabilizing capital flows, exchange rates would be highly unstable – at least in the short run (McKinnon 1986, Ohr 1985, Krueger 1983, p. 40).

The assumption of short-run inelastic imports and exports seems to be quite plausible. However, it should not be overlooked that for the current exchange rate neither the goods which are currently crossing the borders nor the payments which are currently made are important. What counts are the current purchases and sales of foreign exchange. These may happen well in advance of delivery *and payment*. An importer who receives foreign goods today and immediately pays for them may have bought the required foreign exchange half a year or a year ago. Similarily, a contract that is made today, which involves delivery and payment in half a year may immediately lead to a foreign exchange transaction conducted by the party which has to bear the exchange rate risk. Thus the current rate is relevant for today's decisions on imports and exports. If foreign traders tend to hedge part or all of the exchange rate risk, these decisions in turn feed back immediately on the exchange rate.[1] Put differently, one necessary condition for the emergence of the J-curve effect is that foreign traders do not hedge.

Furthermore, there is a class of goods which are often traded in organized markets just like financial assets: commodities. Commodities arbitrage can react to exchange rate changes also in the very short run, immediately affecting the exchange rate – although not immediately statistically registered trade flows (Bui and Pippenger 1990, p.19, note 14).

Both the elasticity approach and the J-curve proposition implicitly assume that capital flows will adapt more or less passively to the trade balance. Such an assumption may be warranted in a system with fixed exchange rates and capital controls. In such a system, the counterparty to any occurring trade balance is the central bank. However, in a system of flexible exchange rates and international capital mobility, trade deficits have to be matched by private capital inflows. Therefore, it has to be explained how such 'induced' capital flows come about (Krüger 1994, pp. 66-71, Krugman 1993, pp. 33-9, Ohr 1985). As Krugman (1993) and Ohr (1985) have shown, 'induced' capital flows may be the result of expected exchange rate changes. If a currency depreciates sharply, due to inelasticities, under the assumption of rational or adaptive expectations investors will expect a subsequent appreciation. Therefore, the expected return rises and capital flows into the country with the depreciating currency, thus financing the trade deficit (ibid., p. 301).

---

[1]   Trade flows which are statistically recorded may indeed display a lagged reaction. But as long as the foreign currency transactions which are connected with these trade flows have been conducted already in the past, these flows are not relevant for today's exchange rate (Machlup 1980).

This theory of induced capital flows could be used as a theoretical underpinning for the competitiveness approach. However, there are some caveats. First, investors have to be confident that all or part of the observed depreciation is only temporary. This surely is the case when effects such as the J-curve effect are indeed an important empirical phenomenon. But can investors expect a recovery of the exchange rate when the depreciation is due to a decline in competitiveness? The worsening of international competitiveness may be a long-lasting phenomenon which could drive the exchange rate further down in the future. Therefore, it seems more likely that capital is going to flow out – not in. That means that a decline of international competitiveness may be accompanied by a current account surplus.

The argument presented by Ohr also presupposes the existence of a large amount of investors which put some confidence into their exchange rate forecasts. This assumption is questionable. The large and mostly unpredictable exchange rate fluctuations seem to have reduced the amount of speculators who have strong views on future currency movements and who are willing to commit large amounts of capital to currency speculation (Group of Thirty 1980, p. 25, Brown 1983, pp. 113-36, McKinnon 1986).[1] Same economist blame monetary policy for this lack of speculation. It is argued that the unpredictable shifts in monetary policy have increased the risk of currency speculation so much, that most speculators have withdrawn from the market (McKinnon 1986, Brown 1983, p. 129).

Overshooting. Dornbusch's overshooting model (Dornbusch 1976) is probably the best known approach to explain excess volatility. In the overshooting model a situation is described in which prices in financial markets adjust faster than prices in goods markets. Under this assumption changes in monetary policy cause an 'overshooting' (or 'undershooting') of the exchange rate from its long-run equilibrium level. In the long run, purchasing power parity is fulfilled. In the short run, there can be deviations however. Therefore, the model can generate short-term real exchange rate changes, whereas in the long run nominal shocks can cause only nominal exchange rate adjustments.

The Dornbusch model has the advantage that the possible amount of overshooting is easily measurable. In this model deviations of the exchange rate from its long-run equilibrium level (for instance real exchange rate changes) are equal to the interest rate differentials. Since interest rate differentials are usually much smaller than real exchange rate changes, the Dornbusch model can at best explain a small part of the observed volatility of real exchange rates (Homburg 1989). To give an example: The real

---

[1]   Exceptions are very short-term speculations such as intra day speculation and, of course, one way speculation against fixed exchange rates.

appreciation of the US$ *vis-à-vis* the D-Mark was 29.1 per cent in 1981 and 13.5 percent in 1984. At the same time interest rate differentials between Germany and the US amounted to 1.9 per cent and 3.4 per cent respectively. Thus, the Dornbusch model cannot contribute very much to the explanation of such striking phenomena as the remarkable real appreciation of the US$ in the first half of the 1980s.[1] Furthermore, the model suffers also from theoretical ambiguities (Lüdiger 1989). It is, for example, not clear why economic agents adjust instantaneously in the foreign exchange markets, but not in the capital markets. While expected inflation and exchange rate changes influence the spot exchange rate they do not affect the interest rate. Hence, the Fisher effect does not apply in the Dornbusch model. If expected inflation would be immediately priced into interest rates, there would be no overshooting

The overshooting model shows that exchange rate adjustments do not necessarily need to be smooth over time. However, since purchasing power parity is assumed in the long run the ultimate cause of exchange rate changes is a change in fundamentals (monetary policy). Asset market models go one step further. Exchange rate changes are mainly traced back to changes in expectations. What matters are not fundamentals but rather 'news' about (real or supposed) fundamentals (Frenkel 1981). Therefore, it becomes possible, at least to a certain degree, to explain exchange rates independently of fundamentals. In this case, the exchange rate might become a factor which independently determines competitive positions.

The asset market approach. In asset market models short-term exchange rate development is explained independently of goods and capital flows. Thus, just like in the elasticity approach exchange rates are exogenous variables for international goods markets. But exchange rate changes are not simply assumed like in the elasticity approach. They are mainly derived from changes in expectations or in the structure of asset supplies.[2] Asset market models treat the exchange rate just like any other asset price (Frenkel 1981, Mussa 1984). The foreign exchange market is modelled like other organized asset markets where prices are mainly determined by expectations over fundamentals – or, as Keynes has pointed out, by expectations over expectations (Keynes 1936/64, p. 156).[3] These expectations are formed on the basis of the existing knowledge. If markets are efficient all existing knowledge about present and future economic conditions should be reflected in the current asset price. Consequently,

---

[1]   It has also been argued that the expected pattern ('Gestalt') of a jump of the exchange rate and a subsequent revision cannot be observed in reality. See Goodhart 1988, p. 437.

[2]   Well known examples are Branson 1977, Kouri 1976 and Frenkel 1981. Frenkel 1983 provides a comparison of the monetary and the asset market models.

[3]   See also Neumann and Klein 1982 on this point.

price changes are mainly due to new information ('news') and cannot be predicted (Frenkel and Mussa 1985, p. 726).[1] Since the market has to digest new information continuously, prices change nearly all the time. These price changes do not necessarily have to reflect correct information. Incorrect news can influence exchange rates as well.

Adjustment in the event of unexpected news is modelled as stock adjustment. If new information affects the expected relative return of assets denominated in different currencies, an immediate reaction in financial markets follows. Investors will try to restructure their portfolios in favour of those assets whose relative return improved. This causes an exchange rate change. Since asset markets are assumed to react much faster than goods markets, the latter are excluded from the short-run analysis. Savings and investment are excluded as well, because their size is negligible in the very short run.[2] Flows of goods and capital are included only in the long-run analysis (Branson 1977).

In the Branson model, just like in the Dornbusch model, there is a reversion of the exchange rate towards purchasing power in the long run.[3] Thus, a very similar pattern of exchange rate changes arises. Sharp jumps are followed by slow reversions towards purchasing power parity. However, in order to explain a protracted appreciation like the dollar appreciation in the first half of the 1980s, one would have to assume a pattern of serial correlated positive news for the dollar – not a very convincing idea (Koromzay, Llewellyn and Potter 1987, p. 27).[4]

The emphasis of the significance of expectations seems to support the notion that exchange rates can be explained independently of fundamentals. But it has to be remembered that expectations relate to fundamentals. In the short run, the variability of expectations may be quite large.[5] But with time passing, flow adjustment will become more important for price formation

---

[1]   Empirical studies did not find much support for this hypothesis. See Almekinders and Rovers 1994. Such empirical studies are difficult to interpret however, because the observer hardly knows which news is really new and which is anticipated. See Neumann a nd Klein 1982.

[2]   It remains unclear, however, why the flow variables (exports and imports) do not have any effect on the exchange rate. This has been criticized by Tobin 1982b, p. 188: 'A model whose solution generates flows but completely ignores their consequences may be suspected of missing phenomena important even in a relatively short run, ...'.

[3]   However, in contrast to the Dornbusch model, the Branson model allows for long-run deviations from PPP. Long-run equilibrium is defined by a zero balance on current account (trade balance = net interest payments) which implies that wealth is constant. This condition allows for deviations from PPP in the short run and in the long run. However, short-run deviations are larger (and in opposite direction) so that there is a tendency for the exchange rate to reverse towards PPP.

[4]   Therefore, Branson gives more weight to the fiscal deficit in the US than to the possibility of a portfolio shift in order to explain the dollar appreciation (Branson 1985).

[5]   Expectations can also be wrong for a certain period of time. If investors realize expectations to be false, they will adjust them. This adjustment also leads to a correction of the exchange rate.

and it will become evident whether expectations were correct or not. In these models as well, what matters are fundamentals.[1] Interpreting exchange rate without regard of fundamentals is possible only in a short-run analysis. Flows of goods and services can be neglected only over very short periods.[2] But, even if the asset market approach can improve the understanding of short-term exchange rate variability, it does not have much to say about misalignments. And, as has been pointed out, the latter are much more important.

Bubbles. Can exchange rate changes be explained as a bubble-like phenomenon? In the literature, two kinds of bubbles are distinguished: rational and non-rational bubbles. An early version of a model with rational bubbles which can start, burst and restart was presented by Blanchard (1979). However, Diba and Grossman (1988) show that a rational bubble cannot burst and restart. Either an asset is from the moment of emission on a bubble path or it is not.[3] Whether or not rational bubbles are possible at all is still an open question. Tirole (1982) shows that in a model with infinitely lived traders there can be no bubbles. But this result was not confirmed in an overlapping generations model (Tirole 1985). Thus, rational bubbles can at best explain long-term overvaluation, but not volatility. The possibility of rational bubbles is put further into question by Blanchard and Fischer who point out that a number of factors may reduce the likelihood of rational bubbles considerably (Blanchard and Fischer 1989, p. 223, see also Krüger 1994). First of all, a high elasticity of supply either of the asset in question or a close substitute can make the emergence of a bubble virtually impossible. Related to this point is the argument that bubbles are less likely in cases where fundamentals are relatively easy to ascertain. And finally, bubbles can be ruled out when the asset price is subject to a terminal condition like for example in the case of bonds. What does this imply for the possibility of exchange rate bubbles? Blanchard and Fischer cite exchange rates as an example for assets, with little understood fundamentals. This would enhance the likelihood of exchange rate bubbles. On the other hand, unless one subscribes to extreme 'elasticity pessimism' an exchange rate bubble would create huge current account reactions. Thus, there would be an elastic supply reaction[4] which severely reduces the

---

[1]   Most economists are sceptical about the possibility of bubbles in foreign exchange markets. See, for example, Obstfeld and Stockman 1985, p. 973.

[2]   And even in short periods, this may be problematic. See the Tobin quote above and Krüger 1994.

[3]   Their argument is based on the fact that there can be no negative bubble. Given that an investor can always walk away from an asset, the value of the asset cannot become negative.

[4]   Economists like Marshall 1922, Haberler 1933, Machlup 1950 and Sohmen 1969 have presented a number of convincing arguments which show that 'elasticity pessimism' is not well founded. See also Stern, Francis and Schumacher 1976.

likelihood of an exchange rate bubble – especially when the size of foreign trade is taken into account.[1] Given these arguments, possible candidates for rational bubbles seem to be only assets of minor importance such as cited by Tirole (1982, p. 1179): 'stamps, coins, paintings, diamonds, some land etc.'.[2]

The second approach to the explanation of asset price volatility is not based on rational expectations. Rather, some market participants are assumed to respond 'to changes in expectations or sentiment that are not fully justified by information' (Shleifer and Summers 1990, p. 23). Such 'noise traders' may destabilize prices. Commonly it has been argued that rational market participants would arbitrage such an influence on prices away, leaving the noise traders with a loss. However, as Shleifer and Summers have pointed out funds for such an arbitrage may be limited when the rational market participants do not exactly know the fundamental value either (Shleifer and Summers 1990, p. 22). In addition, they argue that by destabilizing prices noise traders increase the risk of assets and therefore the returns. Thus, they may not be driven out of the market, even in the longer run. To support their theory, they cite a number of market anomalies (see also Shiller 1990). Most interesting about their approach is the statement that even the rational players, the 'arbitrageurs', may not know the fundamental asset value. Given the poor quality of the predictive capacity of exchange rate models (Meese and Rogoff 1983, Levich 1985), this applies *a fortiori* to the foreign exchange market. Exchange rate fundamentals are not well understood. In such a situation, market participants have to predict not only the influence of fundamentals but also the expectations of other market participants. Thus, the famous Keynesian 'beauty contest problem' arises (Keynes 1936/64, p. 156) and in trying to guess what the market expects 'arbitrageurs begin to look like noise traders themselves' (Shleifer and Summers 1990, p. 26). Thus, it cannot be expected that rational speculators will always keep the exchange rate close to its equilibrium value. However, just like in the case of rational bubbles, deviations from equilibrium prices are also depending on the (flow-) reactions of demand and supply (Krüger 1994). So, even if the beauty test problem is the cause for some of the exchange rate volatility, its impact is limited by the fundamentals.[3]

---

[1]   Tests for bubbles, just like tests for market efficiency in general, face the problem that only a joint hypothesis can be tested: that there are no bubbles and that the model is correctly specified. See Meese 1986 and Flood and Hodrick 1990.

[2]   The question, whether much insight is gained when the fact that fiat paper money has a positive value is interpreted as a bubble will not be discussed here. Menger 1892 and Wärneryhd 1989 propose to interpret money as a social convention.

[3]   Sometimes, it seems to be forgotten that fundamentals may also have a direct effect on price, not just an indirect effect via expectations.

To sum up: theoretical reasoning supports to a certain extent the presumption that short-term exchange rate volatility is only partly related to changes in fundamentals. However, there is widespread agreement that the effects of short-term exchange rate variability should not, and in effect did not, damage international trade very much. More controversial is the judgement about longer run developments. The considerable changes of real effective exchange rates have been witnessed with great concern. Many observers have attributed these changes to other forces than fundamentals, namely unstable expectations and destabilizing speculation in foreign exchange markets (see for instance Krugman 1989). However, this interpretation does not seem to take into account how volatile the exchange rate environment was. Furthermore, the theories which are meant to explain such deviations are applicable in the short run rather than in the long run. Therefore, if longer run phenomena are analysed, the exchange rate should not be treated (like in the competitiveness approach) as a more or less exogenous variable for goods markets.

Both, the competitiveness approach and the elasticity approach suffer from the fact that they simply assume a certain exchange rate or an exchange rate change. Therefore, the exchange rate is an exogenous variable in these models, even when flexible exchange rates are assumed. The asset market approach, on the other hand, explicitly derives the exchange rate within the model. Short-run exchange rate changes are interpreted as the result of financial market activity. This has led some economists to claim that the determination of exchange rates has little to do with real phenomena and depends nearly exclusively on uncertain preferences and expectations (McKinnon 1988, p. 86, Vehrkamp 1992). Thus, the asset approach seems to provide a justification for the treatment of the exchange rate as being exogenous for the goods markets.

A theoretical basis for the competitiveness approach requires also a theory of capital flows. As has been shown, inelastic trade and stabilizing expectations can provide a theoretical model of the interaction of exchange rates, trade flows and capital flows which could explain why a current account falls into deficit when the international competitiveness declines. However, this would imply that speculators put their money into those countries whose competitiveness is declining, hoping to gain from a recovery. It is easy to imagine situations where speculative capital flows out rather than in. Therefore, it is at least as likely, that a decline in competitiveness will produce a current account surplus.

c) Conclusions

According to the competitiveness approach, the balance on current account is caused by the competitiveness of an economy. Competitiveness is defined as 'ability to sell'. The aggregate competitiveness of a nation is derived by simply adding up the competitiveness of single sectors or firms. This is problematic for a number of reasons. First, 'ability to sell' does not seem to be an appropriate definition of competitiveness, neither for firms nor for countries. Rather income should be used, or, in the case of firms, profits. Second, the competitiveness of one sector or one firm is not independent of the competitiveness of other sectors or firms within the same country. Therefore, the position of one firm *vis-à-vis* its foreign competitors also depends on the performance of other local firms. Put differently, the problems of one local sector may be due to the successes of another local sector. Third, the postulated relationship between competitiveness and the current account can only be derived using restrictive assumptions. Only in a system with fixed exchange rates and capital controls does a decline in competitiveness or ability to sell lead to a deficit on current account. If capital is mobile, the opposite effect is more likely: declining competitiveness leads to a capital outflow and consequently to a surplus on current account. Finally, the exchange rate is not a variable which can be treated more or less independently of goods markets at least not in the medium or long run.

II. The intertemporal approach: emphasizing locational quality

A. The Theory of Intertemporal Utility Maximization and the Balance of Payments

a) The individual intertemporal calculus
Following the competitiveness approach, trade balances can be traced back to the individual decision whether to buy goods produced at home or goods produced abroad. This decision is assumed to be dependent on the competitiveness of local firms in comparison to foreign firms. Thus, the competitiveness approach focuses only on trade flows. An alternative approach to the explanation of current account balances is the intertemporal approach which is based to the theory of intertemporal utility maximization.[1] Here a trade balance results from the individual decision whether to consume today or to consume tomorrow. Thus, as will be shown, the balance of payments can be traced back on the savings/investment decisions[2] of individuals. This theoretical approach

---

[1]   Intertemporal utility maximization forms the basis of elementary capital theory. See Fisher 1930. Applications to balance of payments theory can be found for instance in: Sachs 1982, Helpman and Razin 1982, Viñals 1986, Issing and Masuch 1989. For a recent survey see Obstfeld and Rogoff 1994.

[2]   In order to develop the capital theoretic foundations of the intertemporal approach of the balance of payments as clear as possible, in this section we abstract from money and central bank reserves. This may look quite restrictive, but is more or less equivalent with a situation of fixed money supply, constant velocity, and flexible exchange rates.

gains the more relevance, the more the globalization of international capital markets proceeds.[1]

Each individual can use his periodical income either for present consumption or he can spread consumption over several periods. Present income can be saved in order to raise consumption in the future. Suppose that an individual consumes part of his present income and saves the other part. The savings can be used in two ways: the individual can invest in his own household or in his firm or he can lend it to other households or firms. Of course, the existence of net lenders presupposes net borrowers, that is people who consume and invest more than their periodical income. Thus, instead of saving, an individual can consume or invest more than his periodical income only if somebody is prepared to lend. However, the individual can spend less than his future income on consumption because he has to pay off the loan in future periods.

The decision to save and the decision where to invest the savings is the result of simple utility calculus analogous to the decision between two goods. To the extent that the marginal utility of consumption tomorrow exceeds the marginal utility of consumption today, the individual will save. These savings will be invested at home (abroad), if the market interest rate is lower (higher) than the return on investment at home. If, instead, the individual can raise his intertemporal utility by borrowing, his current consumption will exceed his current income. His calculation whether to be a net debtor or a net creditor depends on the interest rate he has to pay relative to his individual discount rate. Thus, net borrowing is a function of the individual discount rate r_i and the market interest rate r:

(1) $netB = f(r_i, r)$ r = market interest rate; r_i = individual discount rate

The individual discount rate is determined by the marginal productivity of capital (incl. human capital) and the marginal rate of substitution between consumption today and consumption tomorrow (rate of time preference).

(2) $r_i = h(mp, dC_1/dC_0)$ mp = marginal productivity of capital, dC_1/dC_0 = time preference.

Time preference depends on expected permanent income, age (the position in the life cycle) and wealth.

---

[1] It should be remembered that, during the time of the gold standard, capital markets were highly integrated as well. This also influenced balance of payments theory. As Haberler 1948, p.450, observed, before the second world war, most economists were of the opinion that the current account is determined by the capital account.

(3) $dC_1/dC_0 = k(Y^p, age, W)$ Y^p = permanent income, W = wealth

So, the individual discount rate becomes a function h' of human capital, capital, permanent income, age and wealth.[1]

(4) $r_i = h'(hc, c, Y^p, age, W)$

In equilibrium, marginal productivity of capital has to be equal to the rate of time preference and both have to be equal to the market rate of interest.

(5) $dC_1/dC_0 = mp = r_i = r$

As long as the individual discount rate is above the market rate, the individual will increase borrowing in order to increase consumption or investment. If the discount rate is below the market rate, the individual can raise his utility by additional lending – financed by a reduction of investment or consumption.

Figure 2.4:   Intertemporal utility maximization

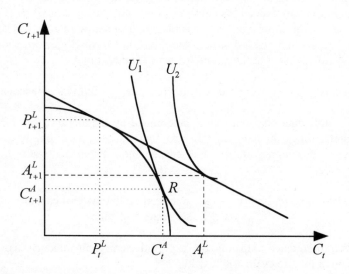

The individual intertemporal utility maximization can also be illustrated graphically (Figure 2.4). Suppose an economic unit which is able to make a

---

[1]   Following standard macroeconomic textbooks, the life cycle hypothesis and the permanent income hypothesis are combined. Compare Dornbusch and Fischer 1990, p. 283.

living by producing and consuming one good. The intertemporal transformation curve has the usual shape which implies declining marginal productivity of capital. There is a trade off between production today and production tomorrow. The capital market is perfect, that is the interest rate is equal both for borrowing and lending. The slope of the capital market line, therefore, is $-(1 + r)$.

Presumed, the economic unit has a very high time preference. In the state of autarky, his Robinson–Crusoe position (Hirshleifer 1970) is R. Consumption in t is C_t^A, whereas the difference to the production possibility is invested. Thus, in $t+1$ he can consume C_{t+1}^A. No lending or borrowing takes place. Now suppose that economic relations to the rest of the world come into being. The economic unit will now be able to raise both absorption in t and in $t+1$, as both A_t^L and A_{t+1}^L show. The individual has to borrow the difference between production and absorption in period t. His capital account is in surplus that exactly matches the deficit on his current account $(A_t^L - P_t^L)$. In period $t+1$, the opposite holds: in order to pay the principal plus interest (deficit on capital account) the economic unit has to show a surplus on his current account $(P_{t+1}^L - A_{t+1}^L)$. The intertemporal utility of the individual has been raised by borrowing a certain amount of the good in t and by paying off this amount plus interest in $t+1$, as the indifference curves U_1 and U_2 show.

Transactions between one individual and the rest of the world, such as borrowing and lending and the purchase or sale of goods, can be displayed in an individual 'balance of payments'. Borrowing and lending is documented in the 'capital account', the corresponding purchase of goods is enumerated in the 'current account'. How are current account and capital account connected with each other? A capital transfer has an impact on both balances (of the lender and the debtor) because it implies the transfer of purchasing power from the individual who saves to the one who borrows.

The recipient has aquired additional purchasing power precisely because he wants to spend more on goods than his income and the lender is only able to lend because he reduced his spending below current income.[1] Capital account surplus (deficit) and current account surplus (deficit) are planned simultaneously.

The fact that current account and capital account are planned simultaneously does not imply, however, that the balance on current account (= balance on capital account) is, on the one, hand determined by factors influencing the intertemporal calculus described above and, on the other hand, by factors influencing the *intra*temporal supply and demand of

---

[1]   If the lender sells assets in order to finance his credit, the purchaser of the assets has to reduce his spending on goods. So, while the lender himself does not reduce his spending somebody else does. Unless the possibility of dishoarding is allowed for, any net lending, that is any command over currently produced goods, is based on consumption forgone (in the wide sense).

goods. Basic capital theory flatly states that current account balances are an intertemporal phenomenon. So, unless a variable influences the relationship between the individual discount rate and the market rate, it will leave the balance on capital account and consequently the balance on current account unaffected.

For instance, if new goods appear in the market which individual A desires very much, the effects on A's balance on current account can be manyfold: first, A can consume less of other goods in order to buy the new good. In this case, the balance on current account is not affected. Second, A can borrow more (save less) in order to buy the good. This would imply a rising current account deficit (shrinking surplus). Third, if A saves more (borrows less) in order to be able to buy the good at some later date the current account surplus (deficit) increases (decreases). Which option A chooses is an intertemporal question. If the appearence of the new good does not affect A's individual discount rate or the market rate, then A's balance on current account will remain constant.

b) Aggregating individual balances to the national balance of payments
The basic capital theoretic approach can be extended from one individual to a group of individuals or a whole country.[1] If there is an integrated capital market within a country (a group) the market rate will be equated to the marginal productivity of capital and the rate of time preference for each individual. Like the discount rate of an individual the market rate of a country or a group depends on human capital, capital, income, wealth and the age structure of the population.[2] In addition, the marginal productivity of (human) capital as well as the savings behaviour (and therefore the interest rate) are influenced by the institutions which govern the interactions between the members of the group and between group members and the outside world. Thus, the discount rate of the group can be represented by the following function:

$$(6)\ r_g = h_g(hc,c,Y^p,age,W,P)$$

where 'P' (politics) represents the institutional factors, and 'age' the age structure of the population.

---

[1]   It is interesting to notice the effects of international capital flows on the domestic net foreign wealth. It increases through a capital export, and it decreases through a capital import. The change in domestic overall net wealth depends on the use of the capital import. If the capital import is used for consumption the net wealth decreases. It remains unchanged if the capital import is invested: Net foreign wealth is less than before whereas the domestic capital stock has grown. In this study only capital flows are considered, changes in total capital stock due revaluations will not be considered. For problems of evaluation of net foreign wealth see Sinn 1990.

[2]   In a closed economy, the value of the stock of physical capital is equal to wealth. In an open economy, however, they may diverge.

Whether or not a country is a net borrower of capital or a net lender depends on a comparison of the internal discount rate with the world market interest rate. If the internal rate is higher (lower) it becomes a net borrower (lender). So, for a whole country just like for a single individual the balance on capital account and consequently the balance on current account[1] is the result of an intertemporal calculus.

(7) $Im - Ex = Cim - CEx = netB = f(r_g, r)$

Figure 2.5:   The marginal efficiency of capital

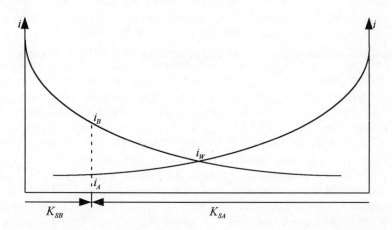

The comparison of internal discount rate and the world market interest rate can be shown graphically in a two-country scenario. Suppose, first of all, two countries in the case of autarky, one of them (country A) relatively capital abundant, the other (country B) rather poor in capital.[2] Due to this difference in scarcity, the interest rate will be low in country A and high in country B. If international capital movements are liberalized, the interest rate differential will give an incentive to export capital from country A where the marginal efficiency of capital is low into country B where marginal efficiency of capital, in contrast, is high (Figure 2.5). Thus, international differences in scarcity of capital can be wiped out by international capital flows which cause imbalances on the capital account and, therefore, imbalances on the current account as well. In the course of

---

[1]   Both, the capital account as well as the current account of a group can be derived by simple aggregation of the individual's accounts. Intragroup flows cancel out and it remains the balance with the rest of the world.

[2]   World capital supply is assumed to be fix.

the capital flow, we obtain the interest rate i_w which in case of perfect capital mobility is the same everywhere.

Figure 2.5 also can be used looking at the supply side of capital. Imagine that the domestic economic units want to increase consumption with GNP and planned investment unchanged. In this case, the supply side is concerned: savings are cut down. This implies diminishing supply of capital at home. Demand exceeds supply, causing the interest rate *ceteris paribus* to rise. The excess demand for capital is to be satisfied by net capital imports.

While the determination of the capital account (current account) is basically identical for a group and for a single individual, the adjustment process in case of changes may be different. From a microeconomic perspective, the 'transfer', that is the conversion of a financial claim into real goods, poses no problem in competitive markets ('immaculate transfer'). First, as has been pointed out already, an individual plans lending (borrowing) and spending on goods simultaneously. Therefore, net capital imports (exports) and net goods imports (exports) are not only equal ex post but also ex ante. Second, for both lender and borrower, prices are given since the supply of goods is infinitely elastic for the individual. Even if the increased demand of the borrower is directed towards other goods than the reduced demand of the buyer, no price changes will occur. Moving from a micro to a macro perspective, the whole matter becomes more complex. While the ex post identity between the current account and the capital account still holds, ex ante planned net borrowing (lending) and planned net imports (exports) do not have to coincide. It is, for instance, possible that individuals of one country wish to borrow more abroad without wanting to buy more foreign goods. In this case the ex ante capital account would not be equal to the ex ante current account. Thus, there would be a disequilibrium in the foreign exchange market. Similarily, goods markets would be in disequilibrium. There would be an excess demand for those goods which the borrowers wish to buy and excess supply of those goods which the lenders do not buy anymore. Since from a macroeconomic perspective changes in the structure of demand may affect relative prices and thus the structure of production the effect of capital flows on the structure of demand has to be incorporated in the model.

The effect of a transfer on the structure of demand and relative prices has already been discussed extensively in the literature about the transfer problem. In the famous controversy between Keynes and Ohlin (Keynes 1929/50 and Ohlin 1929/50) the inclusion or non-inclusion of reparations as an argument of exports and imports marked the decisive difference between Keynes and Ohlin. Once capital flows are treated as autonomous, that is guided by expected returns and not by other components of the balance of payments, the similarity of the transfer problem in the case of reparations and in the case of capital flows becomes evident.[1] In both cases absorption has to be reduced in the paying/lending country. This happens via taxation in the case of reparations and via private saving in the case of capital flows. The receiving country, on the other hand, can increase absorption above income. One of the main points of Ohlin's argument was that the reduction of absorption in the one country and the increase in absorption in the other would be sufficient to bring about part of the real transfer – reducing the necessary amount of real exchange rate changes. Although Keynes was not unaware of this argument (Keynes 1929/50, pp. 161-2) he chose to neglect it during the further cause of his argument where he empasized the necessity of large real exchange rate changes in order to bring the real transfer about. Thus he omitted the direct effect of the capital flows (reparations) on net exports in both countries.

In the light of the extended period which followed and which was characterized by capital controls and trade restrictions, it is not surprising that Keynes's approach survived, while Ohlin's argument was mostly neglected. However, given the current conditions of increased capital mobility it should not be forgotten that economic agents can buy more imports and exportables when they are net borrowers abroad. Therefore, net capital exports should be included as arguments of net exports. Thus, the capital flow itself which represents a shift of purchasing power from lender to borrower countries, usually will induce a flow of goods in the same direction, even if the exchange rate is constant. Only to the extent that the induced flow of goods is smaller in value than the flow of funds do exchange rate changes become necessary.

In order to analyse the relationship between capital account and current account further, a supply side model will be developed which incorporates two goods (tradeables and non-tradeables) and Marshall's destinction of the short run and the long run.

c) A supply side interpretation of national accounting
The use of an intertemporal full employment model has certain implications for the interpretation of some well known accounting identities from the national accounts. These are often used in connection with specific theories, namely Keynesian macroeconomics.[2] For example, the notion that a surplus on current account is expansionary is often based on the well known identity (equation 8):

(8) $Y = C + I + G + (Ex - Im)$

---

[1]   Ohlin treats both cases as 'transfers of buying power' (Ohlin 1929/50, p. 172).
[2]   Sachs 1981, p. 213, shows how various balance of payments theories can be illustrated, starting from the same national accounting identity.

Usually, it is assumed that the variables on the right hand side of equation (8) may vary more or less independently of each other. Clearly, if either consumption (C), investment (I), government spending (G) or the export surplus $(Ex\text{-}Im)$ are increasing, it should be expected that the national income (Y) is increasing as well. Interpreted like this, equation (8) is not only an identity but also an equation which explains the determination of Y. National income is traced back to consumption, investment, government spending and their respective causes.

The implicit assumption underlying this interpretation is that aggregate demand (Y^D) is smaller than full employment income (Y^*).

$$(9)\ Y^* > Y^D = C + I + G + (Ex\text{ - }Im)$$

Supply is constrained by demand and prices are sluggish in the short run. Therefore, employment and income are below their full employment levels.[1] In this situation, demand changes cause supply changes, thus causing changes in real income (Y^r).

$$(10)\ dY^D = dY^S = dY^r$$

Only as Y^D approaches Y^*, prices will be affected as well. Thus, there is a straight line leading from changes in C, I, G and $(Ex\text{-}Im)$ via changes in Y^D to changes in Y^r.

A second assumption underlying the Keynesian model is that aggregate demand is not constrained by monetary factors. Using the quantity equation, nominal demand can be related to money.

$$(11)\ Y^D = vM \qquad (v = \text{velocity}, M = \text{money supply})$$

If the variables on the right hand side of equation (8) are supposed to determine Y^D, they also have to determine the velocity v or the quantity of money M. In the former case, the resulting behaviour of velocity would be quite peculiar: velocity would always adjust to desired spending.[2] However, this assumption about the determination of velocity does not only violate the standard formulations in money demand functions. In addition, it is also highly implausible because it implies that any increase in expenditure is financed by dishording and any reduction of spending leads to hoarding. Thus, it describes a world of infinitely elastic money demand where borrowers can borrow unlimited amounts of money at a given interest rate

---

[1]   The assumptions underlying the Keynesian balance of payments theory are explained in Meade 1951.

[2]   Formally, velocity could be characterized as follows: $v = f(C,I,G,Ex,Im)$ with $dv/v = dX/Y$ $<=> (dv/v)/(dX/X) = X/Y$ (with $X \in \{C,I,G,Ex,Im\}$)

('liquidity trap'). However, such a behaviour of velocity seems extremely unlikely (Laidler 1993, pp. 150-2).

The latter case in which demand determines the money supply is more realistic. For instance, Meade (1951) assumes that central banks peg the interest rate. In this case, the money supply would be endogenous. Desired increases in aggregate spending would be accommodated by money supply changes.

However, the identities of the national accounts can also be interpreted differently, from a supply side view. Such an interpretation would incorporate Say's Law and the quantity theory of money. Say's Law implies that production takes place to earn incomes and incomes are earned to be spent (either on consumption goods or investments). Therefore, there is no such thing as a general tendency for 'overproduction' or insufficient demand.[1] Aggregate supply and demand are not only equal ex post. They are also equal ex ante.[2] And unless there are supply side distortions, both are equal to the full employment income Y^*.

(12) $Y^D = Y^S$ *ex ante*
(13) $Y^D = Y^S = Y^*$

The quantity theory of money is closely related to Say's Law. This theory assumes that the velocity of money is relatively stable.

(14) $Y^D = v^* M$ (v^* being a stable function of a relatively small set of variables)

Monetary disturbances are therefore mainly traced back to money supply changes. Put differently, if the money supply is stable, it can be assumed that there will be no major monetary disturbances. Therefore, the quantity theory can help to justify the application of Say's Law in situations where monetary policy is relatively stable. This does not mean that one has to deny that there can be differences between aggregate demand and aggregate supply. However, these have to be traced back to monetary disturbances, changes in the money supply or money demand (hoarding or dishoarding). So, invoking Say's Law provides a kind of benchmark model. Deviations from this model, due to monetary disturbances, always have to be explained carefully.

---

[1]   The classical economists were well aware that there could be deviations from Say's law during the business cycle. But they considered this to be a short-run phenomenon which is not relevant in the medium or long run (Sowell 1974, pp. 33-66). Since the present study is not concerned with problems of the business cycle, this position is adopted. For a similar view see Sachs 1981, p. 215.

[2]   In the Keynesian model, there is also ex post equality of supply and demand because unemployment reduces supply to the (lower) demand level.

Coming back to equation (8), what would be a supply side interpretation? To answer this question, we have to incorporate equation (13) into equation (8) yielding equation (15):

(15) $Y^* = C + I + G + (Ex - Im)$

Aggregate income is assumed to be given, or better, is assumed to be determined by other factors, 'supply side factors'. In this case, changes in absorption or foreign net demand $(Ex-Im)$ do not affect income. As long as Say's Law applies, any change in absorption is exactly equal to changes in net exports (equation 17) , so that aggregate demand remains constant.

(16) $Y^* = C + I + G + (Ex-Im) = Y^D = A + (Ex-Im)$

For a given Y^* it follows that

(17) $dA = -d(Ex - Im) <=> dA = -d(CEx - CIm)$

Substituting the capital balance $(Cex - CIm)$ for the trade balance $(Ex - Im)$ in equation (16) and rearranging terms, yields equation (18):

(18) $Y^* + CIm - CEx = C + I + G$

This equation can be interpreted as the 'finance constraint' (Tsiang 1989) for an open economy. It implies that any excess of spending over full employment income must be financed by foreign borrowing and any shortfall of spending is due to net capital exports. Absorption is not interpreted as the sum of the supposedly independent variables C, I and G but is simply equal to income plus net borrowing.

This point leads us back to the intertemporal interpretation of current account balances. It shows that the usual assumption that current account surpluses have an expansionary effect on the economy while current account deficits are depressing national income is not compatible with a supply side model. In a world in which Say's Law holds current account surpluses simply reflect the fact that investment and/or government spending is less than would have been the case otherwise.[1] This becomes even more evident, when equation (19) and (15) are equated, yielding (20):

(19) $Y^* = C + S + T$

---

[1]   If savings are interest elastic, consumption as well is lower than would have been the case otherwise.

(20) $C + S + T = C + I + G + (Ex\text{-}Im)$[1]

Subtracting C from both side and rearranging we get

(21) $(S - I) + (T - G) = (Ex - Im)$

Equation (21) shows that a decline in absorption, due to rising savings or declining government deficits, will be offset by an increase in net exports. Equally, an increase in absorption, due to rising investment or increasing budget deficits, leads to a decline in net exports. This result follows from the finance constraint. If there are no hoarding/dishoarding activities or changes in the money supply, any increase in absorption has to be financed in the capital market and any decrease leads to an additional supply of funds.

d) Traded and non-traded goods and the real exchange rate
The preceding section presented an explanation of current account balances which focuses on individual intertemporal maximation. According to this approach, the capital account determines the current account. So far, it has been left open how the current account balance adjusts to the capital account balance. In a one good world, such an adjustment would be without complication. Since absorption is reduced in the capital exporting country by the amount of the capital export and increased in the capital importing country by an equal amount, the transfer of capital would be affected without any price or exchange rate changes being necessary. This is simply a restatement of one of the results of the debate about the transfer problem, where it was shown that a transfer will leave the terms of trade and the exchange rate (or alternatively reserves) unaffected, if the recipient of the transfer spends the money on those goods which are demanded in less quantities by the payer of the transfer.[2] The assumption that only one good exists ensures that just this is the case.

If there are two goods, the basic equations have to be modified. Absorption is still equal to income plus net capital imports. However, it is split now in demand for tradeables and demand for non-tradeables. Thus we get:

$$(22)\ Y + (Cim - Cex) = A = A_T + A_N$$
$$= (C_N + C_T) + (I_N + I_T) + (G_N + G_T)$$

Under this assumption, those goods which savers in A are willing to foresake and those goods which investors in B would like to buy do not necessarily have to be the same. Especially in a world in which non-traded goods exist, it is highly unlikely that the goods basket will be equal. Rather the reduction in demand in A will partly affect traded and partly non-traded goods. Similarily, the increase in consumption in B will partly be directed at non-traded goods. Therefore, it cannot be expected that the financial flow will be translated into a real flow at constant prices. Exchange rates (or reserves and correspondingly money supplies) and goods prices may have to change. The size of the necessary exchange rate change depends a) on the marginal propensity to consume traded goods, b) the flexibility of prices of traded and non-traded goods, c) the price elasticity of demand, d) the elasticity of supply. The latter two points are closely connected with the influence of time and will be elaborated further below.

In models with traded and non-traded goods the relative price between these two groups is of special importance. This relative price is known as the real exchange rate. However, this is not the only definition of the real exchange rate. In the literature different definitions of the real exchange rate can be found (Krugman and Obstfeld 1994, pp. 419-21, Edwards 1988, pp. 47-77). These definitions have in common that nominal exchange rate changes are corrected for price level changes. They differ, however, in the price indices which are used. On the one hand, indices are used which only include prices (or costs) in the tradeables sector. This is the case, for instance, in studies analysing 'price competitiveness'. On the other hand, broader price indices are used which include the prices of non-tradeables as well. Examples for the latter are consumer price indices or deflators of the national product. If a broad price index is used a real exchange rate change can also be interpreted as a change in the relative price of tradeables and non tradeables.[1] A real appreciation (depreciation) indicates a rise (decline) in the relative price of non tradeables. Unless explicitly stated differently, this latter definition of the real exchange rate will be used throughout the text.

e) Marshallian dynamics: the short run and the long run
During the last two decades, there have been large shifts in the net flows of capital and goods, often within very short periods. If such shifts are to be analysed, it is useful to distinguish between the short run and the long run.[2] The short run is characterized by a fixed size and structure of productive

---

[1]   A precise definition of the real exchange rate can be found, for instance, in Heitger 1983, pp. 8-10: $e_r = (Pt/Pn)^a/(Pt^*/Pn^*)^{a^*}$ with e_r: real exchange rate, Pt: price of tradeables, Pn price of non tradeables, a: share (in % of GDP) of non-tradeable goods, *: foreign variables. If the law of one price holds, changes in Pt and Pt^* are proportional. In this case, changes of the real exchange rate must be due to different price changes in the prices of non-tradeables.

[2]   This paragraph is based on Marshall 1920/1961, pp. 306-15.

capacity and given preferences. Therefore, in the short run prices may have to carry the main burden of adjustment. As time is passing, factors may be put to different uses, the capital stock may change due to investment in new plant and restructuring of the old equipment (Salter 1959, pp. 236-8, Meyer 1938). For example, when the OPEC reduced the supply of oil in 1973, world market prices were raising sharply. However, the higher prices intensified the search for oil and oil substitutes. Therefore, investments in these areas increased considerably. After a few years, these investments had the effect of increasing the oil supply (and the supply of substitutes) and reducing prices.

Similarily, it is also quite likely that the elasticity of substitution in demand is higher in the long run than in the short run (Stockman 1980, p. 691, Meyer 1938). Substitution in demand may also require investment. To use the oil price example again: when oil became more expensive people started to buy smaller or more energy efficient cars, they were investing in insulation, etc. Again, these investments were carried out over a certain period of time and affected the market price of oil only with a considerable lag.

If the initial shock is severe and the elasticity of substitution in production as well as in consumption is relatively low, prices will have to carry the main burden of adjustment and react strongly in the short run. As supply and demand adjust to the new conditions, prices slowly recede towards the initial level (however not all the way). So, in a way, the price 'overshoots' its long-run equilibrium level. As will be shown, such mechanisms are also at work when exchange rates are affected by monetary or real shocks.

To distinguish the short run from the long run, in the following it will be assumed that the short-run transformation curve for traded and non-traded goods is reduced to a point, so that the supply of tradeables and non-tradeables is fixed. In the longer run, however, substitution is possible and the transformation curve is represented by a concave slope.

f) Capital movements in a supply side model
In the preceding sections, we derived the determinants of the capital account (current account) from a simple intertemporal calculus and the open economy budget restraint. The principle determinants of the capital account which were derived are: human capital, capital, wealth, the age structure of the population and economic policy.

The factor which has received most attention in the literature so far is the capital stock (Siebert 1987). Since the marginal productivity is *ceteris paribus* high in capital-poor countries, it is argued that capital should flow from capital-rich to capital-poor countries. Such a net capital flow would help the capital-poor countries to catch up with the capital-rich countries. In this scenario capital would steadily flow between countries and adjustment would be smoothly spread out over decades (Siebert 1987). However, such capital flows have not been quantatively important in the last decades which were characterized by large capital movements between industrialized countries. To explain such flows, the age structure and the pension system seem to be more plausible candidates. Furthermore, given the rapid changes in capital and current account balances economic policy seems to have played a major role. Therefore, we do not focus on smoothly proceeding long-run phenomena such as catching up processes which may take decades. Instead, we are trying to analyse the repercussions of exogenous changes in the determinants of the capital account, such as economic policy measures and changes in the age structure.[1]

Our model consists of two capital markets, which determine net capital movements, the markets for tradeables and non-tradeables which determine the relative prices of tradeables and non-tradeables in both countries (the real exchange rate) and the money markets which determine the price level. Given the budget constraints for both countries, capital and goods market equilibrium implies foreign exchange market equilibrium with the nominal exchange rate given by the arbitrage condition $P_T = eP_T^*$.

Capital Markets:

(23) $I - S = CIm - CEx = f(r,r^*)$ local capital market[2]
(24) $I^* - S^* = CIm^* - CEx^* = f^*(r,r^*)$ foreign capital market

Goods Market:

(25) $N^S(P_T/P_N) = N^D(P_T/P_N;A)$ Local market for non-tradeables
(26) $N^{*S}(P_T^*/P_N^*) = N^{*D}(P_T^*/P_N^*;A^*)$ Foreign market for non-t.'s
(27) $T^S(P_T/P_N) + T^{*S}(P_T^*/P_N^*) = T^D(P_T/P_N;A) + T^{*D}(P_T^*/P_N^*;A^*)$
                                                 World market for tradeables

where

$N^S(N^{*S})$ is the supply of non-tradeables,
$N^D(N^{*D})$ the demand for non-tradeables,
$T^S(T^{*S})$ the supply of tradeables,
$T^D(T^{*D})$ the demand for tradeables.

---

[1]   Contrary to intuition, changes in age structure may take place within a few years. See Table 4.1.

[2]   Determinants of savings and investment are derived in section A.a) of this chapter and chapter 4 respectively.

Money Market:

$(28)\ PY = vM$ with $P = \alpha P_N + (1 - \alpha)P_T$

                        $<=>$ $P_T = (P - \alpha P_N)/(1 - \alpha)$

$(29)\ P^*Y^* = v^*M^*$ with $P^* = \beta P^*_N + (1 - \beta)P^*_T$

                        $<=>$ $P^*_T = (P^* - \beta P^*_N)/(1 - \beta)$

Budget constraints:

$(30)\ Y + CIm - CEx = A_N + A_T$

$(31)\ Y^* + CIm - CEx = A^*_N + A^*_T$

Foreign Exchange Market:

$$(32)\ T^S(P_T/P_N) - T^D(P_T/P_N;A) = CEx - Cim$$
$$= T^{*D}(P^*_T/P^*_N;A^*) - T^{*S}(P^*_T/P^*_N)$$

with

$$(33)\ e = P_T/P^*_T.$$

which, in combination with (28) and (29) yields (34)

$$(34)\ e = \frac{P}{P^*}\frac{1-\beta+\dfrac{\beta}{b}}{1-\alpha+\dfrac{\alpha}{a}}$$

with

$$a = P_T/P_N\ ,\ b = P^*_T/P^*_N$$

In the initial equilibrium, ex ante and ex post rates of return are assumed to be equal in both countries. Therefore, there are no net capital flows. In both countries the conditions for an intertemporal utility maximum are fulfilled. The market interest rate, which is the same for borrowers and lenders, is equal to the marginal rate of time preference of all individuals and to the marginal rate of return on investment. Since the effects of a rising capital stock on the capital account will not be analysed here, it is assumed that net savings and net investment are both zero. Exports are equal to imports and the law of one price holds (that is $P_T = eP^*_T$). In the goods markets of both countries the marginal rates of substitution between tradeables and non-tradeables in production and consumption are equal to the inverse of the relative price (Figure 2.6).

Figure 2.6:   Relative prices in autarky

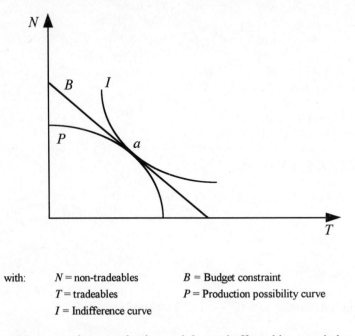

with: N = non-tradeables B = Budget constraint
          T = tradeables P = Production possibility curve
          I = Indifference curve

How are prices, production and demand affected by a capital movement? As has been shown in the first part of this chapter, net capital movements are determined in capital markets. Their size is a function of autarky rates of return. Capital flows from countries with low autarky rates of return to those with high autarky rates of return. These autarky rates of return are determined by time preference, the age structure, the stock of physical capital, wealth, income and economic policy. It is especially economic policy which can change abruptly and in a decisive way, affecting the relative scarcity of capital in a country. In the following, a shock will be assumed (for instance, a deregulation measure) which raises the autarky rate of return in the local economy relative to the foreign autarky rate of return. This causes a net capital inflow. A net capital flow raises absorption (equation 22) by an equal amount.

$$(22)\ Y + (Cim - Cex) = A = A_T + A_N$$
$$= (C_N + C_T) + (I_N + I_T) + (G_N + G_T)$$

A rise in absorption may increase the demand for tradeables and non-tradeables in equal proportions (iso-elastic demand; I_1 in Figure 2.7). The demand for tradeables may rise stronger than the demand for non-tradeables

(I_1'') or the demand for non-tradeables stronger than the demand for tradeables. Finally, there is the possibility that one of the goods is inferior so that demand declines in absolute terms (I_2 illustrates the case of traded goods being inferior). As long as non-tradeables are not inferior goods, an increase in capital imports will therefore always imply an excess demand for non-tradeables. The opposite is true for the lending country. An increase in capital exports, financed by less spending at home, will always lead to an excess supply, unless non-tradeables are inferior goods. If we interpret tradeables and non-tradeables as wide baskets of goods, it is extremely unlikely that demand for one of the baskets declines with rising absorption.

Figure 2.7: Capital movements and the structure of demand

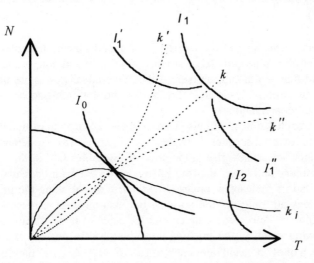

Therefore, in the following, it will be assumed that any increase in absorption increases the demand for both goods and any decrease reduces it for both alike.

(35) $dA_N/dA > 0$

If capital flows increase the demand for non-tradeables in the receiving country and reduce it in the demand of the lending country, capital movements affect the goods market in both countries. With the supply fixed in the short run and dA_N/dA positive there is an excess demand for non-tradeables in the local country (36)

(36) $N^S(P_T/P_N) < N^D(P_T/P_N; A)$

and an excess supply of non-tradeables in the foreign country (37).

(37) $N^{*S}(P^*_T/P^*_N) > N^{*D}(P^*_T/P^*_N; A^*)$

This causes changes in the relative price of tradeables and non-tradeables. In the receiving country non-tradeables get relatively more expensive and in the lending country they get relatively cheaper. Thus, given that a capital inflow increases the demand for non-tradeables and a capital outflow reduces the demand for tradeables, a capital inflow lowers the relative price of tradeables, that is causes a real depreciation.

(38) $\dfrac{d\left(\dfrac{P_T}{P_N}\right)}{dA} < 0$

Depending on the size of the increase in demand for non-tradeables the real appreciation can be quite large or close to zero. In addition, it has to be kept in mind that – although unlikely – it is theoretically possible that an increase in absorption leads to a lower demand for non-tradeables and hence to a real depreciation.

Usually, a capital inflow will also lead to higher absorption of tradeables, an outflow to lower absorption of tradeables. However, raising demand for tradeables does not cause a rise in the price of tradeables (P_T) in the capital importing country and lower demand in the capital exporting country does not cause a fall of tradeables' prices (P^*_T) there. For one thing the price of tradeables does not only depend on local but also on foreign demand and supply conditions. And second, given that the price of non-tradeables rises in the receiving country, the price of tradeables has to decline, if money supply and money demand are unchanged[1] ($P_T \downarrow$). And in the lending country the price of tradeables has to rise ($P^*_T \uparrow$) because in this country the price of non-tradeables falls. Such a simultaneous rise and decline in the price of tradeables can only be brought about by a change of the exchange rate.

The same result can be derived with the help of the equilibrium condition for the foreign exchange market. In equilibrium, the net capital import has to be equal to net imports. If the net capital import is ex ante smaller than the net import of goods, there is an excess demand for local currency and the exchange rate appreciates. Consequently, tradeables are becoming

---

[1]   Alternatively, it could be assumed that monetary policy holds the price level constant, neutralizing any effects of money demand changes on the price level.

cheaper in the capital importing country and more expensive in the capital exporting country. This stimulates demand for tradeables in the capital importing country and reduces the demand for tradeables in the other country. The excess demand for local currency is reduced to zero when the exchange rate has appreciated sufficiently to adjust the trade flow to the capital flow.

$$(32)\ T^S(P_T/P_N) - T^D(P_T/P_N;A) = CEx - Cim$$
$$= T^{*D}(P^*_T/P^*_N;A^*) - T^{*S}(P^*_T/P^*_N)$$

If production is fixed in the short run, these price changes will be relatively large in the short run. As time passes, factors will be moved into other sectors, adjusting the structure of supply to the structure of demand. Therefore, in the longer run, part of the price adjustment is reversed. If tradeables and non-tradeables were perfect substitutes in supply in the longer run, the old price structure would be restored. If substitutability is not perfect, that is, if the transformation curve is concave, the initial price changes will only be partly reversed.[1]

So far, we assumed that the balance on capital account is determined in capital markets without taking exchange rate expectations into account. Once exchange rate expectations are introduced, changes in the spot rate may affect the expected rate of change and therefore relative rates of return of local and foreign investments. For instance, if it is true that rising capital imports lead to a strong appreciation in the short run which is partly reversed in the long run, capital movements would be reduced because the initial appreciation would trigger the expectation of future depreciations (compare the part on the J-curve effect in the chapter 2.I.B).

Yet, we choose not to incorporate exchange rate expectations in the model. For one thing, including exchange rate expectations would not fundamentally alter the results. Introducing rational expectations would simply lead to smaller capital flows and less exchange rate volatility. More fundamentally, we think that our model shows how difficult it is to form reliable exchange rate expectations. If our model catches some important traits of reality, the exchange rate effect of capital movements depends on the marginal propensity to buy tradeables and the marginal rate of substitution in the production of tradeables and non-tradeables. Both, figures may vary over time and are hardly observable. Furthermore, when capital flows do not change once and for all, but are volatile, adjustments to various shocks are overlapping, making the prediction of exchange rates nearly impossible. Finally, the behaviour of foreign investors during the rise and decline of the dollar during the 1980s suggests that investors' exchange

---

[1]   In the long run, as foreign wealth accumulates and foreign interest receipts are rising, the exchange rate will appreciate further. See Figure 2.8.

rate expectations were not significantly influenced by movements of the spot rate. In spite of the immense appreciation, the interest rate differenial between the United States and, say, Germany remained fairly constant (compare case study USA).

Figure 2.8:   Short-run and long-run effects of a capital outflow

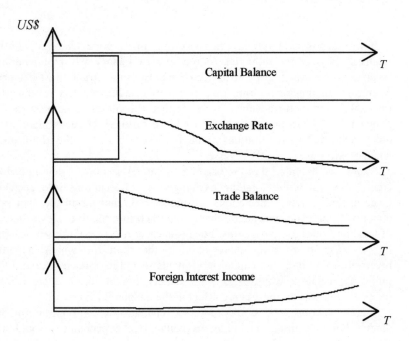

B. The Adjustment under Flexible Exchange Rates

In the following, the working of the model will be demonstrated for a number of shocks. The purpose of this exercise is twofold. For one thing, to fully understand and evaluate the model, it has to be shown how it describes the adjustment in the case of various shocks. Second, it helps to highlight the differences to the competitiveness approach. Consequently, not only those shocks will be examined which are causing changes in the balance on current account in intertemporal models, but also those which according to the competitiveness approach affect the current account. Furthermore, the model will be extended to include monetary shocks and it will also be applied to a fixed exchange rate system.

The effects of four different shocks will be analysed in a two country setting using the well-known Salter diagram (Salter 1959). The two countries are labelled 'United States' and 'Germany'. There are three goods: a non-traded good in each country (N and N^*) and an internationally traded good (T), which is produced and consumed in both countries. The D-Mark and the dollar price of the traded good are tied together by the law of one price ($P_{TDM} = eP_{T\$}$).

The following shocks will be analysed below:

- an increase in the marginal efficiency of capital
- a demand shift towards traded goods
  - with given savings (given time preference)
  - with reduced savings (increased time preference)
- an increase of the money supply.

a) Adjustment in the case of a rise in the marginal efficiency of capital
Initially, the current account is assumed to be balanced.[1] Aggregate income equals aggregate spending (point *a* in Figure 2.6):

$$(39)\ Y = (C_N + C_T) + (I_N + I_T) + (G_N + G_T)\ \text{and}\ Ex - Im = Cim - CEx = 0$$

A rise in the marginal efficiency of capital in the home country (US) relative to the foreign country (Germany) implies that expected returns of investment in the US are relatively higher. If capital flows are unrestricted, this will lead to an inflow of capital. Such a net capital inflow enables the Americans to spend more than their income (shift from *a* to *b*).[2]

$$(22')\ Y + (Cim - CEx) = (C_N + C_T) + (I_N + I_T) + (G_N + G_T)$$
$$= A_T + A_N$$

Germans can increase their net capital exports only if their demand for investment and consumer goods declines, that is when th0ey spend less than their income. Therefore, German demand for traded and non-traded goods declines.

$$(40)\ Y^* + (Cim^* - Cex^*) = (C^*_N + C^*_T) + (I^*_N + I^*_T) + (G^*_N + G^*_T)$$
$$= A^*_T + A^*_N$$

---

[1]   In the following, it will be assumed that initially the net foreign asset position is zero so that there are no receipts on foreign assets. International transfer payments will also be assumed to be zero. Therefore, the balance on current account is equal to the balance of trade and services.

[2]   This is sometimes refered to as 'living above their means'.

Thus, the foreign exchange market is effected in two ways by the net capital import. First, the demand for dollar rises, because of the capital inflow. Second, since part (or all) of the capital import is spend for imports the D-Mark demand (dollar supply) is rising as well. Foreign exchange market equilibrium is given by:

(41) $Ex(P_T/P_N, A) + CIm = Im(P_T/P_N, A) + CEx$

Figure 2.9:   Short-run adjustment in the case of a capital inflow

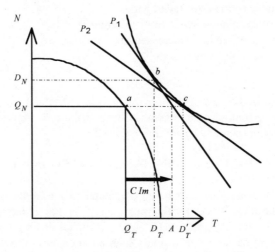

If the Americans wish to buy the same goods which the Germans used to buy before they increased their capital exports the exchange rate will not be affected by the capital flow to the US. This would be the case when the propensity to import is equal to one. Germans would only reduce their demand for traded goods and Americans would only increase the demand for traded goods. Under this assumption, the increased demand for dollars by German capital exporters would be met by an increased supply of dollars by American goods importers (Meyer 1938, p. 135, Samuelson 1980).

It is fairly safe to assume, however, that a shift of purchasing power from Germany to the US will also affect the structure of world demand. It is highly plausible that the marginal propensity to import is lower than one, so that Americans will also demand more non-traded goods. In this case, the increase in the demand for traded goods $(D_T - Q_T)$ is smaller than the net capital import $(A - Q_T)$. At the existing exchange rate their is an excess demand for dollars. The dollar demand of German capital exporters is higher than the dollar supply of American goods importers. At the same time there is an excess demand for American non-tradeables (D_N - Q_N) and excess supply of German non-tradeables. Therefore, the dollar is appreciating, the price of American non-tradeables is raising (the combined effect is mirrored by the shift from P_1 to P_2) and the price of German non-tradeables is falling. Taken together, this implies a real appreciation of the dollar. The magnitude of the appreciation depends on the income and the price elasticity of American and German demand for traded goods.

In the longer run, not only demand elasticities are important, but also supply elasticities. Resources will be diverted from the tradeables to the non-tradeables sector (shift from a to e in Figure 2.10) if the relative price of non-traded goods rises in the US (Ohr 1991, p. 108). This is mirrored by a shift in opposite direction in Germany, where resources are shifted into the tradeables sector. However, these adjustments usually require a certain amount of time.[1] The faster the resource shift and the higher the elasticity of demand are, the smaller will be the exchange rate effect of a capital movement. If demand is inelastic and the structure of supply relatively rigid the dollar appreciation has to be relatively strong to restore equilibrium in the foreign exchange market. In any case, the exchange rate will adjust sufficiently to bring about the real transfer which corresponds to the net capital import.

Notabene, although the appreciation of the dollar in this example is caused by a capital inflow, it does not occur independently of goods markets. Similarly, it does not cause 'distortions'. Quite the contrary: it guides the goods flows which have to follow the capital flows. As Sievert put it: 'International money lending is always at the same time international goods lending' (Sievert 1986, p. 338, our translation). As a rule, Americans do not borrow abroad to hold (hoard) additional foreign money. They are borrowing in order to buy more goods. Net borrowing allows them to spend more than the national income. The additional spending becomes visible in a current account deficit. Therefore, the claim that a current account deficit reduces the demand for local goods, is unjustified.

For American exporters, however, such a real appreciation must appear to be an unwarranted disadvantage, distorting their international competitiveness – a view which is often shared by economists. They interpret the real appreciation as an exogenous event, which weakens the competitive position of exporters and thus 'causes' a current account deficit. This view is not very convincing, however, because it leaves the question unanswered why foreigners should finance the deficit and why the exchange rate appreciated in the first place. It is not the exchange rate

---

[1]   If there are idle resources or above average stocks in the non-tradeables sector, these resources can be employed and the stocks are depleted before resources have to be shifted out of the tradeables sector. In this case, the price of non-tradeables would rise less and the nominal appreciation would have to be stronger to bring about the required real appreciation.

which autonomously influences international competitiveness. Rather, the opposite is true. As has been shown, in the case of a net capital import the appreciation of the dollar has to be the higher, the higher the share of American goods in the demand function of the capital importers is. This share tends to increase with rising competitiveness of American firms. But the exchange rate adjusts always enough to bring about the necessary adjustment of demand and supply. The tradeables sector cannot escape the necessity to adjust. Trade policy, like export subsidies and import restrictions, do not effect the necessity to relocate the national resources.

Figure 2.10:   Long-run adjustment in the case of a capital inflow

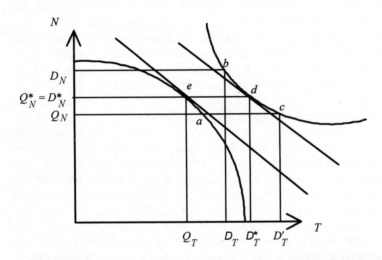

In the case considered in this paragraph, exchange rate changes are not the cause of real adjustments in the economy. Rather, they are the symptom of an exogenous change of some fundamental variable. If the described real adjustments are politically undesired, it will not be very helpful to make the exchange rate the target of economic policy. For this would be about as helpful as manipulating the thermometer when one does not like the weather. Attempts to lower the American deficit on current account by 'talking down the dollar' are therefore bound to fail.[1] More to the point, although not necessarily recommendable, are the following measures: reduction of the federal deficit, promotion of individual saving,

---

[1]   As could be witnessed in 1994, such an attempt may reduce the international reputation of the US-dollar and thus lead to higher interest rates. To the extent that higher interest rates curb net borrowing, 'talking down the dollar' may have an indirect effect on the balance on current account, albeit at a price (higher interest rates), which was hardly anticipated.

discouragement of investment. Such measures would reduce the inflow of foreign capital and thus the current account deficit. However, the question remains, whether this would be good for the US.

As adjustment proceeds in the US towards higher production of non–traded and lower production of traded goods (adjustment in Germany mirrors this process) the real appreciation of the dollar slows down. The restructuring of the American production leads to a (relative or absolute) decline of capacities in the tradeables' sector. This causes the import demand curve to shift outwards. At the same time restructuring in Germany increases capacities in the tradeables' sector. Therefore, export supply is rising. This implies that the demand for D-Marks is rising and the demand for dollars is falling. Even if the capital inflow is sustained, the dollar appreciation will eventually come to a halt and finally be reversed.

This process is reinforced by adjustments on the demand side. Since the elasticity of demand (in absolute terms) is higher in the long run than in the short run, the exchange rate change which is required to redirect demand becomes smaller over time (Stockman 1980, p. 691). However, it cannot be expected that the exchange rate will fall back on its initial level. This would be the case only if tradeables and non–tradeables were perfect substitutes in the production.[1] The real depreciation which follows the initial appreciation shows that adjustment is under way. The declining presence of American firms in the tradeables sector causes the real depreciation. In this stage, exchange rate changes are driven by real adjustments.

Once again: if the US becomes a net capital importer, there will be an initial appreciation and a subsequent depreciation. The reason for this pattern lies in the fact that the adjustment of supply and demand in goods markets require a certain period of time. If supply and demand are inelastic in the short run, a comparatively strong real appreciation is required. The more the adjustment processes are completed, the more becomes the initial appreciation superfluous and the dollar depreciates. The transitory real appreciation can be interpreted as a kind of 'transfer–bridge' which facilitates the goods transfer following the capital transfer.

The exchange rate of the dollar in the 1980s is a case in point (Hoffmann and Homburg 1990). In the early 1980s, the US experienced a radical change in economic policy. Taxes were lowered and a number of deregulation measures were passed. This raised the marginal efficiency of capital. At the same time, public capital demand rose to cover the raising budget deficits. Both factors caused capital inflows to rise. The US became a net importer of capital and the US current account turned into deficit. At the same time the dollar appreciated considerably. Many economists and politicians were concerned about this development and blamed the dollar

---

[1]   In this case the transformation curve between tradeables and non-tradeables would be a straight line. See Hoffmann and Homburg 1990, p. 63.

appreciation for the current account deficit. The dollar appreciation was interpreted as a phenomenon which independently influenced the competitiveness of the US economy. However, this interpretation cannot explain why the dollar appreciated and why foreigners invested large amounts of capital in the US.[1] It is simply assumed that the current account deficit was somehow 'financed'. Therefore, this explanation is not convincing. Rather, the current account deficit should be traced back to the capital inflows which were caused by changes in economic policy. The real appreciation of the dollar was just a part of the adjustment process as has been described above.

A closer look shows that the actual pattern of the balance of payments and the exchange rate developments conform to the pattern which was derived theoretically. In the years 1982-84, net capital imports rose strongly and the current account turned passive. Simultaneously, the dollar appreciated in nominal and real terms. In the following years net capital imports and current account deficits remained on a relatively high level. However, the dollar did not continue to appreciate. From 1985 to 1987, it depreciated considerably (see case study USA).

b) Adjustment in the case of a rising import demand and constant saving
In the competitiveness approach, current account balances are traced back to demand changes, supply changes or protectionist measures. Using the example of a demand shift in a two country world, in the following paragraph it will be analysed how such changes affect the current account. At first, saving, investment and consumption will be held constant. Consumers in the US simply shift from non-traded to traded goods. Since locally produced and foreign produced goods are perfect substitutes, such a shift is equal to an increased demand for imports.

Initially, the current account is assumed to be balanced (point *a* in Figure 2.11). A rise in the demand for traded goods (shift from I_0 to I_1), leads to an excess demand for traded goods in the US market ($W_T - T_0$) and to an excess demand for D-Marks. Consequently, the dollar price of traded goods is rising and the dollar is depreciating (movement from P_0 to P_1). In addition, the price for non traded goods in the US is falling because there is an excess supply ($N_0 - W_N$).[2]

---

[1]   The claim that the dollar depreciation was due to a portfolio shift in favour of dollar assets (Frankel and Froot 1986, Bordo and Schwartz 1989, p. 251) is not very convincing because in the period discussed US interest rates were substantially higher than in most important surplus countries (Japan and Germany). An exogenous shift out of Japanese and German assets would have raised interest rates in these countries relative to US interest rates. For a similar conclusion see Branson 1985, pp. 146-7.

[2]   Germany, on the other hand, is not affected. The exchange rate change and the change of the dollar price of the traded goods are offsetting, keeping the D-Mark price constant.

Figure 2.11:   Adjustment in the case of a demand shift

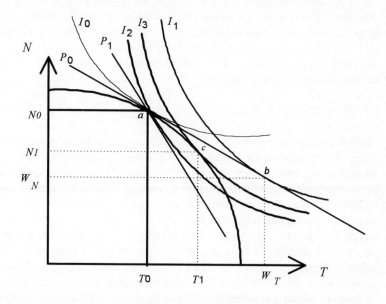

In the short run, the supply of traded and non-traded goods is fixed and the transformation curve is given by $N_0/a/T_0$. Therefore, adjustment can be brought about by price changes only. The price movements persist until the demand for traded goods in America is sufficiently reduced to match the supply. The short-run equilibrium remains in point *a* where the indifference curve I_2 touches the transformation curve. Compared to the initial equilibrium only the relative price of tradeables and non-tradeables (the real exchange rate) has been changing.

But in the long run, factor shifts between sectors are possible and the transformation curve has the usual form, known from the text books. The relative price change in the US will also trigger supply responses. These require some time, however. Due to the demand shift and the depreciation, the relative price of tradeables has increased. The dollar has depreciated in real terms. Therefore, resources from the non-tradeables sector will be directed towards the tradeables sector. The supply of tradeables (i.e. goods which compete with imports and can be exported) rises and the supply of non-tradeables declines (shift from *a* to *c*). This reduces import demand and raises exports. Both factors in turn lead to an appreciation of the dollar.[1]

---

[1]   The long-run equilibrium price is given by the slope of the tangent in c. This slope lies between the the initial price P_0 and the slope of P_1. To keep the diagram manageable this slope has been omitted.

Again, there is a pattern of short-run exchange rate adjustment which is partly reversed in the longer run.

If the capital account is balanced and not affected by the shift in the structure of consumer spending, the exchange rate will always adjust to keep the current account balanced. Unlike in fixed exchange rate regimes, there is no mechanism which provides automatic financing for desired current account deficits.[1] If there are no net capital imports goods, imports have to be paid by goods exports.

c) Adjustment in the case of a rising import demand and a reduction in
   saving

Shifting consumer spending from non-traded goods to traded goods does not effect the balance on current account. However, if Americans reduce their savings to buy more goods, this result may not hold any more. A reduction in savings will cause interest rates to rise, if investment demand is not reduced by the same amount. Foreign capital is attracted and the US becomes a net capital importer.[2] Just as in the first example (increase of the marginal efficiency of capital), the exchange rate reaction depends on the structure of demand. If the additional demand which is financed by capital imports leads to a higher demand for non-traded goods, the dollar will appreciate. In this case, the dollar has to appreciate until the dollar demand of foreign capital exporters is matched by the dollar supply of additional American goods importers, that is until the net capital import is equal to a current account deficit. The appreciation causes further adjustment of supply and demand in both countries, as has been described above.

At this point, the question may be raised, whether the last example confirms the thesis that the capital account determines the current account. After all, it was a rise in the demand for foreign goods which ultimately caused a net capital inflow and a current account deficit. Therefore, it might be stated that in this case the current account determined the capital account. This interpretation, however, does not take into account the various alternatives. If Americans wish to consume more foreign goods, they have various options to 'finance' the purchase of these goods. As has been shown, more consumption of foreign goods can be financed by a reduction in the consumption of local goods. Another possibility would be to work more and raise incomes in order to be able to buy more foreign

---

[1]   If investors are speculating on reversals of exchange rate changes there exists a kind of financing mechanism. Compare the paragraph about the J-curve effect in chapter 2.I.B.

[2]   If the foreign capital supply is completely elastic there will be no interest rate rise and no reduction of investment. However, it is questionable whether foreign capital will be as readily available in the case of rising consumption as in the case of a rise in the marginal productivity of capital. Therefore, it seems likely that the capital supply is not completely elastic, even for a small country and that interest rates will rise and investment will decline. In this case the net capital import and the increase in overall demand will be smaller (Dluhosch 1993).

goods. A reduction of saving or increase of debts is a conscious decision against the other two possibilities. It is a decision for more consumption today and less tomorrow.

d) Adjustment after an increase of the money supply
So far, only real shocks have been analysed. An increase in the money supply is a monetary shock. Accordingly, the accounting identities of part B of this chapter have to be modified.

$$(20') \ S + T + dM = I + G + H$$

with H = net hoarding.

In addition to savings and taxes, money becomes another source to finance expenditures. In case of a monetary shock, adjustment could be brought about by instantaneous price changes. Real variables would be unaffected and money would be neutral. However, prices usually do not adjust instantaneously and money supply shocks cannot be treated as random events.[1] In the real world money is not distributed via helicopter but enters the economy in the form of additional credits. Therefore, monetary shocks are likely to have real effects, at least transitory.[2]

There is no clear cut relationship between money supply increases and the balance on current account. The results which can be derived theoretically depend on the underlying assumptions. Results may also vary with the length of the observed period. It will not be attempted to give a detailed account of all the possible outcomes of a money supply increase.

If the money supply is increased in the US the additional money can be used either:

– for the purchase of goods and services or
– for the purchase of assets.

The former will be the case, if, for example, the Fed finances increased government spending (Bordo and Schwartz 1989). The latter can be expected when the Fed lowers interest rates unexpectedly. These two possibilities are not mutually exclusive. They usually occur together. But in order to show the different consequences, they will be analysed separately.

---

[1]   Fellner 1982 and Haberler 1980 criticize the idea that there exists a clear division between 'systematic factors' which can be anticipated and 'random factors' which cannot be anticipated. Monetary policy is a case in point. Time and again, measures of the central banks seem to be something like an 'expected surprise'.

[2]   Long-run neutrality of money is emphasized by proponents of the monetary approach to the balance of payments. But they are prepared to admit that money does have short-run real effects. See for instance Blejer and Frenkel 1987, Bordo and Schwartz 1989.

The first case can be considered as the 'standard case'. Economic agents use the additional money to purchase more goods. If the additional purchases include foreign goods the demand for foreign exchange increases and the local currency depreciates. If the determinants of capital movements are unaffected by the money supply increase (admittedly a big 'if') or if capital is internationally immobile, the depreciation will keep the current account balance constant. In this case, money would not affect the current account balance. Whether or not the structure of production (traded vs. non-traded goods) will be affected depends on the relative speed of price adjustment. If the prices for traded goods adjust faster – due to exchange rate changes – there is an incentive to switch production towards traded goods. In the long run, however, the structure of production is not affected.

If capital is internationally immobile, local individuals can only buy local assets. In this case local interest rates will decline. The balance of payments and the exchange rate are not directly affected. However, as soon as the asset sellers spend their earnings, the same results appear as in the case above. If capital is internationally mobile local individuals will not only buy local but also foreign assets. This leads to a net capital export. The net capital export causes a surplus on current account and a depreciation.[1] The higher the degree of capital mobility is, the larger will be the capital outflow and the smaller will be the effect on local interest rates. Under perfect capital mobility there will be no interest rate reduction of the home country. In any case, however, money supply increases will cause a current account surplus if capital is internationally mobile. This outflow will be accompanied by a real depreciation. Prices in traded goods will rise strongly and resources will be shifted into the tradeables sector.

This effect is not permanent, though. Due to the increased money supply and the depreciation local prices have to rise. A rising price-level reduces the real money supply. This causes a tendency towards higher interest rates, which reduces the capital export and the current account surplus. In the long run, these will fall back on their initial levels. The exchange rate depreciation and the price level increase will remain.[2]

Finally, there is the possibility that a money supply increase triggers expectations of higher inflation. If this is the case individuals will try to avoid losses due to inflation. Foreign assets are a possible shelter against

---

[1]   In this example, there will be a depreciation in any case because the net capital export is not financed by a reduction of local demand, but by an increase in the supply of money.

[2]   Many variants of this case can be found in the literature, for instance the famous 'overshooting-model' by Dornbusch or the Mundell–Fleming model. See Mundell 1968 and Dornbusch 1976. It would take too much space to give a thorough analysis of these models. But it should be mentioned that the main difference between the Dornbusch model and this model lies in the assumptions regarding interest rate determination. Dornbusch assumes, like most other macroeconomists, that interest rates are determined in the money market and can be set by central banks. In this text, however, the interest rate is assumed to be determined in capital markets.

local inflation. Therefore, it can be expected that most or all of the additional money will be used to purchase foreign assets. In addition, individuals will try to reduce their holdings of local bonds and shift into foreign bonds.[1] In this case, the money supply increase causes a net capital export and an interest rate increase. Once again, the net capital export is equal to the current account surplus, and the local currency depreciates. In the long run, the current account and the capital account should fall back on their initial positions.

Although the consequences of a money supply increase depend on the underlying assumptions, the effects on the current account are always the same: in flexible exchange rate systems an increase of the money supply either does not affect the current account or leads to current account surpluses. The increased demand for foreign goods is always neutralized by exchange rate adjustments.

C. Adjustment in Fixed Exchange Rate Systems

In a pure system of fixed exchange rates the nominal exchange rate is permanently fixed. Therefore, nominal exchange rate changes are not part of adjustment processes. This does not mean that there are no real exchange rate changes. It is not possible to fix the real exchange rate simply by fixing the nominal exchange rate. In the long run, in a fixed exchange rate system the capital account balance matches the current account balance, just like in flexible exchange rate systems. In the short run, there is not such a tight relationship, however. If central banks intervene in the foreign exchange market to defend the existing parity the balance on capital account will differ from the balance on current account.

(42) $Ex - Im = Cex - CIm + dR$ with dR = increase in foreign reserves

Therefore, equations 15 and 18 have to be modified:

(18') $Y + (Cim - CEx) = C + I + G + dR$
(15') $Y - dR = C + I + G + (Im - Ex) = A$ in case of $(CEx - CIm) = 0$

Net capital imports which are not spend on foreign goods lead to an increase in international reserves (18'). Similarily, absorption can be increased above income – even if net capital flows are zero –, if reserves are reduced (15'). In this case dR is negative and $-dR$ is positive.

---

[1]   Of course, this is not possible for the group of investors as a whole. An investor can only sell an asset if another buys it. Therefore, only gross savings are available for capital exports. See Stützel 1978, p. 135, note 1.

But in the long run, it is still true that a net capital transfer induces a net goods transfer, that is a current account surplus. As in the preceding paragraph, four different shocks will be discussed:

- an increase in the marginal efficiency of capital
- a demand shift from traded to non-traded goods
    - with constant savings (constant time preference)
    - with declining savings (rising time preference)
- an increase of the money supply.

a) Adjustment in the case of a rise in the marginal efficiency of capital[1]
Once again, the capital account and the current account are assumed to be balanced. If the marginal efficiency of capital increases in the US, the demand for dollars will increase stronger than the supply of dollars, just like in a flexible exchange rate system. Supply and demand will increase by equal amounts only if capital imports are used exactly in the same way as before. If this is not the case and capital importers plan to spend a higher proportion on non-traded goods in the US, there will be an excess demand for dollars (excess supply of D-Marks). In this case the central bank has to intervene and purchase the excess supply of D-Marks. Thus, the current account deficit is smaller than the net capital import, the difference being equal to an increase in foreign reserves. The change in foreign reserves, in turn, is equal to a change in the money supply.

In contrast to a system of flexible exchange rates, there is no mechanism which ensures that the financial transfer (net capital import) is always equal to the real transfer (current account deficit). The adjustment of the capital account to the current account requires time. As in a flexible exchange rate system, adjustment is brought about by a real appreciation. But since the nominal exchange rate is fixed, a real appreciation is due to a rise in the price of non-tradeables. This price rise is caused by the increase of the money supply. If the relative price of non-tradeables rises, higher factor income in the non-tradeables sector will be the result and factors will be shifted from the tradeables to the non-tradeables sector. The supply of non-tradeables is increased and the supply of American tradeables is reduced. American demand for tradeables depends more and more on foreign supplies. This leads to an increased demand for D-Marks, and the excess demand for dollars declines. The central bank has to purchase less D-Marks and the expansion of the money supply is reduced. The whole process continues until the net capital import is matched by a current account deficit – just like in a flexible exchange rate system.

---

[1]   Using the case of Switzerland and Spain, these processes are analysed in some detail in Willgerodt 1964 and Dluhosch and Krüger 1991.

Spain provides a good example for the adjustment process just described (see case study Spain). Economic reforms and the entrance into the EMS led to a large increase in capital inflows. This led to increasing current account deficits and an increase in foreign reserves. As a result money supply increases could not be reduced as much as desired. Inflation remained above EMS average. The Spanish peseta appreciated in real terms.

Real adjustment processes in a fixed exchange rate system are quite similar to those in a flexible exchange rate system. By fixing the nominal exchange rate the competitiveness of the tradeables sector in the capital importing country cannot be preserved. Under flexible exchange rates competitiveness is eroded by a nominal appreciation, whereas under fixed exchange rates it is eroded by increased competitiveness of the non-tradeables sector which bids factor prices up. In both cases the non-tradeables sector grows at the cost of the tradeables sector.[1] This is brought about by a decline in the price of tradeables (flexible exchange rates) or the increase of the price of non-tradeables (fixed exchange rates).

b) A demand shift from non-traded to traded goods (constant savings)
If, starting from a balanced capital and current account, Americans are demanding more traded goods, the central bank has to sell D-Marks to stabilize the exchange rate. In a system with flexible exchange rates, a depreciation of the dollar would keep the current account balanced. However, in a fixed exchange rate system an increased import demand can cause a current account deficit because of the intervention mechanism. But this is possible only to a limited degree. First, central bank reserves are limited. And second, central bank sales of D-Marks lead to a reduction of the money supply in the US. This in turn reduces demand – including demand for imports. If intervention duties are symmetric, the money supply in Germany will be increased at the same time, raising demand in Germany. In addition, there will be a change of relative prices. Due to the initial reduction in demand for local goods and the effects of a reduction in the money supply, non–tradeables will become relatively cheaper in America. Therefore, resources are shifted into the tradeables sector and the supply of export goods and import substitutes rises.

This process is mirrored by the situation in Germany. There the increased money supply leads to an increase of the prices for non–tradeables, and resources are shifted into the non–tradeables sector. These adjustment processes in both countries continue until the current account is balanced and central bank intervention ceases. If demand elasticities are low and supply structures are rigid, central banks have to intervene with large amounts and changes in the money supply will be correspondingly high.

---

[1]   In a growing economy the tradeables sector does not necessarily have to shrink. A reduction of the growth rate may usually be enough.

This would lead to relatively large price changes and real appreciations or depreciations. High elasticities in supply and demand, on the other hand, would facilitate a rather smooth adjustment.

c) A demand shift from non–traded to traded goods (reduced savings)
Just like in the analysis of a flexible exchange rate system a change in the consumption pattern has to be distinguished from an increase of consumption which is financed by lower savings. If investment demand is unchanged, lower savings will induce a capital import. Whether or not this is accompanied by an increase of foreign reserves and a monetary expansion depends on the structure of demand. If the rise in consumer spending is directed exclusively towards tradeables higher capital imports are matched by higher goods imports and the exchange market stays balanced. Interventions by central banks are unnecessary. If, however, part of the additional demand is directed towards non-tradeables, the additional import demand is smaller than the capital import, and there will be an excess demand for dollars. The central bank has to sell dollars, thus increasing the money supply. This will lead to further adjustments, as described above. In the end, the net capital import will be matched by a current account deficit.

d) Adjustment after an increase in the money supply
Just like in a flexible exchange rate system, additional money can be used:

– for the purchase of goods, or
– the purchase of assets.

If individuals use the additional money to purchase more goods, demand for traded and non-traded goods alike is increasing. An increase in the demand for non-traded goods causes prices to rise. An increased demand for traded goods causes a current account deficit immediately because part of the additional demand will be directed at foreign goods.[1] This current account deficit is financed by the central bank which has to sell the necessary amount of foreign exchange to protect the exchange rate. Thereby, part of the monetary expansion is reduced. If the foreign central bank has to intervene as well, the foreign money supply is increased. The structure of production will be affected only to the extent that price increases for traded and non–traded goods differ. The contractionary effect of the interventions on the local money supply and the expansionary effect on the foreign money supply serve to reduce the current account deficit.

---

[1]   Often, it is assumed that a precondition for the deficit is a rise in the local price level relative to the foreign price level. This assumption is criticized by Meyer 1938 and Samuelson 1980 who show that the price of traded goods is rising in both countries simultaneously.

The adjustment processes come to an end when the current account is balanced and the additional money has been divided between both countries – with the effect of a higher price level in both countries.

If the monetary expansion leads to an increased demand for assets, there will be tendency for local interest rates to fall. Since local and foreign assets can be assumed to be nearly perfect substitutes in a fixed exchange rate system an immediate capital export will be the result. Normally, this will lead to a reduction of central bank reserves, partly offsetting the money supply increase. In the foreign country, interventions lead to an increase of reserves and the money supply. Thus, in this case monetary expansion is equalised in both countries by capital movements. This shows that in a fixed exchange rate system money supply shocks can be transmitted from one country to the other, without significantly changing the balance on current account.

Usually, an increase in the money supply will lead to higher goods demand as well as higher asset demand. In an open economy this leads to additional demand for foreign goods and assets. Goods imports and capital exports both increase at the same time and there will be a current account deficit and a net capital export, a constellation which is possible only in fixed exchange rate systems. As a consequence, there will be a marked reduction of reserves of the local central bank and a strong increase in reserves of the foreign central bank. The monetary change is transmitted rapidly to the foreign country.

E. Conclusions

In a flexible exchange rate system the current account is determined by the capital account. Exchange rate changes play an important role in facilitating adjustment of the current account to the capital account. The necessary adjustments of the real and/or nominal exchange rate can be considerably large. Due to the wide variety of possible shocks, there is no clear-cut relationship between exchange rate changes and the current account. Large exchange rate fluctuations may be accompanied by more or less stable balances on current account and large changes in current account balances may be witnessed without major exchange rate changes. Furthermore, a given balance on current account – say a deficit – may be accompanied first by an appreciation and later on by a depreciation. As has been shown, this does not mean that the exchange rate fluctuates independently of fundamentals.

In a fixed exchange rate system, the current account balance and the capital account balance do not have to match. Divergences are made up by changes in reserves. Reserve increases or decreases lead to adjustment processes, which ultimately cause the equivalence of the capital account and the current account balance. However, adjustment may require a long period of time. The length of the adjustment period depends on the amount of reserves of the deficit country and the willingness of the surplus country to accumulate reserves. This willingness is usually limited. Central banks of deficit countries, on the other hand, can intervene in the foreign exchange markets only if they have accumulated reserves before.[1] Therefore, reserve increases and decreases tend to be offsetting in the medium or long run. If interventions in one direction occur only temporarily then in the longer run it is also true for fixed exchange rate systems that the balance on current account is determined by the balance on capital account. In the adjustment process real exchange rate changes are of crucial importance and can be expected to be stronger in the short or medium run than in the long run.

The possibility that the current account and the capital account may change somewhat independently over shorter periods has a strong impact on economic theory. Time and again, it is stated that the balance on current account is determined by competitiveness, in the sense of ability to sell.[2] This assumption which is valid in fixed exchange rate systems only for shorter periods is even applied to flexible exchange rate systems. However, this is not possible because there is no mechanism of automatic deficit financing in a flexible exchange rate system.

The idea that current account surpluses are *per se* positive, current account deficits negative, is also widely accepted. This idea was developed in times with fixed exchange rates and capital controls. As has been shown, a decline in competitiveness may lead to a loss of reserves and a subsequent reduction of the money supply. The reduction in the money supply has deflationary consequences which cause unemployment when wages are sticky. This is probably why current account deficits are still assumed to be negative. However, we do not live in a world with tight capital controls any more and fixed exchange rates have been abandoned in many cases. Therefore, in most cases current account deficits are the result of net capital imports which by no means have to be judged as negative.

It has to be emphasized that these results have strong implications for the interpretation of exchange rate volatility. As has been shown, the size of exchange rate adjustments, due to real and monetary shocks, depends on the openness of an economy (represented by the relation of the tradeables to the non-tradeables sector) and the flexibility of the economy as a whole (Frankel 1986, Ragnitz 1989). If the tradeables sector is large, if factors are mobile and internal barriers are low, real adjustments will be accomplished relatively fast and easy. This limits the amounts of necessary exchange rate changes. This points to the importance of economic policy. Improving the supply side conditions by reductions in tariff and non-tariff barriers,

---

[1]   In addition, there may be the possibility to borrow from other central banks or the IMF.

[2]   A general critique of this kind of balance of payments theories can be found in Willgerodt 1961, 1978 and in Heyne 1989.

deregulation, etc., is an important measure to increase the responsiveness of the economy to price changes. Thus, it can help to reduce exchange rate variability.

3. Measuring Price and Non-Price Competitiveness

I. A closer look at the current account: regional and sectoral imbalances

The theoretical analysis has shown that there is no strong relationship between the balance on current account and the competitiveness of an economy, in the sense of ability to sell. Nevertheless, on the basis of the competitiveness approach some indicators have been derived in order to measure the international competitiveness of an economy and to explain the balance on current account. High surpluses and high or growing market shares are, for instance, seen as of evidence for high competitiveness whereas, following standard wisdom, deficits and low market shares confirm low international competitiveness. Particularly sectoral deficits and low market shares in high-tech industries are assessed negatively. The following chapter is dedicated to the critical discussion of some of these indicators.

A. The Regional Structure of Trade

One main indicator of international competitiveness is the bilateral current account balance *vis-à-vis* other countries. In general, showing a surplus is treated as an equivalent to being more competitive than the other country.[1] In this section we will focus on the trade balance which is the most thoroughly researched part of the current account. Moreover, there are reasons to concentrate on the trade balance. First, public transfers are usually not affected by reasons related to competitiveness. The basis for transfers often are purely political decisions. Second, trade in services is still a small, although a growing fraction of overall trade. Moreover, the reasoning for trade as well as services is basically the same. Hence we concentrate on trade in goods to keep the argument simple. Let us now take a look at the most important trading countries which are the OECD-members, one oil-exporting country, namely Saudi-Arabia and some developing countries in Asia and Latin America. Table 3.1 shows the bilateral trade balances of 21 countries *vis-à-vis* each other and the national total trade balances for the year 1992.

---

[1]   A very bizarre example of this view is the 'success story' of Baden-Württemberg, a German state. Its state governor, Mr. Teufel, announced in 1992 that the state of Baden-Württemberg had a surplus in its bilateral trade with Japan in 1991 which he interpreted as a sign of high competitiveness.

Table 3.1:   Bilateral trade balances of 21 countries in 1992

	Aus.	N.Z.	Arg.	Brazil	Mex.	Can.	U.S	Hun.	FCSFR	Ger.	France
Australia		604	13	-52	9	199	-5213	n.a.	n.a.	-1566	-350
New Zealand	-100		n.a.	n.a.	103	-5	-587	n.a.	n.a.	-145	-43
Argentina	-35	n.a.		-1668	33	-14	-1877	n.a.	30	-352	-307
Brazil	8	n.a.	1262		732	-144	1186	n.a.	n.a.	44	218
Mexico	-40	-81	-64	-69		-259	-11472	n.a.	n.a.	-1995	-757
Canada	-43	-28	1851	-2121	4473		23250	n.a.	n.a.	-1055	-1058
United States	4963	n.a.	n.a.	-97	n.a.	-10333		n.a.	n.a.	-8468	-1033
Hungary	13	n.a.	n.a.	-94	n.a.	10	21		-185	358	0
Former CSFR*	n.a.	n.a.	-141	-1571	2225	27	-84	44		-590	74
Germany	1116	n.a.	n.a.	-1032	584	56	423	37	631		6921
France	14	-291	n.a.	-1081	243	722	-4629	n.a.	n.a.	-3931	
United Kingdom	632	n.a.	n.a.	-970	n.a.	-564	-2578	n.a.	n.a.	-7084	-1348
Italy	36	n.a.	248	-804	n.a.	46	2614	-145	32	-4544	-1187
Spain	-108	n.a.	-180	n.a.	-489	-209	-4240	n.a.	n.a.	-6240	-2832
Saudi Arabia**											
China***											
India****	-358	n.a.	n.a.	n.a.	n.a.	-86	1036	6	100	-279	-154
Indonesia	-667	-99	n.a.	n.a.	n.a.	-170	597	0	n.a.	-1163	-321
Hong Kong	525	-26	214	-281	492	1581	18453	n.a.	n.a.	3508	396
Korea	-1742	-388	-375	-633	733	56	-146	n.a.	n.a.	-864	-399
Japan	-4791	-595	197	-1706	2562	-536	43849	n.a.	n.a.	9587	930

bn US$

* = 1990, ** = no data available

*** = data not usable, ****= 1991

Source: United Nations 1993, own calculations.

Table 3.1 (continued):   Bilateral trade balances of 21 countries in 1992

	UK	Italy	Spain	Saudi	China	India	Indon.	H.K.	Korea	Japan	Total
Australia	-847	-166	81	-298	-320	381	411	690	1302	2870	1693
New Zealand	162	-109	15	-130	-50	22	80	101	262	115	620
Argentina	-28	-180	95	24	-42	-8	66	-166	-385	-322	-2673
Brazil	850	750	582	-1196	404	n.a.	n.a.	210	427	106	15515
Mexico	-371	-859	343	n.a.	-501	-63	-62	-341	-8	-2156	-20607
Canada	-877	-482	0	-198	-167	196	168	-472	-508	-2778	11794
United States	1143	-4146	2282	-4129	-20004	-2152	-2136	-1715	-2752	-52611	-84501
Hungary	-107	320	59	n.a.	-24	-6	-11	n.a.	-39	-166	-437
Former CSFR*	73	40	8	n.a.	-149	68	n.a.	n.a.	n.a.	-65	-1152
Germany	5781	2416	6825	1280	-3796	92	600	-314	-365	-14944	21967
France	2831	-150	3868	-994	-2108	-48	445	848	-113	-5590	-6800
United Kingdom		-1129	2618	1757	-924	142	-395	-1391	-497	-9200	-32079
Italy	966		2989	-89	-1282	-283	-253	1706	190	-986	-10267
Spain	-2357	-2795		-632	-1103	-175	-224	-37	-587	-4041	-35170
Saudi Arabia**											
China***											
India****	-46	177	151	n.a.	27		80	538	-73	291	-5343
Indonesia	125	25	77	-269	644	-146		627	189	4739	3273
Hong Kong	1798	-239	677	382	-10372	-423	-119		-3767	-15210	-3916
Korea	485	-479	306	-2856	-1071	-40	-357	5033		-7857	-5443
Japan	7739	-249	2471	-5331	-5000	-557	-6643	18662	6218		106936

bn US$

*   = 1990, ** = no data available

***   = data not usable, ****= 1991

Source: United Nations 1993, own calculations.

Interpreted according to the competitiveness approach, the most competitive countries seem to be Japan, Germany, Saudi Arabia and Brazil since they have the highest trade surpluses. The US, Spain, the UK and Mexico should be seen as relatively uncompetitive since they have the highest trade deficits. Seeing Brazil as one of the most competitive economies in the world with the British or American economies behind, might already raise doubts about the validity of this concept. The competitiveness approach is even more suspect when focusing on the bilateral imbalances.

Four examples may illuminate the shortcomings of the competitiveness approach.[1] The first is the case of Canada. Its total trade balance is in surplus. Nevertheless, its bilateral trade balance is in deficit with all countries except for the US, India, and Indonesia. This should not be interpreted as evidence in favour of the hypothesis that Canada is only competitive in comparison with these three countries. Instead, the Canadian product range fits the US demand very well whereas the preferences of Canadian citizens are met by products from all other countries.

The second case will help to clarify this point. The citizens of Saudi Arabia import goods from all over the world but they export only into a few countries of destination. Thus, according to the competitiveness approach, Saudi-Arabia is competitive only *vis-à-vis* a few countries, namely those depending on oil. This, however, stands in contrast to the fact that the overall current account of Saudi Arabia shows a surplus. Tracing back the current account surplus to the competitiveness approach, one would come to the conclusion that the Saudi-Arabian economy is a very competitive one if compared with the rest of the world. This contradiction can be solved by looking at the structure of trade flows which is explained by quoting the principle of comparative advantage rather than referring to an overall competitiveness. Due to the geological conditions Saudi Arabia has comparative advantages in the production of oil. Consequently, more than 80 per cent of Saudi Arabian exports are mineral fuels (SITC 3). Since the elasticity of demand for oil in most other countries is low, export earnings depend heavily on oil prices. The earnings are used to pay for imports from all over the world. The import structure, naturally, is different from the structure of exports. A glance at the bilateral trade balances *vis-à-vis* Japan and Germany may strengthen the argument. Japan does not provide those goods, the citizens of Saudi Arabia prefer. Therefore, its trade balance *vis-*

---

[1]   One has to make strong reservations about the data used in the table. First, bilateral export data of country A do not match exactly the bilateral import data of country B, since normally exports are calculated f.o.b., whereas imports are computed c.i.f. Second, the UN data are based on national accounts which, of course, are not all of the same quality. One can find huge divergences in both the level and the direction of trade balances. For example, Argentina and Korea reveal both a deficit in trade *vis-à-vis* each other. The Chinese data are not reliable at all.

à-vis Saudi Arabia shows a deficit. On the other hand, because Germany can provide these goods, its trade balance with Saudi Arabia is in surplus. The comparative advantages of Japan do not allow its entrepreneurs to sell enough goods to Saudi-Arabian citizens in order to match the Japanese imports from Arabia. The German comparative advantages, instead, fit the demand of the Saudi citizens. Therefore, the German bilateral trade balance is in surplus.

This leads to the third case. The competitiveness approach suggests that Germany is more competitive than Saudi Arabia and that Saudi Arabia is more competitive than Japan. Yet, a look at Table 3.1 shows that the Japanese trade balance with respect to Germany is in a huge surplus. From the point of view of the competitiveness approach this demonstrates the higher Japanese competitiveness. So we have an intransitive order. The same occurs in the fourth case which shall be cited here: Australia has a trade surplus with respect to Japan; Japan, in turn, has an overwhelming trade surplus *vis-à-vis* the United States, while the US itself has a surplus in trade with Australia. These two examples cannot be explained by simply referring to international competitiveness.

To draw a conclusion, it is by no means a problem if the bilateral trade between two countries shows an imbalance. Trade takes place because of different comparative advantages of nations, because of product differentiation, and because of differences in preferences. Even in a world where no net capital flows take place, bilateral trade imbalances can appear due to those reasons. If Japanese citizens strongly prefer Australian products and Australians like goods from the US whose citizens, on the other hand, prefer Japanese products, the situation will be exactly the one prevailing in 1992 (Table 3.1). *A fortiori*, there is no need to worry about a situation like this.

There is another important reservation in this view of competitiveness. The world trading system is multilateral, that is the markets are integrated in general, whereas the bilateral approach rests on the assumption that markets are separated from each other. However, competition between German and Japanese firms does not take place only in these two countries but all over the world, such as for instance in the United States and in France. Accordingly, a bilateral imbalance cannot deliver a true picture of the competitiveness of the firms located in both countries, unless markets are isolated from each other by trade barriers or capital controls. Nonetheless, even if the latter would apply, it would be impossible to give a precise testimony on the true international competitiveness of any of the two because of the distortions. The existing international trade barriers and capital controls, however, are not that segmenting. The markets of the major industrialized countries are fairly integrated. That makes bilateral imbalances interdependent.

As shown above, the real exchange rate facilitates the adjustment of the current account to the capital account. If the balance on capital account is determined by intertemporal decisions, it is not affected by changing trade flows. A growing trade surplus *vis-à-vis* one region reduces *ceteris paribus* the surplus *vis-à-vis* another. This can be demonstrated by using a simple example. Supposed the US demand shifts from German products towards Japanese. This reduces the bilateral German surplus in the trade balance towards the United States. Presumed the capital flows do not change, the D-Mark depreciates, and the Japanese yen appreciates. In the course of this revaluation, Japanese exports to Germany decrease, and German exports to Japan increase. Hence, the bilateral German trade deficit towards Japan also decreases, although neither in Germany nor in Japan anything has changed. Following the competitiveness approach, one would argue that German competitiveness has improved. Instead, the cause was a loss in competitiveness of some German firms in the United States.

People often accuse trade policy of being responsible for bilateral trade imbalances. An illustrative example is the actual US–Japanese trade conflict which reached a peak during the first half of 1995. In the United States it is taken for granted that the huge imbalance on the overall current account is due to a lack of openness of Japanese goods markets. Consequently, the Japanese administration is urged to open Japanese markets. Although there is no evidence that the Japanese markets are relatively closed (Saxonhouse 1993, Bhagwati 1994) let us imagine what happens if import barriers in Japan are lowered significantly with everything else staying the same. The consequence will be a rise in the demand for commodities made in America, thus increasing Japanese imports from the United States. Therefore, the demand for US$ will also climb, and the dollar appreciates. Yet, the appreciation causes an increasing demand for Japanese products in the United States. As long as trade policy does not alter the determinants of the capital account, the bilateral trade imbalance will not change. The US deficit would be still as high as before. However, the volume of trade would increase.[1]

To sum up: in a multilateral trade system bilateral trade imbalances cannot be judged as a sign of a country's lack of international competitiveness. They are, instead, a result of international capital flows and of the exploitation of comparative advantages. Emphasizing bilateral imbalances and thus justifying trade policy measures bears the danger of a relapse into the bilateralism of the thirties with fatal consequences for world-wide growth and employment.

---

[1]   Import barriers can be interpreted as a tax on international trade. When this tax is lowered both, exports and imports, are going to rise.

B. Sectoral Imbalances and Comparative Advantages

a) The causes of trade and trade imbalances

Does the examination of sectoral imbalances improve our understanding of competitiveness? One reason for international trade to take place is the existence of international differences in factor endowments. It is worthwhile for a country to specialize in accordance with its comparative advantages. As the Heckscher–Ohlin model is based on perfect competition with homogenous goods in the absence of transaction costs, it is adequate to explain interindustrial trade. In the industrialized world however, most of the trade is intraindustrial which, in general, is explained in different ways.[1] First, the Heckscher–Ohlin framework can be used by relaxing its assumptions concerning transaction costs. Thus, for instance border trade can be traced back on transportation costs which can be higher as tariffs or non-tariff barriers respectively. Second and more important, products are not completely homogenous. In a framework of monopolistic competition with static and/or dynamic economies of scale, trade will be very much intraindustrial.[2]

Both explanations imply that trade takes place voluntarily and only when both partners think of it as advantageous. This, however, does not imply that every transaction is automatically a good deal for both sides; errors are made, expectations fail. But in general, international trade reflects the wishes and preferences of the participants.[3] Keeping this in mind, distinct sectoral trade imbalances cannot be interpreted as undesirable if no trade barriers and distortions exist.[4] Rather, the opposite seems to be true. Sectoral imbalances in countries' current accounts are due to comparative advantages and product differentiation, since firms in different countries spezialize in different goods. Even if individual countries would show no overall current account imbalances, sectoral imbalances would exist due to the international division of labour. Sectoral as well as regional trade imbalances are the expression of the international gains from trade.

b) Some thoughts about the pattern of specialization

With respect to international competitiveness it may be interesting to analyse how different countries would specialize according to comparative

---

1   For an exhaustive overview see Grubel and Lloyd 1975, part II.

2   For a simple model of intraindustrial trade see for instance Krugman and Obstfeld 1994, chapter 6, and Kenen 1994, chapter 7.

3   Theoretically, one can think of very special cases in which one country does worse compared to autarky. However, dynamically, consumption possibilities usually will be enlarged substantially as can be seen by the much better performance and higher living standards in countries pursueing an outward oriented strategy.

4   However, even if distortions do exist, it is usually the very country in which the distortions prevail that suffers also the drawbacks in international trade. Hence, the removal is in the interest and the realm of national economic policy. See Markusen et al. 1995, pp. 142-58.

advantage and how they actually do. There surely are certain regularities in the international division of labour which are due to differences in the factor endowment of different countries. The knowledge of these regularities may allow for an assessment of sectoral imbalances. This might not be what the proponents of the competitiveness approach have in mind. Rather, it serves as an indicator as to where competitive positions are distorted by national economic policy. For this purpose it is useful to divide the different industries and products according to their factor intensities in three groups called Ricardo goods, Heckscher–Ohlin goods, and Product Cycle or Schumpeter goods (Hirsch 1974, pp. 66-9). Ricardo goods are produced drawing primarily on the natural endowment of a country, that is the climatic and geological conditions or natural resources. The comparative advantage in the classical example given by Ricardo – wine in Portugal and cloth in Britain – is derived from differences in productivity due to such factors. Contemporary examples are agriculture and mining. Goods that need either a high share of labour or of capital are called Heckscher–Ohlin goods. They are characterized by the usage of differences in factor intensities. The production function is assumed to be identical everywhere in the world. In case of Heckscher–Ohlin goods the comparative advantage, in other words the location of production, depends only on ex ante differences in relative factor prices reflecting differences in factor endowment. By and large, the following products can be subsumed to Heckscher–Ohlin goods: leather, clothing, footwear, wood and paper manufactures and optical instruments. The third group contains products that need a relatively high share of a third factor of production, namely human capital (Vernon 1966). They result from research and development (R&D) activities. Hence, they are called Schumpeter goods. It is useful to divide the Schumpeter goods further into two groups, the first of them called immobile Schumpeter goods. In this case, R&D and production have to be carried out at the same place as there are local economies of scope. Examples are machineries, cars, aircrafts and aerospace products. The second are mobile Schumpeter goods; here R&D and production can be separated spatially (Vernon 1979). An illustrative example is a semiconductor which is produced in five steps. Four of those steps need high technical skills whereas one (the fourth step: assembling) is very labour intensive. Therefore, it takes place in a labour abundant country with comparatively low average wages (offshore assembling).[1] Other types of mobile Schumpeter goods are some chemicals, electronic products, office machines and data processors.[2]

---

[1]   For a detailed survey on semiconductor production see Bletschacher and Klodt 1992.

[2]   This categorizing is somewhat rough since the aggregation has been done on a two-digit level (SITC).

A highly industrialized country like Japan, the United States or Germany can be expected to have a comparative advantage in the production of Schumpeter goods as it is relatively well endowed with human capital. Thus, the trade balance of these countries should be in surplus as far as Schumpeter goods are concerned, and in deficit with regard to Ricardo and Heckscher–Ohlin goods. However, industrialized countries are under pressure from developing countries with respect to mobile Schumpeter goods. For although developing countries do not have the technological potential to promote such goods, some of them have the corresponding locational quality for the production process.

There is another source of adjustment pressure on the industrialized world. Comparative advantages can change over time, for instance, when the technology of Schumpeter goods becomes common knowledge and is standardized. This can be the case as the product passes different stages of a product cycle. As long as the share of human capital in production is high, the industrialized country has the comparative advantage. When the production function is standardized, the share of human capital incorporated is low enough to move production to a country which is endowed with relatively more labour or capital. Hence, a product can shift from a Schumpeter to a Heckscher–Ohlin good.[1] This is an important challenge for the developed countries. For, if they want to keep their living standards and even more so, if they want to hold the pace with which their real income increased in the past, they are permanently forced to use their relatively high share of human capital productively.

C. High tech products and the current account

The argument just presented suggests that the specialization pattern should mirror comparative advantages. But, does this also mean that it is necessary to have a trade surplus in high tech products for keeping a high standard of living? Many observers claim that this is necessary. Especially in Europe there has emerged a very intensive and emotional debate on this issue. Whereas, during the 1960s, it was the American challenge (Servant-Schreiber 1967) which made the people feel uneasy, in the mid-1980s it has been the Japanese challenge (Seitz 1991) that has caused growing concern. In these debates, the current account or at least the trade balance are frequently used as an indicator for the size of the alleged problem. It is argued that a sectoral trade surplus in high tech products – however defined – is necessary to preserve the countries' overall ability to sell, not to speak of keeping the living standard.

---

[1]   Basic cars can be seen as an example for the product cycle (Klodt, Schmidt et al. 1989, pp. 29-31).

Table 3.2:   *Bilateral and multilateral trade balances in high tech*
industries: the German case in the 1980s (Mio D-Mark)

	1982	1984	1987	1988	1989	1990
a) Multilateral balances						
Data processors	-495	-1426	-1668	-2938	-4103	-5720
Consumer electronics	13	-1248	-1054	-1578	-1452	-3733
Telecommunications	1302	1255	1669	933	651	450
Semiconductors	-719	-1011	-1251	-318	-418	-762
Other component parts	537	809	800	1609	1730	1450
Materials (e.g. silicon)	-112	-134	-143	-190	-181	-157
Aircrafts	-827	812	-1233	-1355	-2197	-137
Spacecrafts	n.a.	n.a.	n.a.	114	631	-2447
Components	24	-463	-820	-158	-486	1792
b) Bilateral balances						
Data processors	-246	-842	-1834	-1868	-1898	-2504
Consumer electronics	-2172	-2650	-2213	-2142	-2065	2120
Telecommunications	-286	-361	-591	-743	-892	-793
Semiconductors	-174	-785	-511	-1009	-1405	-1142
Other component parts	-3	33	1	-128	-160	-176
Materials (e.g. silicon)	55	83	46	46	55	57

Source: Statistisches Bundesamt (e), own calculations.

Indeed, bilateral and multilateral trade deficits do exist with regard to high tech in the western world. Take the German example during the 1980s. Both multilateral trade and bilateral trade *vis-à-vis* Japan was in deficit as Table 3.2 makes clear. The interpretation of the data, however, is rather ambiguous as illustrated by aircrafts and spacecrafts. The sign of the balance switches more than once. Does this mean that the competitiveness of the German aircraft and spacecraft industries is changing annually? Probably not. The German industries are part of the European programme with Airbus Industries as the main enterprise. The allocation of production, therefore, seems not to follow cost advantages; rather it seems to be determined politically (Freytag 1995b). Moreover, since aircrafts are very costly, a large-scale order of the Lufthansa, the German airline which does not include only home made aircrafts will cause a deficit on the sectoral trade balance.

Although sectoral balances do not provide much information about international competitiveness, many claim that the situation in high tech trade is different from traditional products. Traditional trade theories are said not to be appropriate to explain trade taking place in highly innovative products. Therefore, the trade deficits in this range of products are seen as alarming indicators for the diminishing competitiveness of both Europe and the US *vis-à-vis* the world, especially with regard to Japan and some so-called Asian tigers.[1] Two lines of argument have been stressed which also gained attention as a basis for policy interventions designed to balance the trade in high tech industries. The first is a political one, referring to some popular theses. The second is an economic one, which can be traced back to new directions in theoretical thinking.

The first one has its roots in the popular fear of insecurity of supply with essential goods when relying on markets only. If a country did not maintain its own production of certain commodities, so the argument goes, it would become more and more dependent on foreign suppliers. In times of international crisis, supply would not be guaranteed. Especially a few products, for instance food and energy, have been protected, quoting this argument. Nowadays, high tech products like semiconductors, data processors and biotechnological goods are seen as a part of infrastructure, necessary for civilization staying alive (Seitz 1991, pp. 337-41). Therefore, following the security argument, it is not enough to trust market relations. Instead, the state should protect these industries so that there is at least a minimum supply available. Of course it is justified to worry about the supply of important goods. The task of the economist, however, is to judge the efficacy of the methods and the costs incurred for achieving this goal. From this standpoint, any aim at more autarky is to be rejected. Instead, the best way to become independent is through liberalized international trade. While international integration increases interdependence and consequently dependence on others in general, it reduces the dependence on specific suppliers (Freytag 1995a, pp. 14-20).

Besides this political argument, two economic theories are used to argue in favour of interventions in high tech markets. Roughly speaking, one can distinguish the theory of strategic trade policy and the new growth theory, both of which are based on a similar reasoning. They draw on economies of scale, either intratemporally or intertemporally. Whereas the first deals with above average rents in oligopolistic markets due to barriers to entry,[2] the second refers to spillovers of research and development activities.[3] Although they offer some theoretically appealing insights, they do have their shortcomings (Krugman 1987). First, they do not sufficiently take general equilibrium effects into account. Second, they are not much of a help when

---

[1]   For the US see for instance Magaziner and Reich 1982, Thurow 1992 and Tyson 1992.

[2]   See for instance the pioneering works by Krugman 1984, Brander and Spencer 1985 and Dixit 1984.

[3]   Examples are to be found in Romer 1990, Grossman and Helpman 1990 and Aghion and Howitt 1992.

it comes to economic policy, even if the theoretical analysis seems to provide a clear cut policy recommendation. The information requirements are far too high to be sure of achieving the desired results when pursuing trade or industrial policy. This critique holds both for the strategic trade policy and new growth theory models.[1]

Nevertheless, notwithstanding these shortcomings, both lines of argument, the political one and the theoretical one, are in use world-wide in order to impose trade barriers. The European Union has provided itself with a range of policy instruments to be applied on trade in high tech (anti-dumping measures, the new trade policy instrument, Article 130i Maastricht Treaty, Common Technology Policy). The US use Section 301 and Super 301 in order to protect some of their industries.

Of course, it is possible to reduce a sectoral deficit by imposing import barriers and promoting exports. But it is only possible on the behalf of other industries; their position will be worsened via currency appreciation or via rising prices when they are downstream industries as a number of examples impressively show.[2] Most likely, the diminished surplus in one high tech industry will cause a higher one in another. Thus, governments should resist the temptation to protect high tech industries through trade and industrial policies. They are not only ill suited for achieving the very goals aimed at but also have their costs. The best way to cope both with the structural change resulting from pressure by developing and the newly industrialized countries and growing competition caused by high tech producers from industrialized countries is to open markets and to trust competition unless there really exists market failure.

II. Further indicators of the ability to sell

The discussion of trade balances has not provided helpful and consistent results as regards ability to sell. When looking at the overall trade balance of 21 countries, we could not interpret the balances as evidence in favour of the competitiveness approach, since this kind of analysis gave the impression that, for instance, Brazil is an economy more competitive than the United States. The results of an analysis of bilateral trade balances made even less sense. In more than one case, we obtained an intransitive order of 'competitiveness', when we compared the bilateral trade balances of three countries *vis-à-vis* one another. Sectoral balances have to be seen as the expression of making use of the international division of labour. Therefore, trade balances are no reliable indicators of international competitiveness interpreted as ability to sell.

---

[1]   For a detailed critique see Bletschacher and Klodt 1992.
[2]   See chapter 5.II.C.

This result is not too much a surprise. Consequently, efforts have been made to improve the measuring of competitiveness. In this chapter, we analyse three such indicators, namely the index of revealed comparative advantage, world market shares and real exchange rates. For this purpose, we discuss them theoretically and calculate them for some OECD countries. As will become clear soon, they have their merits for certain aspects of international relations, but they are very difficult for the analysis of overall competitiveness of countries, to say the least.

A. Revealed Comparative Advantage (RCA)

The concept of revealed comparative advantage (RCA) is based on the classical theory of international trade and comparative advantage. Since it is very difficult to work out comparative advantages in a trade model (Balassa 1965, pp. 100-3), the trade performance of a country's industries is used for this purpose. To calculate the so-called RCA index, the ratio of sectoral exports and imports is divided by the ratio of national exports and imports (equation 43). This makes it possible to analyse the international competitiveness of specific industries, either in comparison with other industries or in a dynamic shape. The index is calculated as follows:

$$(43) \quad RCA = \ln \left(\frac{\dfrac{EX_i}{IM_i}}{\dfrac{\sum_i EX_i}{\sum_i IM_i}} \right)$$

where EX_i = exports of industry i
       IM_i = imports of industry i

The standardization is helpful to compare different branches, even if they differ widely concerning size. The approach of sectoral balances does not provide these insights. The RCA index is to be interpreted in the following way: a positive RCA of industry i seems to reflect a comparative advantage of the industry as the ratio of sectoral exports and sectoral imports exceeds the ratio of all exports and all imports. If both ratios equal each other, the index will be zero. The industry, obviously, has a comparative disadvantage as the index is negative.

Nonetheless, there are some serious objections regarding the RCA index. First, all distortions that are incorporated in trade flows and in the trade balance are also incorporated in the RCA. In order to draw correct conclusions, it is necessary to have complete information of the trade policy applied to all industries. Moreover, an implicit assumption of the analysis is that the country's exports are subject to the same level and structure of protection in every country of destination (Donges and Riedel 1977, p. 69). This is by no means self-evident. Second, it is important to distinguish export proceeds from profits. If a firm sells at a low price in order to yield a high rate of capacity utilization or to stay in the market, profits will be poor or even negative. In this case, the international competitiveness of the firm seems to be low rather than high.

Third, these calculations echo the past; they are ex-post oriented. However, the evaluation of future developments should be the main focus of competitiveness indicators. Yet, information about the past does not allow any definite statement about the future. Fourth, international competitiveness is reflected not only in exports. Home market sales are important too. The confinement to export is likely to underestimate the real competitiveness of an industry as the case of the German car manufactures immediately after the German unification demonstrates: exports did not grow from 1989 to 1990 whereas imports grew about 25 percent; the RCA index decreased from 0.81 to 0.66. At the same time the total turnovers of German car producers increased by some 8 percent. Thus, the German car sellers proved to be internationally competitive when the (up to 1989 repressed) demand for cars in Germany (mainly in the former GDR) expanded. Fifth, some statistical problems may arise. The index is sensitive to the level of aggregation and to the year which has been chosen (Donges and Riedel 1977, p. 69). Too high an aggregation can conceal different advances within an industry. Too low an aggregation can provide too much, but not the relevant information. The time chosen for calculating RCA indices is important because the impact of business cycles has to be taken into account.

In spite of these reservations, the revealed comparative advantages provide a better insight into international competitiveness of certain industries (not of the economy as a whole!) than the concept of sectoral imbalances since all these objections apply for sectoral balances, as well. Especially for two reasons the RCA index has to be favoured. First, the standardization can help to compare several industries. Moreover, the sectoral balances are also a function of capital flows. The standardization adjusts the RCA index for changes in capital flows.

We have calculated the RCA for five countries in 1992 (Table 3.3). The result is compatible with the principle of comparative advantages. Regarding the products analysed, Spain has comparative advantages only in the production of some Ricardo goods, some Heckscher–Ohlin goods, and road vehicles. This is to some extent surprising. In general, the other four countries have comparative advantages in the production of Schumpeter goods. Japan is another interesting case because inter-industry trade is predominant.[1] The statistics do not show any exports of Ricardo goods. Therefore, no RCA could be computed although huge imports take place.

Table 3.3:   Revealed comparative advantages for Germany, Spain, the US, Korea and Japan 1992, two-digit-level SITC.

	USA	Japan	Korea	Spain	Germany
Ricardo goods					
SITC 01 Meat and Preparations	0,58	n.a.	n.a.	0,46	-0,965
SITC 03 Fish and Preparations	-0,326	n.a.	1,12	-1,004	n.a.
SITC 05 Vegetables and Fruits	0,14	n.a.	-0,353	-1,759	-2,011
SITC 11 Beverages	n.a.	n.a.	n.a.	0,61	-0,739
SITC 12 Tobacco and Manufactures	n.a.	n.a.	n.a.	n.a.	0,11
SITC 32 Coal, Coke and Briquettes	n.a.	n.a.	n.a.	n.a.	n.a.
SITC 33 Petroleum and Products	-1,939	-3,606	-1,865	-1,08	-1,894
Heckscher-Ohlin goods					
SITC 61 Leather	n.a.	n.a.	0,35	0,56	n.a.
SITC 65 Textile Yarns, Fabrics, etc.	-0,117	0,07	1,18	0,01	0,06
SITC 67 Iron and Steel	-0,693	0,88	0,41	0,55	0,08
SITC 84 Clothing and Accessories	-1,85	n.a.	3,3	-1,07	-1,142
SITC 88 Photo Eqp., Opt. Glasses, etc.	-0,453	1,04	-0,345	-1,43	-0,085
Immobile Schumpeter goods					
SITC 71 Power Generating Equipment	0,34	1,38	-1,2	-0,21	0,4
SITC 72 Machines for Special Ind.	0,56	1,46	1,47	-0,46	0,95
SITC 73 Metalworking Machinery	0,15	1,44	n.a.	-0,24	0,76
SITC 74 General Industry Machinery	0,43	1,35	-1,09	-0,27	0,67
SITC 78 Road Vehicles	-0,495	2,1	1,54	0,632	0,51
SITC 87 Precision Instruments	0,85	0,37	-1,48	-0,786	0,43
Mobile Schumpeter goods					
SITC 51 Organic Chemicals	0,35	0,03	-0,667	-0,403	0,26
SITC 52 Inorganic Chemicals	0,41	-1,19	n.a.	-0,125	0,22
SITC 58 Plastic Materials, etc.	1,1	0,8	0,53	-0,157	0,32
SITC 59 Chemical Materials	1,12	-0,42	n.a.	-0,811	0,53
SITC 75 Office Machines, ADP Eqp.	0,03	1,23	0,64	-0,649	-0,693
SITC 76 Television Receivers	-0,054	1,84	1,47	-0,588	-0,343
SITC 77 Electric Machinery	0,12	1,15	0,3	-0,127	0,27

Source: United Nations 1993, own calculations.

Anyhow, Japan clearly has a comparative disadvantage in the production of Ricardo goods. Korea has a comparative advantage concerning mobile Schumpeter industries, and disadvantages concerning immobile Schumpeter industries. Germany has comparative advantages in the fabrication of immobile Schumpeter goods, and has disadvantages concerning mobile Schumpeter goods (except for chemicals). These results fit the theoretical

---

[1]   For more details see the case studies, chapter 5.

considerations. On the other hand, it is difficult to explain why Germany and Japan seem to have comparative advantages in the production of textiles and iron and steel. The results for the United States seem to reflect the principle of comparative advantages more closely than results for other countries. The RCA is mainly positive regarding Schumpeter goods and negative concerning Ricardo and Heckscher–Ohlin industries.

All these results confirm the predictions of the classical theory of international trade. It is nearly impossible for a country to achieve positive sectoral external balances for all industries. It is in the logic of international trade to export some goods and to import others. It should be obvious that modern industrial countries without natural resources import huge amounts of petroleum. Nobody would call for higher trade barriers towards oil imports in order to diminish the sectoral trade deficit. Naturally, some results of international trade are not caused by comparative advantage only. Trade barriers often disturb international trade relations in a serious manner. Therefore, it is not convenient to complain about sectoral deficits without taking a closer look at the factor endowment and the trade policy applied.

B. Market Share Analysis

Another way to evaluate the international competitiveness of countries is to calculate market shares of its industries in world trade. Rising market shares of the industries are in general judged as proof of increasing international competitiveness. The crudest method is to calculate world market shares of national industries. For this purpose the national exports of an industry are divided by all exports of this industry world-wide.[1] The turnovers of firms on their home market are not considered. This can be a serious problem if an industry in a big country satisfies the total demand at home. Its world market share is underestimated in such a case.

We compared the world market share of the three most important trading nations, the United States, Japan, and Germany during the 1980s. American enterprises lost market shares in many industries, no matter whether Heckscher–Ohlin or Schumpeter goods are considered. The German firms could maintain their shares in most of the industries; both in Heckscher–Ohlin goods and Schumpeter goods. The Japanese situation is quite different: its firms lost shares in Heckscher–Ohlin industries and conquered market shares in both mobile and immobile Schumpeter industries. Having the theory of the product cycle in mind, the Japanese case seems to fit best to the theoretical predictions. An industrial country should take up the challenge of structural change by inventing new products and by giving up the production of Heckscher–Ohlin goods.

---

[1] We use only OECD data since they are relatively credible and since the trade within the OECD covers almost all world trade.

Table 3.4:   *World market shares in the 1980s (per cent)*

		1981	1984	1986	1987	1988	1989
Heckscher-Ohlin goods							
Germany							
SITC 61	Leather	17,5	15,8	14,3	14,8	14,3	12,3
SITC 65	Textile Yarns, Fabrics, etc.	15,3	16,5	18,8	19,2	19,5	19,8
SITC 67	Iron and Steel	17,2	16,6	18,7	19,2	18,4	18,2
SITC 84	Clothing and Accessories	13,8	13,8	15,3	14,6	15,2	14,8
SITC 88	Photo Eqp., Opt. Glas., etc.	12,1	11,7	13,7	13,5	13,5	12,9
Japan							
SITC 61	Leather	7,5	7,9	6,1	4,9	4,8	4,6
SITC 65	Textile Yarns, Fabrics, etc.	16,2	15,9	12,8	11,1	10,2	9,8
SITC 67	Iron and Steel	27,9	27,5	22,9	20,8	20,9	18,6
SITC 84	Clothing and Accessories	3,3	3,2	2,2	1,5	1,7	1,6
SITC 88	Photo Eqp., Opt. Glas., etc.	32,7	33,7	34,8	32,4	33,3	31,7
United States							
SITC 61	Leather	10,0	13,2	10,2	9,9	12,6	12,3
SITC 65	Textile Yarns, Fabrics, etc.	9,9	7,1	6,0	5,8	6,7	7,0
SITC 67	Iron and Steel	4,8	2,6	1,8	2,0	2,7	4,2
SITC 84	Clothing and Accessories	7,2	4,2	3,3	3,2	4,5	5,6
SITC 88	Photo Eqp., Opt. Glas., etc.	14,9	14,1	7,4	6,7	6,7	3,2
Immobile Schumpeter goods							
Germany							
SITC 71-74	Machinery	18,9	19,8	23,3	23,9	22,6	21,9
SITC 78	Road Vehicles	21,0	19,1	21,8	23,4	22,8	23,1
SITC 87	Precision Instruments	17,4	17,1	20,1	21,0	20,4	19,6
Japan							
SITC 71-74	Machinery	13,4	15,8	15,8	15,1	16,1	16,2
SITC 78	Road Vehicles	27,2	27,4	28,7	26,6	25,4	24,7
SITC 87	Precision Instruments	9,2	11,6	11,5	11,1	12,8	13,4
United States							
SITC 71-74	Machinery	24,0	20,2	15,0	13,9	15,0	15,7
SITC 78	Road Vehicles	13,0	12,7	9,9	9,8	9,7	10,3
SITC 87	Precision Instruments	30,8	29,2	25,7	23,9	25,4	26,1
Mobile Schumpeter goods							
Germany							
SITC 51-2, 58-9	Chemicals	19,0	19,3	20,9	21,1	20,4	19,9
SITC 75	Office Mach., ADP Eqp.	11,7	8,9	11,2	10,8	9,1	9,3
SITC 76	Television Receivers	10,6	8,3	10,5	11,8	10,4	10,2
SITC 77	Electric Machinery	18,1	15,6	18,9	19,2	18,0	17,9
Japan							
SITC 51-2, 58-9	Chemicals	5,8	6,2	6,3	6,4	6,5	6,6
SITC 75	Office Mach., ADP Eqp.	15,7	22,6	24,8	24,7	26,0	25,7
SITC 76	Television Receivers	48,5	54,6	52,2	47,8	48,3	45,3
SITC 77	Electric Machinery	20,9	25,4	23,7	23,3	24,9	25,5
United States							
SITC 51-2, 58-9	Chemicals	19,8	18,5	14,9	14,1	14,7	16,4
SITC 75	Office Mach., ADP Eqp.	35,4	33,3	26,0	25,3	26,7	25,4
SITC 76	Television Receivers	11,6	10,5	9,3	9,7	11,1	12,7
SITC 77	Electric Machinery	18,5	22,5	17,3	17,3	18,3	19,1

Source: OECD (a), own calculations.

The faster this process of innovation and imitation takes place, that is the faster knowledge is transmitted, the more important it becomes for an industrial country to react immediately.[1] It seems as if the Japanese enterprises successfully faced the structural change in the 1980s whereas the German firms did not do equally well. The case studies (chapter 5) shed further evidence on this point.

However, again, the calculation of world market shares is a rather shaky basis in one, albeit important, aspect. A high market share does not necessarily imply a high return on investment. Therefore, the concept has been modified in some ways. The first method to mention is the constant-market-share (CMS) analysis.[2] Using this analytical tool, attempts have been made to separate the changes of a country's world market shares into a structural and a competitive component in order to work out a CMS norm. By taking the structural changes on the market into account, one can consider how the national market share would have developed without changes in the national firms' competitiveness. The structural changes can be either regional or they refer to certain goods. In addition, not values, but volumes are considered. Due to such structural changes the market share will change, too, even in cases in which the competitiveness of domestic firms did not vary. Therefore, it would be inappropriate to draw conclusions about the national competitiveness of nations just because market shares have changed. An example illustrates the relevant argument. Suppose the market volume for product x is diminishing. Yet, if the country under consideration can keep its market share constant, a proponent of the CMS analysis would argue that national competitiveness did not decrease. However, its overall share in international trade would have declined.

Because of the serious drawbacks of this concept we did not compute any constant market shares. First of all, it has proven very difficult to calculate the market shares correctly. The level of aggregation of products is too high for a precise consideration of structural changes. In addition, it is nearly impossible to isolate all distortions due to trade barriers. There is another, even more substantial aspect in the CMS analysis: resolving varying market shares for structural changes can give a wrong picture of a country's ability to face the structural change. For, as has been pointed out, it makes no sense to talk of competitiveness being unchanged when the respective markets are on the decline. In this case, holding one's market share indicates that structural change has not been managed satisfactorily. It hence can demonstrate a lack of competitiveness to hold market shares on declining markets. In other words, losing market shares on declining

---

[1] Of course, structural change is a challenge for all sectors: a world being thus dynamic not only calls for a high flexibility of its factors of production, but also for a quick reaction of its policy makers.

[2] See for instance Leamer and Stern 1970, chapter 7.

markets and gaining on increasing markets can be a sign of strong performance of a country's industries. In addition, the results are not robust with respect to the sequence in which the calculation is done. Therefore, it is not appropriate to eliminate the international structural change from the analysis of world market shares. A third shortcoming of the approach is the focus on volumes. Instead, the economically relevant variable of competitiveness as interpreted by us seems to be the return on investment. Holding market shares constant or even gaining market shares is worthless, if they are achieved at the price of diminishing profits or even losses. Especially for these last two reasons, we refrain from calculating CMS.

In contrast to the CMS, another method to compute market shares emphasizes markets that grow very fast (Sachverständigenrat 1988). Whereas the CMS tries to neutralize the effects of structural changes on the competitiveness of local firms, this method stresses how they cope with structural changes. A country that has high and growing market shares on the fast growing markets is seen as very competitive. This approach is future oriented whereas the above mentioned RCA, for instance, is ex-post oriented. By using this new approach one can hope to obtain a forecast of domestic firms' competitiveness in the future.

However, this approach also suffers from crucial shortcomings. Just like in the case of the other indicators, there are statistical problems. In every group of commodities, say on the two-digit-level, there can be concealed many subgroups with highly different growth rates. Therefore, one can easily imagine even a deep aggregated analysis providing misleading results. If these results were used in order to give policy recommendations, for instance where to subsidize R&D efforts, a distorting and suboptimal policy would be implemented. Moreover, having a high market share on a growing market does not give any information about profits. As mentioned above, it is by no means a sign for high competitiveness, if a firm has high market shares, as long as it does not earn high profits. Market shares, in general, cannot be interpreted easily. No standard exists about an optimal market share for countries with a certain factor endowment and so on. Hence, we do not compute any adjusted market shares.

To sum up, all these indicators do not tell enough about competitiveness, at least not about the competitiveness of nations as a prerequisite for high incomes and growth. The method to compute RCA indices can give an impression of where a country has its comparative advantage. Nevertheless, one has to keep in mind all the reservations made above, especially the relevance of trade barriers. The analysis of market shares, adjusted or not, has even more serious drawbacks.

C. Real Exchange Rates

In the competitiveness approach, the real exchange rate is considered to be a variable which can exogenously influence the competitiveness of a country and its current account balance. Therefore, investigations of the 'price competitiveness' are mainly concerned with the relationship between competitiveness and real exchange rates (Turner and Van't dack 1993, Orlowski 1982, pp. 11-39). This relationship is analysed for those enterprises which are – in fact or potentially – competing with foreign firms. Such enterprises can be found in the tradeables sector. Obviously, in this sector it is important for enterprises to be able to produce at lower costs than foreign competitors. If locally produced goods are too expensive, local suppliers stand to be competed out of the market. Therefore, for these suppliers it is especially important how high their costs of production are in comparison to firms in other countries. Interpreted in this way, price competitiveness can be measured with the help of real exchange rates. In this context, however, real exchange rates are not defined in the same way as in chapter 2.II. Since the competitiveness of local producers in the tradeables sector is analysed only, prices for tradeables are used to derive real exchange rates. Such real exchange rates indicate a real appreciation if locally produced traded goods have become more expensive than goods which are produced in foreign countries. This can be due either to higher price increases (lower price decreases) or to a nominal appreciation. Since a real appreciation is associated with relatively higher prices, it is interpreted to indicate a worsening of the competitive position of local producers. Just the opposite is true for a real depreciation which implies a relative decline of costs and an improvement of the competitive position of the local economy.

Yet, the theoretical concept as well as its empirical application have certain weaknesses. The selection of suitable price indices for the calculation of real exchange rates proves to be extremely difficult, since prices of non-traded goods as well as prices which are distorted by government intervention should not be included (Orlowski 1982, pp. 18-20).[1] Even more important is the theoretical criticism. As far as homogenous goods are considered,[2] it should be impossible either for local or for foreign suppliers to raise prices unilaterally. If consumers consider local and foreign

---

[1]   Turner and Van't dack 1993, p. 28, argue however, that goods which are potentially tradeable should be included.

[2]   From the point of view of the demanders, homogenous goods are identical. Thus they can be treated as perfect substitutes. Price differences for such goods can persist only to a very limited extent and the 'law of one price' is a good approximation of reality in this case. However, there are only very few goods which fit into this category. Examples are raw materials and certain intermediate products. The bulk of international trade is in heterogeneous products which allow for much wider price differences (Isard 1977).

goods to be identical, they will only buy the cheaper goods. Thus, those producers which have increased prices either have to lower them or they won't be able to sell anything. The matter is quite different, if local goods and foreign goods are considered to be different. In this case divergent price developments are possible to a certain degree. However, in this case, it is questionable whether a real appreciation can be interpreted to indicate a decrease in competitiveness and a real depreciation an increase in competitiveness (Turner and Van't dack, 1993 p. 28). If, for instance, local producers are able to increase the demand for their products (via advertising, quality improvements, better service, etc.) they can charge higher prices without losing market shares. The increased demand for local goods may even translate into a nominal appreciation. The combined effect of price increases and the nominal appreciation is equal to a real appreciation. But it would not make sense to interpret this real appreciation as a decline in international competitiveness, however defined. Given the increased willingness to pay for local goods, rather the opposite is true: the real appreciation indicates an improvement in international competitiveness.

To avoid these shortcomings of price indices, often cost indices are used to calculate real exchange rates. Since wages are the most important cost component and since other costs are hard to measure, usually indices describing the development of labour costs are employed.[1] In order to account for productivity changes most economists use indices of unit labour costs (Turner and Van't dack 1993, pp. 32-5). A real appreciation calculated on the basis of unit labour costs implies that labour costs – calculated in the same currency – have been rising faster than in foreign countries. Therefore, a real appreciation is interpreted as an indicator of a decline in ability to sell.

However, several factors make it very difficult to interpret real exchange rate indices which are based on unit labour costs. First, it cannot generally be presupposed that the development of labour costs in the local and the foreign economy takes place in sectors where nearly identical goods are produced. 'Unit' labour costs can only be used to compare the cost situation in different countries, when the units are equal. If the goods involved are heterogeneous, stronger rises in costs (lower declines) can also be due to quality improvements. In this case, a real appreciation cannot be interpreted as an indicator for a deterioration in competitiveness. Second, productivity is endogenous. If real wages are pushed upwards, productivity will adapt via reductions of employment. In such cases average productivity may rise. But this would be the result of a lack in competitiveness of certain suppliers – not of an increase in competitiveness (Turner and Van't dack 1993, pp. 33-4.). Third, it has to be kept in mind that labour costs are an important but not the only cost factor (Deutsche Bundesbank 1994, pp. F 52-4, Turner

---

[1]   Labour costs are discussed in more detail in chapter 4.IV.C.

and Van't dack 1993, p. 33). Therefore, the development of unit labour costs may not give an unbiased picture of the development of the entire costs of production. If, for instance, labour is substituted for capital, there will be a tendency for labour unit costs to decline. Capital costs on the other hand are rising. Finally, the prices of imported intermediate goods are also not included in labour cost indices.

Figure 3.1:   Real exchange rates, Germany

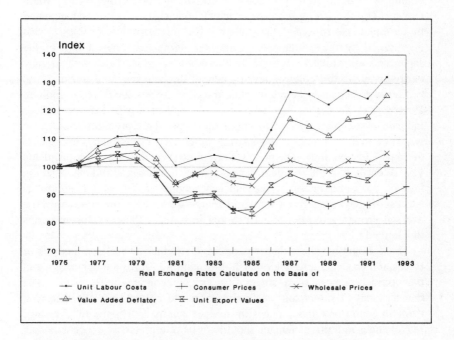

Source: IMF (a), Deutsche Bundesbank (b), own calculations.

The development of various real exchange rate indices for the German economy clearly shows how difficult these indices are to interpret. The first thing that is immediately evident is the marked difference in the development of the various indices. Although they exhibit a similar pattern, indicating a real appreciation in the late 1970s, a real depreciation in the early 1980s and again a real appreciation in the middle of the 1980s and at the beginning of the 1990s, the levels are strongly divergent. For the period from 1975 to 1992, the index which is based on unit labour costs in manufacturing indicates a real appreciation of more than 30 per cent, while the index which is based on consumer prices indicates a real depreciation of 10 per cent. Other indices for real exchange rates are lying between these two extreme cases. Clearly, without additional information it is hardly possible to interpret this divergent development of real exchange rate indices.

One interpretation which has been put forward is that the divergent development reflects the relatively strong productivity growth in the non-tradeables sector (Turner and Van't dack 1993, p. 46). In contrast to most other countries, in Germany productivity in the non-tradeables sector has been rising faster than in the tradeables sector (ibid., pp. 98-102). If the non-tradeables sector provides inputs for the tradeables sector the latter is bound to benefit from productivity growth in the former. This would explain why the strong increase in unit labour costs was not accompanied by an equal rise in export unit values.[1] The role of non-tradeables is also highlighted by the example of Japan. The large real appreciation of the Japanese yen which is derived on the basis of wider price indices may partly be due to the sluggish development of the non-tradeables sector.[2]

This argument may help to explain the gap between the different indices. However, it does not help to answer the question whether the indices indicate a rise or a decline in competitiveness. This problem arises even when the indices are not as far apart as in the case of Germany. In the case of Japan, for example, all indices show a marked real appreciation of the yen. According to the competitiveness approach this would indicate a strong loss of competitiveness of the Japanese economy. Given the enormous success of Japanese firms in world markets and the comparatively high average growth rate of the real national income, such a conclusion seems ill-founded.

These examples show that it is doubtful whether an isolated analysis of prices and costs can provide enough information to form a judgement about the competitiveness of a single firm or an economy as a whole. The development of prices and costs always has to be analysed together with demand conditions and changes in product quality. Furthermore, exchange rate changes and price changes should not be interpreted as exogenous data whose development is more or less independent of the real side of the economy. This may be appropriate for a short-run analysis. As the analysed period is extended, this procedure becomes more and more problematic. As the Council of Economic Experts in Germany put it: 'In the medium run fundamental changes which affect the competitive position of an economy have a stronger influence on the real exchange rate than in the short run.' (Sachverständigenrat 1988, paragraph 150; our translation). In a longer run

---

[1]   Turner and Van't dack 1993, p. 46, also propose that German exporters may not have been able to increase prices in international markets when German wages rose. Given the long and steady increase of the gap between unit labour costs and unit export values, this is hardly plausible.

[2]   One important Japanese non-tradeables sector with relatively low productivity increases is retailing.

analysis changes of prices and exchange rates have to be derived from fundamental changes. To simply assume that they independently influence the competitive situation of an economy is not justified. Therefore, at least in the longer run, the real exchange rate should be viewed as the result of competitiveness and not as its determinant.

4. A Different View of Current Account Balances: Locational Quality

I. International competition for mobile resources

Up to now, we discussed a variety of indicators which are supposed to measure international competitiveness. All of them – including the real exchange rate – did not allow very valid and helpful conclusions. This reflects the problem of applying the analytical concept of ability to sell from a firm to a whole economy. Whereas a firm can go bankrupt, an economy as a whole cannot. In a firm, the whole staff can become unemployed which is inconceivable for the complete labour force of a country. Only some of the workers will become jobless in the course of a structural change. Either new opportunities will offer new jobs or the real wages in the old industries will decline. The factors of production in an economy can be adjusted to new circumstances. Moreover, there are factors which are internationally (but not between firms) immobile, for instance land and (by and large) labour force. They are not able to 'disappear' from an economy in the same way as they are able to leave a firm.

Because of the lack of factor mobility the performance of industries or firms is interdependent. A structural crisis in one industry leads to sectoral unemployment. The whole national labour market is put under pressure. On the other hand, an improvement in the performance of one industry leads to higher wages and/or an appreciation of the national currency. Thus, the international competitiveness of other industries decreases. Therefore, in order to look at international competitiveness it is not useful to analyse an industry or a firm individually.

Having the interdependence in mind, another concept of international competitiveness seems much more convincing in order to explain current and capital account balances. This is the concept of locational competition, that is competition for investment between countries (Fels 1988a). Capital as a factor of production has reached a very high degree of international mobility, at least if compared with labour. Decreasing costs of information and communication have made the process of production more decentralized. Nowadays, it is possible to produce simultaneously in more than one country; research and development can be separated locally from production (mobile Schumpeter goods). Hence, international locational competition is on the rise. The immobile factors in different countries compete for the mobile ones, mainly capital. The capital owners invest where they can reach a high return on investment – compared to other places and other assets. The immobile factors are beneficiaries of the

86

investment, too, because their income, employment, and economic growth, in general, depend among other things on the stock of capital in the respective country. Therefore, locational quality has been gaining more and more importance in economic policies during the last decade.[1]

Using the concept of locational competition, the traditional interpretation of current account balances is no longer valid. Rather than being an indicator of high competitiveness, a current account surplus may indicate that the capital owners estimate the international competitiveness of the location to be low. Thus, a current account deficit would indicate high and a current account surplus low competitiveness. But this interpretation also does not always hold because a net capital account deficit can have many reasons:

- the tendency to save more or to consume less,
- an increase of the marginal return on investment abroad,
- economic policy at home disturbing the mechanism of relative prices which is a disincentive to invest, or
- international transfer by the government.

Yet, keeping these reservations in mind, it seems to be possible to gain information about the locational quality of a country by looking at net capital flows.

II. Some notes on the structure of international capital movements

As should have become clear, the interpretation and normative judgement of the capital balance is by no means unambiguous. Neither is a net capital inflow *per se* positive nor is a net capital outflow to be judged negatively without looking at the facts behind the balance. Therefore, the capital account is to be examined with respect to three structural features:

- the maturity of the capital flows,
- the share of foreign direct investments (FDI) in capital flows, and
- the level of privately motivated flows as compared to those of the public.

Looking at capital imports, a high share of long-term capital imports, a high portion of FDI and mainly private debtors, are generally meant to reflect a high locational quality. Concerning capital exports, high long-term capital exports, especially FDI by private agents, often is considered to be a

---

[1]   In 1994, the German government passed a law which was meant to enhance locational quality ('Standortsicherungsgesetz').

sign for low locational quality at home which makes investors engage abroad. Is this a generally valid interpretation?

We now turn to the first feature: one can distinguish short-term and long-term capital flows; short-term flows are statistically defined as the purchase or sale of an asset with a time to maturity of less than one year. All other assets are said to be long-term ones. The longer the borrower can use the capital, the better he can schedule. From his point of view, it seems persuasive that long-term capital flows are to be preferred. Moreover, the maturity of an asset can show how venturesome the investor is and how much confidence he has in the borrower. A long-term asset shows a lot of confidence of the investor. But one has to distinguish between the legal life of an asset and its real maturity. Capital assets are internationally tradeable in many cases so that the maturities can be transformed to a large extent. Therefore, a formally short-term asset can be intended to be a long-term one and vice versa. The transformation can be done by a person or by a country.

Switzerland is an example for transformation of maturities. In 1988, Swiss banks imported net short-term capital (7 bn SFR), whereas at the same time they exported net long-term capital to the amount of 2.6 bn SFR (Statistisches Bundesamt (b)). If one believes in the above-mentioned hypothesis, this should be interpreted as a sign for a lack of locational quality. Therefore, growth and employment in Switzerland should be low which is not the case. Long-term growth is comparable to other OECD countries, with a very high per capita income. Moreover, there is nearly full employment. The same thing could be witnessed in Japan in the late 1980s. Between 1983 and 1989 Japan's cumulated net long-term capital exports amounted to US$ 620 bn, which was more than US$ 200 bn above the current account surplus. The difference was made up by net short-term capital imports (Tavlas and Ozeki 1992). But, Japan is not an example for an uncompetitive economy. These two examples make clear that the maturity structure of capital flows cannot be interpreted easily. Moreover, one can imagine an inverse structure of interest rates being an incentive for investing mainly in short-term assets without any considerations about locational quality. In the case of Japan, Japanese banks financed the long-term lending of dollars with short-term borrowing of dollars (Turner 1991). Therefore, the maturity of international assets itself does not have much of an explanatory power for the locational quality and the potential growth in real income and employment of a country.

Normally, the second criterion, the volume of FDI, is said to have more explanatory power in measuring locational quality. Besides capital, it is technological know-how, management quality and marketing knowledge that is crossing the borders. This technological transfer can cause positive externalities in the recipient country if it includes a better training of the workforce. Real GNP is growing faster than the entrepreneur's profits. This effect has been especially emphasized for developing countries (IMF 1985,

p. 9). But often FDI are used to buy a firm or a participating share without a net increase in producing capacity. In this case they do not automatically create new jobs.

In order to judge locational quality on the base of FDI flows, another reservation is very important. One has to ask why foreign direct investment takes place. If it is used to bypass trade barriers it will be impossible to draw any conclusion on the locational quality of the recipient country. If the investment takes place in order to set up a distributional network only a few new jobs will be created. After the German unification there was a tendency for investing in distributional networks. The privatization was most successful in the range of trade and commerce. But not many new jobs were created. Besides that, domestic market oriented foreign direct investments incorporate a high risk for the investor.

In order to compare FDI with portfolio investments concerning their impact on growth and employment it is important to examine how the domestic capital markets inside and outside the recipient countries work. Under perfectly working capital markets it makes no difference whether the capital inflow is an FDI or a portfolio investment. The borrower who is creditworthy is able to borrow on international markets on the same terms as any foreign investor. It makes no difference if capital flows between industrial countries are FDI or portfolio investments, if two conditions are fulfilled. First, the transfer of technological and management skills should not play an important role and second, most controls of capital movements between those countries have to be abandoned. Both is the case.

The situation is quite different, if the capital markets are working imperfectly. For in this case it proves difficult for domestic entrepreneurs to raise a credit on international capital markets. Foreigners face a very high risk in making a portfolio investment. Thus, the only way to raise growth and employment in a country with foreign capital is by FDI. Such is the situation in many developing countries and in the former communist countries of Central and Eastern Europe. This shows that a high proportion of long-term capital inflows including FDI relative to short-term flows does not necessarily imply high locational quality. It may simply be a reflection of poorly working internal capital markets. Similarily, a large volume of short-term inflows may be due to high competitiveness of local banks which also become active in international maturity transformation (Krüger 1995).

The third criterion to judge international capital flows concerning locational quality or potential growth and employment distinguishes between private and public borrowers. Normally, a private borrower is forced to spend the funds in an efficient way because of the necessity for repayment which has to be done by using own resources. Public debts can be treated less carefully, although the discharge of public debts is obligatory, too. The funds to fulfil this obligation can be raised more easily than in the case of a private debtor, either at the expense of the taxpayers or by reducing the claims of the savers. Public choice theory suggests that public spending is by far not as efficient as private spending.[1] Nevertheless, public spending for investment – for instance in infrastructure – is often necessary as intermediary goods for private investors. Hence, they can be valued as very beneficial. Consequently, not every public expenditure has to be condemned, in quite the same way as not every kind of private spending is desirable, for instance consumption financed by fresh capital without intertemporal considerations.

Second, presume a net capital export. The above considerations do not play a key role in the calculation of a lender. The main determinant of capital exports is the expected return on investment. One can imagine a situation in which a public asset is preferred to a private asset, although under certainty the expected return of a public asset is lower, but under uncertainty the risk of private investment is higher due to an inappropriate economic policy abroad. The investor has to fear expropriation or growing tax burdens, for example.

Another indicator for a good locational quality of a country may be the share of private foreign lenders. The more private agents are involved, the better the locational quality can be assessed. On the other hand, the higher the share of foreign public institutions among the lenders is, the more the locational quality can be questioned because the loan can be the result of political negotiations and has nothing to do with high expected returns on investment.

To sum up, examining the maturity of capital flows does not make it easier to assess a capital account deficit with regard to growth and employment. The better international capital markets work, the more comfortably maturity transformation can take place. Moreover, the distinction of portfolio investments and foreign direct investment does not help to consider locational quality of the recipient country when capital markets work well. Only the distinction of private and public investments makes an evaluation easier: the more a country is able to attract private capital and the more the loans are used for investment instead of consumption, the higher the locational quality of this country should be estimated.

III. The international supply of capital

A. Age, Savings, and the Current Account: Theoretical Reasoning

In order to explain international capital flows with factors of supply it is necessary to focus on savings in different countries. Relatively high or even

---

[1]   See for instance Niskanen 1971.

growing savings at home *ceteris paribus* cause a net capital export which leads to a current account surplus. To illustrate the importance of the level of savings for the current account, one only needs to refer to the United States, Japan, and Germany. The savings of the US were diminishing in the early 1980s. Since then, their current account exhibits a persistent deficit.[1] In Japan and Germany savings increased in the mid-1980s accompanied by a rising current account surplus in both countries.

According to neoclassical thinking, the level of savings is determined by the interest rate, given the individual discount rate. A rising real interest rate causes savings to increase. From a Keynesian point of view the reason for an individual to save is slightly different: a tie between income and consumption is modelled with savings as a residuum. The higher the income is, the more the individual saves. Both concepts are theoretically unsatisfactory and have proved empirically not to be solid (Hoffmann 1989, pp. 55-7). A model which is better suited to explain the savings behaviour of economic agents is the life-cycle model (Modigliani 1986) which is based on the intertemporal utility maximization approach as discussed in chapter 2 of this study. The individual has a lifetime utility function which he maximizes in the well-known way under a budget constraint over many periods. The budget constraint contains the heritage from the generation of his parents and the discounted income of all years of his life minus his planned bequest to the following. Saving would be unnecessary if the periodical income exactly would match the planned periodical consumption every year. Such a synchronization is rather unlikely. Quite the contrary, it seems probable that the periodical income of the first and the last years in a human being's life is lower than preferred consumption, whereas his periodical income exceeds his planned consumption when he is in his middle age. To overcome these divergences the individual will lend against his human capital in his youth, will save in order to pay back this credit and create wealth when middle-aged, and will dissave after his retirement.[2]

It is easily possible to apply this idea to a whole economy: the higher the share of middle-aged people (from 40 through 65 years) in a country is, the higher are the savings in the economy as a whole. The national savings–GNP ratio will *ceteris paribus* rise in the course of an increasing share of the working population in the economy. More savings is tantamount to a higher supply of capital. A constant demand for capital presumed, the

---

[1]   During the 1970s, the link between savings and the current account was not that strong in these countries. Whereas the level of savings was similar to that in the 1980s, the current account imbalances were by far lower than in the following decade. One should, however, keep in mind that the mobility of capital in the 1970s was much lower than it is nowadays.

[2]   There are two necessary conditions for this model to work in the neoclassical framework: First, capital markets have to work well, even financing the formation of human capital. Second, there is no redistributive state. As we will work out later, these conditions are not fulfilled in many countries.

national interest rate will tend to fall because of the rise in supply. This will change international capital flows since the suppliers of capital want to realize the higher interest rate abroad. Therefore, they export capital which will equilibrate[1] national and international rates of return again, provided the structure of population abroad does not change in the same way. A net capital export can also take place without a change in structure of domestic population. For if the demand for capital is similar all over the world, a significant lower or a diminishing saving rate abroad is sufficient for net capital exports. Vice versa, a decrease in saving at home leads *ceteris paribus* to net capital imports.

These considerations are often called into question. It is often claimed that individuals, in general, are not able to care adequately for their old-age protection. Instead they are said to overemphasize present consumption at the expense of future consumption.[2] Consequently, in most countries there exist state-run old-age protection systems on a pay-as-you-go principle which normally contain some distributive elements besides the protection for old age. Another way to organize an old-age protection is a fully funded system.[3] Under the funding principle the premiums of all employees are invested in the capital market. In this way, every employee is building up an individual capital stock – although he does not have it at his own disposal. After his retirement, the capital stock is reduced for consumption. The elder generation sells its capital, so to say, to the next generation. Therefore, the economy as a whole permanently owns a positive capital stock. Moreover, the installation of a fully funded system does not distort the individual savings decisions.

In contrast, the system on a pay-as-you-go basis does not create a positive capital stock.[4] The premiums of the actual employees are *uno acto* given to the pensioners. Thus, the impacts of the two old-age protection systems on the capital stock of an economy are quite different. Compared with the fully funded old age protection, the pay-as-you-go principle leads to a lower capital stock (Homburg 1988, p. 55). Consequently, in the period in which the capital stock is built up aggregate saving is influenced as well. Therefore, the national level of savings is dependent on the structure of age on one hand and – at least transitory – on the system of old-age protection on the other hand.

---

[1]   This will only be the case, if there are no controls of capital movements.

[2]   The fact that people discount future consumption is cited as supporting evidence. As Homburg 1988, however, shows to discount future consumption does not necessarily mean that man estimates it lower. Instead he argues that the evaluation of present consumption can be dependent on age. A thirty year old man may evaluate a consumption worth one thousand US$ higher than a seventy year old man.

[3]   In principle, both systems could be run by the state or by private firms.

[4]   Nevertheless, no matter which system is used there exists a positive capital stock in the economy which is funded by private or governmental savings.

So far, we have discussed a stationary economy. The regular situation, however, is a growing economy where GNP increases every year. We again distinguish between a fully funded system of old-age protection and a pay-as-you-go system of social security. The results do not change substantially when we suppose a growing economy. Suppose the old-age pensions are growing with the same rate as the GNP. Therefore, premia have to grow at that rate, too. Suppose further that individual savings as a ratio of GNP stays constant over time, that is its absolute amount grows with the same rate as GNP. In a fully funded system, the whole economy saves more than in a system that works on a pay-as-you-go basis, since the premia are added to the capital stock of the elder generation. If the pay-as-you-go principle is applied, overall savings will be reduced, since the premia which are reducing the private savings[1] are used for instant consumption.

B. Age, Savings and the Current Account: Empirical Evidence

Does an empirical assessment provide evidence in favour of these theoretical considerations? In order to answer this question, we take a look at the situation in two net capital exporting countries (Japan and Germany) and in three net capital importing nations (United States, United Kingdom, and Canada) during the 1980s. One has to take into account the share of middle-aged people (from 40 through 64) and the organization of the system of old-age protection as determinants of savings.

During the 1980s, both in Germany and Japan the share of middle-aged people has climbed from under 30 per cent to 32 per cent and 31 per cent respectively (Table 4.1). In the same period gross savings in Germany rose from 20 to 26 per cent, and also increased in Japan, namely from 28 to 34 per cent. Moreover, the 1980s were characterized by high deficits on capital account in both countries. In Germany, net capital exports amounted to more than four per cent of GNP, in Japan it came to nearly four per cent of GNP. The German cumulated deficits (in terms of GNP) are a little bit higher than in Japan, although Japanese gross savings exceed those of Germany significantly (about 9 percentage points). How can these differences be explained? The system of old-age protection in Germany provides less incentive to save individually than the Japanese. Whereas in Germany the maximum pension is 60 per cent of the last income and the minimum insurance time is 5 years, in Japan the pension is only up to the maximum of 30 per cent of the income and it is necessary to be insured for at least 25 years (Holzmann 1990, pp. 152-3). Therefore, in order to have a comparable income after retirement, a Japanese citizen has to save individually more than a German. To sum up, for the net exporting

---

[1]   However, it is possible that increasing premia due to an aging population will change the savings behaviour of the working people.

countries the link between age, old-age protection, and capital outflows seems to be empirically valid.

Table 4.1:   Age structure in five OECD countries

Country/Age		40-59	60-64	65 and elder
U.S.	*1980*	20.4	4.5	11.3
	1991	21.7	4.2	12.5
Germany*	*1980*	25.9	3.8	15.5
	1991	26.4	5.4	15.0
U.K.	*1981*	22.8	5.2	14.9
	1991	23.8	5.0	15.6
Canada	*1981*	20.6	4.0	9.8
	1991	23.0	4.4	11.7
Japan	*1980*	24.9	3.8	9.1
	1993	29.2	5.8	13.6

Shares of groups in per cent; (*) including Eastern Germany

Source: Statistisches Bundsamt (a) and (b), various issues, own calculations.

Nevertheless, this result illuminates only one side of the coin. The situation in net capital importing countries has to be considered, too. If the age-structure in the United States, the United Kingdom, and Canada had developed in the same direction, the argument would no longer be convincing. The share of middle-aged persons in the US is lower than in both Japan and Germany (around 25 per cent) and has been nearly constant in the 1980s which can be seen as a tendency to fall relatively to Japan and Germany. Simultaneously, the gross savings ratio fell from nearly 20 per cent to 15 per cent. The general propensity to consume grew in the US during this decade. The same happened in the United Kingdom: the share of middle-aged persons stayed constant, the gross saving rate fell. In both countries the old-age protection system does not provide an old-age income as high as the German one. Hence, the differences in savings are even more evident. As a consequence, both cases of net capital exporters and net capital importers give a piece of evidence in favour of our argument – but it does not seem possible to explain international capital flows by looking on the supply side only, that is on savings.[1]

First, there are significant differences in saving rates without significant differences in net capital exports or imports. Two examples illustrate this fact: the Japanese savings ratio is much higher than the German one. However, Japan's net capital exports are even lower than those of Germany (in terms of GNP). The United States faced net capital inflows all through the 1980s, the United Kingdom did not start to have surpluses before the mid-1980s. Nevertheless, both countries suffered the same diminishing savings ratio during the whole decade (OECD 1994c). Second, the Canadian case cannot support our argument. The share of middle-aged persons increased during the 1980s, the saving rate fluctuated severely. Nevertheless, the capital imports were very high during the 1980s. This phenomenon cannot be explained by analysing the supply-side of capital only. The scarcity of capital and the level of the interest rates depend in the same way on the demand for capital.

As Hayashi (1986) points out, international comparisons of saving rates have to be interpreted with caution. There are problems concerning at least three issues: first, which sectors are relevant in order to calculate national saving rates? Second, which income is the right one, especially in order to reach an international comparison? The third question deals with durable goods: do they contribute to consumption or to investment? He comes to the conclusion that the US savings are underestimated, since all public expenditures are categorized as consumption, and that the Japanese savings are overestimated, since the depreciations are valued at historical costs (Hayashi 1986, pp. 150-63). Nevertheless, the Japanese savings are still substantially higher than US savings.[2]

IV. The demand for capital

Demand for capital depends on the expected rate of return in a country. At first sight, there exist natural candidates for high and persistent capital inflows: the developing countries. Their capital stock is low and therefore the relative price for capital should be high so that they should be attractive for international investors. As far as scarcity of capital is concerned, it should be clear that capital will, normally, flow from industrial countries to developing countries, that is capital flows from the industrial centre towards the underdeveloped periphery, where the marginal efficiency of capital is higher (Giersch 1986, pp. 17-9.). In the process of development, more and

---

[1]   Moreover, the Canadian case does not support our hypothesis that strongly since the share of middle-aged people rose during the 1980s.

[2]   See also chapter 5.I.

more capital will be accumulated, and the capital stock will grow compared with the labour force. In general, in the course of this process the marginal efficiency of capital will diminish.

In the course of economic development, a country typically passes through a so-called debt cycle (Siebert 1989) which proceeds as follows: a debtor country is regarded as young when the credit is used for local investment. Its capital account is in surplus and its current account is in deficit. A country having a surplus in its trade balance which does not compensate the deficit in its balance on services, caused by the interest payments, becomes a mature debtor. Therefore, the current account is still in a deficit. Although the marginal efficiency of capital has decreased – absolutely and compared to other countries – the capital account is in surplus yet. After the capital stock is built up sufficiently the country starts to pay back the credit; the capital account is in deficit while the current account is in surplus: the surplus of the trade balance exceeds the deficit in the balance on services. As soon as the repayment is completed, the country has become a young creditor country. Its citizens own a positive net foreign wealth. Both the trade balance and the balance on services are in surplus, and net foreign wealth is growing because of the capital account deficit. A country is called a mature creditor country when the net foreign position does not change anymore; the capital account is in balance. The citizens consume more than they produce. The deficit in the trade balance is compensated by the surplus in the balance on services, caused by interest payments from abroad.

The Republic of Korea can be used to illustrate the debt cycle, at least up to the year 1989. At the beginning of the 1970s, the country became a debtor country. During this decade, mainly the state was the borrower. Only afterwards private banks and households started to take up credits in the international capital markets in order to invest at home. In the year 1985 the cumulated debt of Korea reached a peak and amounted to US\$ 42.8 bn (Sinn 1990, p. 173). Until 1989, the current account was in a surplus. It helped to pay up the international credits. Since 1990, the current account is in deficit, again. This does not fit exactly the theory of debt cycles. Nevertheless, the early capital imports were used to invest in order to pay up the credit. According to the above mentioned categories, Korea today may be called a mature debtor country.

A. The Demand for Capital in Developing Countries

Following this approach, it should be expected that industrial countries such as the United States, Japan, and Germany (at least the former Federal Republic) do not experience significant and persistent capital imports. On the contrary, since they are relatively well endowed with capital, one should expect the marginal efficiency of capital to be low, compared to the marginal efficiency of developing countries and, nowadays, of former communist countries (including the former GDR). Their capital stock depreciated in the course of the transformation process. As a consequence, capital from the industrial countries should flow into developing and transforming countries, either as portfolio investment or as FDI.

Empirical evidence does not confirm these considerations. The developing countries are by no means the main net capital importing countries. Foreign direct investments are mainly carried out between industrial countries.[1] This is amazing because the national capital markets in developing countries do not work that well and FDI could overcome this problem. Moreover, developing countries do not attract high portfolio investments either. The German capital balance with respect to developing countries illustrates this phenomenon throughout the 1980s.[2] Only 4.3 per cent of the net capital exports from 1981 to 1991 were flowing into developing countries. During this period, the regional capital balance with respect to developing countries was even twice (1986 and 1990) in surplus. Regarding gross capital exports, only 7.5 per cent are invested in developing countries. Less than 20 per cent of German gross long-run capital exports into these countries were FDI. In addition, most of the loans were given by banks; they provided nearly 100 per cent of short-term loans. Private firms or other investors were not willing to shoulder the risks attached to an investment in these countries. There is another interesting tendency in the German capital balance: the former communist countries seem to be a more attractive location for investors than the developing countries. Their share of all net capital exports has risen in the last years. This tendency is likely to even worsen the situation of the traditional developing countries.

Although capital is (absolutely and) relatively scarce, the lack of private investments is a sign for a very low return on investment, even lower than in industrial countries. Apparently, there are facts that decrease the returns in these countries. Some of them may be due to failures in domestic policies, economic and other policies; some may be due to the behaviour and policy-making in other countries. We will, in short, survey possible reasons for the lack of capital inflows.

What makes the locational quality in developing countries that bad? Concerning domestic policy issues, one can quote the following (Hemmer 1988):

– A central point is the guarantee of property rights. The danger of expropriation makes many potential investors refrain from an engagement in

---

[1]   As for FDI, only 7 per cent of German FDI aimed at developing countries.The share was a little higher on average in most of the OECD countries (Stehn 1991, pp.6-8).

[2]   For all data see Deutsche Bundesbank (a).

such a country. Expropriation may be caused, for instance, by political revolution, foreign exchange controls, and a ban on transferring the capital to the country of origin.

– The same problems occur when the transfer of profits is banned or is at least threatened to be banned. If the investor is not able to dispose of the profits, he will not invest in the country in question.

– In addition, numerous institutional weaknesses, as for instance administrational problems, an autocratic political class[1] and the lack of working capital markets are other reasons not to invest in developing countries.

– Often the existence of very high, nearly confiscating taxes on earnings deters foreign investors.

– Very important is a lack of credibility of the monetary policy in a country. Persistent high and volatile inflation is another reason for not attracting capital. Rather it is a reason for domestic citizens to export capital. Many developing countries have experienced a high capital flight during the last years. One important example was the case of Argentina (Mastroberardino 1994).

– Many developing countries are facing the problem of brain drain, that is a lot of highly educated people leave the country in order to reach a higher income abroad. This is quite costly for the country of origin (World Bank 1983, p. 103), since the country is short of factors of production complementary to the capital imports on one hand and it is short of potential entrepreneurs on the other hand. These qualifications would probably attract capital on the international capital markets. The true costs of 'brain drain' may be the subsidies of the state for a type of education which is too specialized for the need of developing country anyway.[2]

The low level of capital imports, however, lies not only within the responsibility of developing countries. A very important determinant of capital flows is the trade policy of industrial countries towards the developing world. Especially the United States, Japan and the European Community have erected a broad range of trade barriers against products from developing countries since they have comparative advantages in the production of Ricardo and Heckscher–Ohlin goods. In Europe, the US and Japan, these industries are under pressure and have successfully called for protection. The international Multi Fibre Agreement and the Common Agricultural Policy of the European Community are two of many relevant examples for trade barriers. Therefore, as long as the markets in industrialized countries are closed for producers of the Third World, it is

---

[1]   For the political economy in developing countries see Krueger 1974 and 1984.

[2]   Thus, it is doubtful whether it helps a developing country economically to have scientist trained in nuclear physics at some reknown universities in the western world.

not attractive for capital owners to invest there. Although a foreign direct investment in developing countries would be worthwhile under normal circumstances, it does not come about because of the low chances to sell the goods produced with the newly created capital stock on the world market. In other words, the marginal efficiency of capital in developing countries is lowered by trade policy as currently applied in the industrialized part of world.

Since international capital flows nearly shun developing countries, in the following we discuss the demand for capital in industrialized countries. What determines locational quality in industrialized countries? The fundamental economic framework in the industrialized world is satisfactory. Therefore, the locational competition these countries are subject to works by using other, more sophisticated, parameters. Nevertheless, the competition seems to be fierce.

B. Rates of Return on Investment: Some Caveats

Turning from supply to demand, we discussed some indicators of locational quality such as, for instance, the structure and direction of international capital flows. Since it turned out that overall international capital flows as well as their structure form a rather poor indicator, the question arises whether we can do better. The most obvious alternative which comes into mind is the rate of return as usually calculated from national accounts. This seems to offer a method for measuring locational quality in the most direct way.

But unfortunately, here, some caveats are in order too. For a conclusion like this takes for granted that the rate of return thus derived is a reliable indicator of locational quality. However, because of statistical problems such as quantifying the compensation for entrepreneural activity and estimating the replacement costs of the capital stock in operation, this is by no means sure. Therefore, the rate of return as derived by national accounts can only be seen as a rough estimate.

An alternative concept often proposed for estimating the rate of return on investment is to calculate the rate of return directly from the companies' balance sheets.[1] The argument put forward to support a calculation like this is that an increase of the rate of return as derived by national accounts can be primarily the outcome of an increase in the rate of return on monetary assets. Thus, it need not reflect a rise in the rate of return on investment in productive capacities. What is neglected in this case is, however, that the rate of return on monetary assets also depends very much on the rate of return on the productive capital stock, as long as the former reflects interest

---

[1]   For details as well as problems in estimating gross rates of return on the basis of national accounts see Dicke and Trapp 1984.

payments on outstanding debt in the corporate sector. If, however, the rate of return is estimated on the basis of profits as shown on the balance sheet, only the rate of return on equity is considered as relevant. This, however, is too short a perspective. For the attractiveness of a location for investment also depends on the rate of return which creditors can hope to expect.

The rate of return as derived from national accounts has the advantage of being an indicator for the rate of return on investment in general, independent of whether financed by equity or debt. The argument against the use of national account figures, therefore, applies only for the part of gross income from assets which reflect the rate of return on government bonds. Moreover, rates of return which are derived directly from the balance sheets of the private sector have the same shortcomings as the ones which are calculated on the basis of national accounts. Pure profits have to be separated from labour income of the self-employed and costs of replacement have to be estimated, both of which must be deducted from gross figures.

Whichever route one takes, all results derived in estimating the gross rate of return have to be interpreted very carefully. The case in point is that looking at national figures only might give rise to wrong conclusions. Whether a project in the country under consideration is worthwile undertaking or not, depends not only on national aspects alone. In addition, the rate of return expected by market participants from an investment abroad has to be taken into consideration as well.[1] For if the expected rate of return on investment abroad climbs and thus capital exports are on the rise, all those projects in the capital export country which earn a lower rate of return will not be competitive anymore. Although the average rate of return on domestic investment as shown by the statistics has increased, locational quality has declined in relative terms. The reason is that all the firms remaining in the market must at least offer a rate of return which is comparable to the one expected from an investment abroad.[2]

Therefore, only an international comparison of gross rates of return expected from investments in different locations *before* undertaking a decision concerning the location could give a reliable information about a country's attractiveness in terms of locational quality. An ex ante figure like this, however, can not be derived from the statistics.

A closer look at German data will highlight the case in point: looking at the rates of return as calculated from national accounts, Germany seems to

---

[1] Moreover, calculations show capital income gross of taxation. Tax payments, however, are also decisive for the attractiveness of undertaking a project. See chapter 4.IV.D.

[2] An increase in the rate of return abroad works in the same direction as an increase in deficit spending by the domestic government. This is at least the case if the public sector absorbs an ever higher share of world savings, without world savings increasing correspondingly. In the international struggle for mobile capital only those firms will prove to be competitive which can offer a similar or higher rate of return as the government.

have lost ground in the early 1980s.[1] In the late 1980s, however, the rate of return in Germany improved again (Figure 4.1). The latter stands in stark contrast to the hypothesis that Germany has lost in attractiveness as a location for investment during the 1980s and has therefore experienced a surge in net capital outflows, which was accompanied by a correspondingly high surplus on current account. Seeing the huge surplus on current account, this is at least what would be supposed on the basis of the intertemporal approach. Yet, at the same time as the surplus on current account was on the rise in the second half of the 1980s, the rate of return on investment as derived from national accounts climbed too.

Figure 4.1:   *Rates of return according to national accounts: Germany's performance in the 1980s*

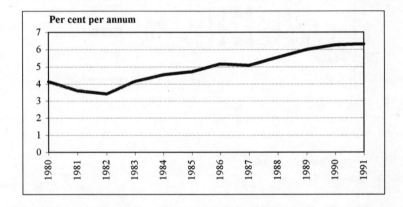

Source: Statistisches Bundesamt (c), own calculations.

If Germany had indeed gained ground in the international competition for mobile resources in the 1980s, the improvement should not only show up in the rate of return, but also in a correspondingly high investment activity. Investment activity, however, was rather sluggish in Germany. Even after the recession of the early 1980s the annual rate of growth in investment remained quite flat. Frequently, real growth rates in investment were well below of those experienced by other major OECD countries.

As Figure 4.2 shows, the success of German firms on world markets in the 1980s was not accompanied by a correspondingly high investment activity. It was not before 1989 that the rate of growth in real investment in

---

[1]   In this case, capital income minus a fictional compensation for management in owner-led firms is related to net productive assets valued at costs of replacement.

Germany was higher than the one which the rest of the OECD countries experienced on average. Thus, investment activity in Germany picked up just at the time as the German current account turned into deficit, namely in 1990/91, and as the rest of the world slipped into recession. Hence, looking at the rates of return only fails to take into account that projects must also earn an internationally competitive return.

Figure 4.2:   *Annual rate of change in real gross investment 1980-1995:*
                Germany, United States, Japan, United Kingdom, total of
                OECD countries

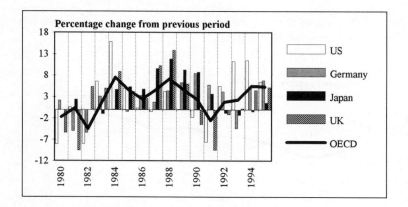

1994/95: Estimates and projections.
Source: OECD 1994c.

To sum up: in principle, rates of return would be the appropriate indicator for comparing capital demand internationally. However, an approach like this faces two difficulties: first, rates of return are very hard to quantify. Second, estimates are ex post figures after international capital flows have taken place. Consequently, we do have to focus on indicators which also give some information about the rates of return ex ante. In the following, we will therefore focus on locational quality and investment activity in a more direct way, namely labour costs, capital costs and budget policy.

C. Labour Costs, Capital Flows and Balances on Current Account

There are many factors which make up for locational quality, for instance political stability, the economic and political constitution, economic policy (such as, for instance, fiscal policy, especially taxation, monetary policy, environmental policy and regulations prevailing), an R&D-friendly

atmosphere, an efficient infrastructure and administration and the qualification of workers.

Notwithstanding the relevance of all the factors mentioned, it is very often labour costs which are stressed in policy-orientated discussions. And even though they are considered as being decisive for locational quality (that is capital account balances) usually, here again arguments are very often put forward which are based on the competitiveness approach: for, generally, they run from labour costs to a country's international price and cost competitiveness and end up in talking about consequences for the overall ability to sell and the balance on current account.

So, let us therefore take a closer look at the role labour costs play for international competitiveness, however defined. What makes labour costs one of the factors most focused on when it comes to international competitiveness is the fact that they differ widely. This becomes most evident when average wages prevailing in less developed countries are compared to those paid in the rest of the world. In principle, the same applies when the major industrialized countries are considered only. Although differences are substantially smaller, the fact that the linkages by international capital and trade flows are much stronger amongst the latter than between the developed and the less developed world seems to make them even more important a factor. For in the case of less developed countries government influenced capital flows form a major part of the linkages provided by international capital flows. Yet, with such a high level of government intervention, capital flows into less developed countries can hardly be regarded as the outcome of individual considerations about the market rate of return.

For sure, labour costs form only one cost component amongst several. Yet, the high share labour costs take in total costs of production and the enormous international differences in gross compensation per hour suggest that labour costs make up an important factor in the international competition for mobile resources. In Germany, for instance, labour costs currently make up for more than a quarter of gross product in mining and manufacturing. Moreover, most of the other factors of production are more mobile internationally than labour. This suggests that in these cases prices are linked more closely together. Consequently, all firms are affected similarly by a change in their costs, wherever they are located.[1]

Yet, it is not sufficient to look only at the direct compensation of workers. Other costs such as social security payments (independent of whether they are laid down in the legislation, in tariff agreements or voluntarily paid) have to be considered as well.[2] Concerning the burden

---

[1]   For details see Fels 1988b, p. 141.

[2]   From an economic point of view, costs of labour market regulations have to be added as well, e.g. extensive job security of those already employed and compensations to be paid in

labour costs pose, it is of no importance whether they are paid either by the employee or the employer.

Table 4.2: *Total hourly compensation for manufacturing workers for a selection of countries, converted at current exchange rates*

	Total hourly compensation for manufacturing workers (wage plus supplementary benefits)	Total hourly compensation for manu facturing workers (excluding social insurance contributions payable by the employers, family allowances and other social security benefits)	
	1991	1992	1993
	US$	US$	US$
Portugal	4,22		
Greece	6,73	4,60	4,24
Ireland	12,11	10,03	9,15
Spain	12,66		
United Kingdom	13,40		
Japan	14,40		
France	15,28		
USA	15,45	11,46	11,74
Italy	17,18		
Canada	17,33	11,99	12,25
Austria	17,49		
Denmark	18,07		
Netherlands	18,58		
Belgium	19,44	10,98	
Finland	20,62		
Sweden	22,09	13,87	10,7
Germany	22,20	14,41	14,39

Source: 1991: World Economic Forum 1993; 1992-93: United Nations 1994; exchange rates: OECD 1994c.

case of an organizational restructuring. They count for fixed costs of employment and thus impede structural change. However, in these cases quantification is much harder to do. On this issue see Giebel 1985, Lazear 1990 and Blanchard et al. 1985 as well as Deregulierungskommission (German Commission on Deregulation) 1991, chapter 8.

In Germany, for instance, additional costs are almost as high as the direct compensation, whereas in several other OECD countries the share of direct compensation in total compensation is much higher. In the United Kingdom, for instance, it came up to 73 per cent in the late 1980s, in the United States to 71 per cent.[1]

If compared in dollars, Germany topped the list in average hourly compensation of workers in manufacturing in 1991, followed by Sweden, Finland and the smaller European countries. Canada, Italy, the United States, France, Japan and the UK were in the pack. Spain, Ireland, Greece and Portugal, although differing widely, formed the bottom line. Looked at from this perspective, the level of compensation seems indeed to reflect net trade flows of the same year: whereas the US was slightly in deficit (US$ 6.9 bn), Germany was even more so (US$ 19.4 bn). Japan more than formed the counterpart by scoring a surplus on current account of US$ 73 bn while at the same time showing the lowest compensation per hour of all of three. Yet, as is well known, productivity has to be considered as well, and frequently countries which rank upon the highest in terms of wages per hour do so in labour productivity too. Therefore, the correspondance of current account deficits (surpluses) and high (low) labour costs is not conclusive.

If differences in productivity are taken into account, thus comparing unit labour costs, there is no clear cut relationship between the average size of labour costs on the one hand and the balance on current account on the other hand.[2] This is not surprising, since consequences of a change in unit labour costs differ depending on whether

- there is an excessive level of compensation in a regime of flexible exchange rates,
- there is an excessive level of compensation in a regime of fixed exchange rates, or
- the regional or sectoral structure of wages does reflect the relative scarcity of labour or not.

a) Differences in wages and the exchange rate regime

Yet, the nominal burden labour costs make up in Japan, the United States and Germany as measured in national currency shows indeed striking

---

[1]   For the different components in total labour costs see Statistisches Bundesamt (d), edition 1991, p. 58. For an overview of labour costs in manufacturing of twenty industrialized countries in 1991 (including perquisites) see Institut der deutschen Wirtschaft 1992a, p. 3. According to the latter, labour costs per hour in West Germany ranked among the highest with 40.48 D-Mark. Further international comparisons can be found in Hemmer 1991 and Salowsky 1991, pp. D 5-7.

[2]   The consequences of labour costs for the balance on current account are examined by Corden 1994, chapter 3 and 15, van Suntum 1986, Orlowski 1982 and Meyer and Willgerodt 1956. For a critical view on competitiveness, trade balances and wages see also Krugman and Lawrence 1993 and Fagerberg 1988.

parallels with the respective development of the balance on current account. In the decade between 1980 and 1990 unit labour costs[1] climbed in nominal terms in Japan as well as in Germany much slower than in the United States (Figure 4.3). Whereas Japan and Germany showed persisting surpluses on current account, the United States formed the counterpart by running high deficits.

Figure 4.3:   Unit labour costs in the business sector: United States, Germany, Japan 1980-1995[2]

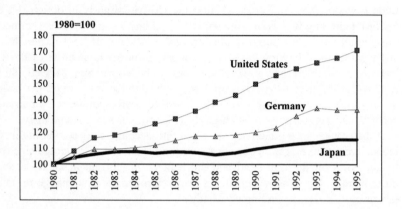

1994/95: Estimates and Projections.
Source: OECD 1994c, own calculations.

This seems to be in support of the commonly made assumption that there is a clear cut relationship running from average unit labour costs on the one hand to the sign and the size of the balance on current account on the other hand. However, the recent swing in the bilateral balance on current account in Germany *vis-à-vis* Japan cannot be traced back to the substantial increase of nominal wages and unit labour costs in Germany as experienced in the early 1990s. Furthermore, as should be apparent from our discussion of the competitiveness approach versus the intertemporal approach, there is no

---

[1]   On the concept of unit labour costs see Sachverständigenrat (German Council of Economic Experts) 1976, paragraph 156. On methodological problems in calculating unit labour costs see Kroker 1990. Problems of calculating and interpreting real exchange rates with regard to competitiveness are discussed, for instance, by Lipschitz and McDonald 1992, Turner and Van't dack 1993 and Marsh and Tokarick 1994.

[2]   Hourly compensation in nominal terms picked up much stronger. However, at the same time as nominal compensation increased, productivity of those employed improved too, so that the rise in unit labour costs was lower than a look at gross hourly earnings would suggest.

theoretical basis for the assumption that labour costs determine the balance on current account.

If competitiveness in costs and prices would shape the balances on current account as well as on capital account, sectors of the economy which are net exporters should in general be those which show relatively low nominal unit labour costs as compared with the unit labour costs of other sectors. However, this is not the case. Again, Germany provides a good example: as Figure 4.4 shows, there is no systematic relationship between the specific unit labour costs on the one hand and net sectoral exports on the other hand. Instead, there are sectors showing high exports on balance in which unit labour costs are above average of the manufacturing industry (engine building, automobile) as well as sectors with unit labour costs below (chemicals).[1]

Figure 4.4:   *Relative unit labour costs in manufacturing and net exports by sector: Germany 1989*

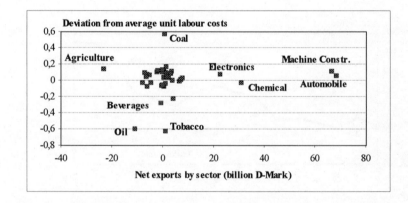

Source: Statistisches Bundesamt (c) and (d), own calculations.

In case of flexible exchange rates, a systematic relationship between unit labour costs and the balance on current account is lacking because the demand for a country's products on world markets not only depends upon the internal development of prices and wages, but also on the exchange rate.[2] Too high a level of wages in the tradeables sector brings about a

---

[1]   Moreover, an approach like this suffers from methodological shortcomings since studies which focus on the consequences of labour costs for net exports do not take into account that market shares within the respective country also reflect the ability to sell.

[2]   See also the study by Deutsches Institut für Wirtschaftsforschung 1992, p. 121, focusing on German labour costs.

depreciation of the respective currency. This becomes visible in inflation-prone countries. In these countries wages usually shadow the rate of inflation as unions try to get a compensation for the purchasing power lost. If firms on average aim at shifting the increase in costs on export prices, demand for tradeables which then are becoming more expensive will decline. Thus, demand for the currency inflating more strongly declines as well. In a regime of flexible exchange rates, high inflation currencies would therefore depreciate *vis-à-vis* other currencies thereby preserving the ability to sell of a high wage country on world markets.[1] Or to say it in somewhat different words: the change in the nominal exchange rate prevents countries with a rather stable monetary framework from gaining in market share on world markets at the expense of countries experiencing a relatively high rate of inflation.[2]

Figure 4.5:   *Real exchange rates based on normalized unit labour costs: United States, Germany, Japan*

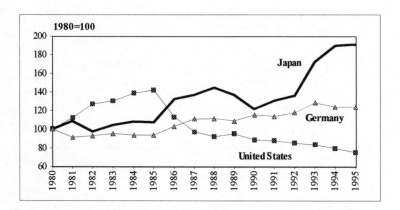

1994/95: Estimates and projections.
Source: 1980-92: IMF (b), edition 1994; 1993-95: OECD 1994c, own calculations.

This shows up, for instance, in the case of Italy: although nominal unit labour costs in national currency increased (primarily because of inflation) by more than twofold during the 1980s, the Italian current account was almost balanced.[3] At the same time, the Italian lira experienced a substantial

---

[1]   Provided that it is indeed a problem of levels only.
[2]   See Orlowski 1982, p. 150, and van Suntum 1986.
[3]   From 1980 to 1991, the consumption price index rose by some 170 percentage points from 100 to 270.5. See IMF (b).

decline in value. If the nominal depreciation is taken into account, it becomes visible that unit labour costs for Italian firms as measured in foreign currency climbed only by some 12 per cent. In the early 1990s the real effective exchange rate based on unit labour costs even declined due to the lira losing substantially in value, although unit labour costs were still on the rise. In the same manner as in case of differences in rates of inflation, flexible exchange rates react to other differences in the level of costs, provided the necessary change in the exchange rate is allowed to take place.[1]

Yet, focusing on real effective exchange rates based on unit labour costs, in the early 1980s differences in labour costs still seem to be in line with the competitiveness approach to the balance on current account: the ability to sell of the US declined rapidly as the real effective exchange rate of the dollar rose sharply. At the same time, unit labour costs in Japan climbed only slightly while the Japanese economy was building up a huge surplus on current account. Germany, lacking any major movement in real effective exchange rates obviously proved also to be more competitive thus being also able to increase net exports substantially. Yet, the competitiveness approach fails to explain the change which took place in 1985/86: balances proved to be persistent or climbed even further, despite the swing in price and cost competitiveness taking place. The intertemporal approach, on the other hand, provides a consistent answer, both for the rise and the decline of the dollar and the real appreciation of the yen and the D-Mark mirroring the former.[2] Evidently, balances on current account of the US, Japan and Germany were not mainly driven by exogenous changes in unit labour costs, but a matter of price and cost competitiveness changing endogenously in the course of adjustment to international capital flows which switch direction in the early 1980s.

Turning back to our question of how exogenous changes in labour costs affect the balance on current account, we have one more qualification to make. Even in case of flexible exchange rates not all movements in the level of wages are compensated for smoothly by the price mechanism thus preserving international competitiveness in the sense of ability to sell. The situation becomes a different one, if those employed not only aim at a compensation for the loss in purchasing power due to inflation but also for the loss in real income due to changes in the exchange rate. For in this case any change in the exchange rate implying a decline in real purchasing power will be made undone by correspondingly higher claims of those employed. Hence, the exchange rate cannot preserve competitiveness on world markets if wage levels are fixed too high (Corden 1994, p. 279). All

---

[1]   For a comparison of unit labour costs in EC countries which takes exchange rates into account see, for instance, Berié and Hofman 1991.

[2]   Another explanation is given by Baldwin and Krugman 1989.

those firms which are not competitive on world markets at such a high level of production costs will have to close down or at least have to shed labour. Technically spoken, the transformation curve of the high-cost country shifts inwards. With production possibilities thus reduced, it might well be that capital flows out, thereby causing a surplus to the balance on current account.

Consequently, the exchange rate only has a chance to preserve the ability to sell in the international sector when there is exchange rate illusion prevailing. If, instead, there is neither money illusion nor exchange rate illusion on the part of those employed and if they still insist on a level of real wages higher than the market can bear, the ability to sell in sectors exposed to international competition will indeed suffer. Contrary to conventional wisdom, high labour costs, preserved by real wage rigidities, will thus have the effect of reinforcing any surplus on current account and of mitigating any deficit. This effect persists as long as capital is looking for new investment opportunities abroad (because of losing paying production possibilities at home) due to a decline in international cost competitiveness. Focusing on non-tradeables, it is evident that too high a level implies that workers must be laid off and investment must be reduced in the course of which capital exports can increase.

As far as the exchange rate of foreign currencies is stabilized via central bank intervention or monetary policy in general – and this applies especially amongst currencies participating in the EMS – it cannot be excluded that labour costs have stronger consequences for the balance on current account. In a regime of flexible exchange rates, fluctuations in the nominal exchange rate can bring about changes of real wages from nominal wages, thus preserving competitiveness. If, however, the exchange rate mechanism cannot work, jobs are more directly exposed to foreign competition. Too high a level of wages in nominal terms will therefore also prove to be too high in real terms. Hence, in this case it is even in terms of national currency that wages cannot any longer be fixed without taking into account what foreign workers receive in payment. National wages increasing on average by more than in other countries, everything else being the same, will not only imply losses in employment but usually also a net outflow of capital and therefore a surplus on current account.[1] Wages increasing in nominal as well as in real terms by more than the market can bear lead to rationalization effects and shedding of labour. Consequently, productivity rises thus putting unit labour costs again in line with those of major competitors.

This result seems to stand in stark contrast to the commonly made argument that market participants might switch towards foreign goods if wages and thereby unit labour costs should prove to be higher than those of

---

[1]   On labour market aspects of the EU see also Sachverständigenrat 1991, paragraph 391.

foreign competitors. From this perspective comparatively high unit labour costs should show up in a reduction rather than in an increase of the surplus on current account. Yet, this is only the case in a system of fixed exchange rates where the central bank automatically finances any trade deficit – running down the accumulated stock of foreign reserves. An often heard popular belief is that of cost competitiveness being jeopardized by too high a level of wages. However, a situation like this must show up in an additional indicator, namely in a nominal exchange rate getting under pressure thus calling for a decline in the national quantity of money and the stock of foreign reserves.[1] In the medium run, real wages should again be more in line with those of foreign competitors because of the decline in money supply making real wage resistance more expensive in terms of employment forgone. If, instead, the contraction in money supply in the course of the central bank intervening is compensated by increasing money supplied via other channels, we have a classic example of an economy being trapped in a vicious circle.

The fact that the competition for mobile resources becomes tougher the more national markets are opened up and deregulated does by no means imply that wages paid in industrial countries will have to decline to levels known in less developed countries just for staying competitive. This is a concern frequently raised in the political arena. The notion that labour will be generally on the losing side is a faulty one. Instead, some workers will experience a rise in their wages whereas others will have to cut claims if they still want to be employed without adjusting to circumstances, that is by moving either sectorally or regionally. Although there can be no doubt that competition becomes stiffer, there will also be premia for all those being more alert than the average. In other words: the wage structure moves closer to the one reflecting true scarcity, no more, no less. Thus, there is no need to talk about wage dumping which has to be met. Wages which are too low compared to scarcities prevailing are pushed up by mobile resources competing for less mobile ones, namely labour. No doubt, now and then, the process of catching up by trade partners can make for personal hardship. Yet, on average, real income is higher than otherwise due to the rise in the division of labour made possible by opening up national markets and speeding up adjustment. Moreover, as long as local economic policy is reliable and capital endowment, human capital included, makes for higher productivity, relative incomes will be higher too.[2]

---

[1] If the declining competitiveness also leads to outflow of capital, the loss of reserves is even larger, putting into question the sustainability of the fixed exchange rate. Such a situation prevailed, for instance, during the recent crisis in Mexico.

[2] Whereas too low a wage on balance not necessarily attracts capital, it might well be that if wages claimed are too high capital will shun the country. What makes for the difference is that in the former case normally there is no ceiling which limits wages from moving upwards to competitive levels reflecting scarcity. In the latter case, however, the very same

b) Distortions in the wage structure and exchange rate flexibility
So far, no generally valid link between labour costs and the balance on current account could be derived. The consequences of labour costs for locational quality and thus for international capital flows very much depend upon the exchange rate mechanism in place and whether wages are too high in real terms or in nominal terms only. Moreover, looking at the aggregates would not do the job. A much closer look is in order. For average unit labour costs can stand for a wide variety of different wage structures. Focusing on averages only can give therefore rather poor results. This applies to economic theory as well as to economic policy. In the case of the former it might well be that a theory is mistakenly rejected because of being inconsistent with the data. Concerning the latter economic policy might refrain from removing labour market regulations although locational quality is calling for action.

Therefore, it is not only averages which matter for locational quality and competitiveness but also the structure of wages. The wage structure becomes all the more important since a structure which is not in line with scarcity cannot be compensated for by changes in the exchange rate. Even if nominal exchange rates are allowed to fluctuate, exchange rate flexibility can only ensure overall competitiveness. The exchange rate mechanism makes sure that the balance of payments is evened out. In the case of nominal exchange rate flexibility the combined accounts of international capital and trade flows are balanced immediately, whereas in the case of fixed nominal exchange rates the balance of payments is evened out in the short run via changes in the balance on foreign reserves and it is in the medium run that also the combined balances on current and capital account will be evened out.

The distortions of the structure, however, remain. Thus, some sectors and firms will gain in international competitiveness whereas others will suffer a setback.[1] If, instead, it is the nominal level only that is affected, no such shifting in competitive positions within the international sector occurs. Yet, there should be no doubt that labour market regulations and the like usually affect the sectors of the economy differently. Labour market distortions are hardly ever only a matter of levels. Nearly always, the wage structure is distorted as well. Although production may shift towards more capital intensive processes, it might well be that capital exports rather than imports are strengthened, since within the boundaries of the full-employment transformation curve the set of paying projects is by definition smaller than in an economy without any distortions.

---

wage that proves to be too high also forms the bottom line which prevents wages from falling to market clearing levels. Otherwise, a correction by outsiders trying to get a footing in the market would follow suit.

[1] See Orlowski 1982, p. 151.

Table 4.3: Qualification and unemployment: West Germany September 1990

Qualification right before entering unemployment	Total of unemployed labour force	as per cent of the unemployed labour force	with professional training	without professional training
Employees	976329	56.5	536214	440115
— non-skilled workers	438492	25.4	113518	324974
— skilled workers	157477	9.1	130258	27219
— lower level employees	184579	10.7	117363	67216
— higher level employees	195781	11.3	175075	20706
— trainees	29204	1.7	19691	9513
— all other employees	26764	1.5	14530	12234
Employment interrupted or never employed	695445	40.3	349487	345958
— employment interrupted	424772	24.6	207795	216977
— without employment until now	270673	15.7	141692	128981
— of which: with school education finished	74145	4.3	43841	30304

Source: Bundesanstalt für Arbeit 1991, p. 539.

The fact that distortions in the wage structure prove to be detrimental to locational quality can be seen in the case of Germany. For a longitudinal section shows that the structure of wages with respect to different qualifications of workers has remained relatively stable since 1970. In the meantime, however, Germany underwent a substantial structural change.[1] It can hardly be believed that structural change takes place without any kind of friction. Therefore, there is good reason to assume that the spread should at least transitorily increase in size until markets have adjusted to the new situation. If the spread is suppressed by regulation, unemployment is the result. A look at the structure of the unemployed labour force right before the one shaped by German unification corroborates the assumption: unskilled workers and persons without professional training as well as those who were temporarily unemployed or who were not employed before are especially hit by unemployment. So, it is quite obvious that the squeezing of

---

[1] See Gundlach 1986, pp. 74-88. See also the econometric studies by Paqué 1991.

the wage scale contributed to firms with a high share of unqualified labour moving abroad.[1]

To sum up: there can be no doubt that labour costs are of utmost importance for employment. As far as the balance on current account is concerned, however, consequences are less clear cut. To the point that exchange rates are flexible, the competitiveness of the export sector thus jeopardized by excessive wages can be preserved via a depreciation of the nominal exchange rate, provided that there is 'exchange rate illusion'. If, instead, nominal exchange rates are stabilized, such as, for instance, within the EMS, jobs are more directly exposed to international competition. Thus, wages cannot be set without taking notice of what is paid elsewhere. Facing competition in a more direct way implies that the level and structure of wages abroad has to be taken into account not only in real, but also in nominal terms. Otherwise, firms are forced to shed labour, eventually they even move abroad for staying competitive. As far as Europe is concerned, the implications of the latter are obvious: as the European Union heads towards Monetary Union, the competition for capital will intensify. Hence, wages neglecting scarcity will more than ever before drive capital out of the country.

Distortions in the structure of wages do have employment effects as well as international repercussions, independent of the exchange rate regime prevailing. However, sharing in the benefits of international integration is only possible if structural change is allowed for. This almost always implies that some sectors of the economy are especially affected by international competition. If they are not able to preserve their competitiveness via lowering their costs and prices, they must shed labour, the result of which can be that net capital exports increase. For even flexible exchange rates cannot compensate for distortions in the structure of wages. They can only preserve the overall competitiveness of an economy in the sense of evening out the balance of payments.

To what extent the international allocation of capital and thereby balances on current account were affected by labour market distortions in the recent past can hardly be estimated. The difficulties arise because of the 'natural' change in the international division of labour and the change in the direction of international capital flows induced thereby taking place at the same time. But, it is not so much the balance of payments effect of labour market distortions which call for labour market reforms. The prime cause for concern is the employment consequences. These point towards labour market institutions which allow for individual agreements and thus for a more flexible wage structure. For it is the task of the parties negotiating a

---

[1]   See Wissenschaftlicher Beirat beim Bundesministerium für Wirtschaft 1990, p. 6, and Deregulierungskommission 1991, p. 133 and especially pp. 144-5.

contract to take care of employment, a task which can never be accomplished by a third party, namely government, in a market economy.

D. Private Demand for Capital: Capital Costs and Investment

Focusing on locational quality, capital costs are also regarded as being of utmost importance. And indeed, although real interest rates internationally moved much closer together since the early 1970s, local capital costs can differ widely due to differences in taxation.[1] Thus, the international allocation of mobile capital can also be driven by international differences in the cost of capital, even if the national propensity to save and gross rates of return should point towards similar conditions for investment.

In the 1980s, many industrial countries have used tax policy as an instrument for actively promoting investment.[2] In the United States and the United Kingdom, tax rates on corporate income have been lowered, depreciation allowances have been increased and tax credits for investment have been implemented.[3] Other countries adopted similar measures.[4] In the meantime, part of the rather generous depreciation allowances in the United States and in the United Kingdom have been withdrawn. Statutory tax rates, however, are still lower than those prevailing in the 1970s. Focusing on tax rates, it was again Germany which hesitated in following the trend. In contrast to the substantial decline in foreign tax rates, Germany lagged behind. For in Germany, the tax rate on corporate income was only lowered by some 6 percentage points, namely from 56 percent to 50 percent. At the beginning of the 1990s, the tax rate on corporate income is therefore higher than in other major OECD countries. The difference in tax rates is still more pronounced if income-independent property and excise taxes are taken into consideration as well.[5]

---

[1]   Expected changes in real exchange rate may also affect the cost of capital (Frankel 1986 and Ragnitz 1989).

[2]   What is not to be considered here is tax avoidance and evasion. In the case of both of which the benefits of public services and the contribution towards their financing might well differ. Whether the difference in incidence of benefits and contributions give (either in a static or in a dynamic setting) rise to distortions will not be discussed any further in this study.

[3]   The balance on current account however behaved differently. Whereas in the case of the United States it was 1982 when the current account turned into deficit, it was not until 1987 that the British current account did so.

[4]   See Bossons 1988, Whalley 1990 and the various studies in Boskin and McLure 1990. For an overview of the changes in tax rates see also Pechman 1988, p. 5, and Institut der deutschen Wirtschaft 1992b, pp. 4f.

[5]   Property must also be considered in case of international comparisions. However, Table 4.4 does not contain property taxes.

Table 4.4: *Statutory corporate income taxes in per cent: G7 countries 1991*

Country	Federal	State	Local	Total	Deductability on Gross Dividends
Germany	50 36^2	- -	13 13	56.5 44.3^2	 36
United States*	34	6.5		38.3	0
United Kingdom*	$34(33)^3$	-		$34(33)^3$	25
Japan*	37.5	-	12 + 6.49	49.98	0
France	34 42^2	- -	- -	34 42^2	 33.3
Italy	36	-	16.2	47.83	36
Canada*	28.84 $(23.84)^1$	12.9 $(11.9)^1$	 $(35.74)^1$	41.74 20	20

(*) Small businesses or firms with profits smaller than a certain level are subject to a lower tax rate
[1]   Manufacturing
[2]   Distributed dividends
[3]   As planned
As far as the state and local level is concerned, numbers refer to averages.
Source: OECD 1991b, p. 71.

Nevertheless, international comparisons of tax rates can only give a rather vague picture of the impact of tax policy on the attractiveness of a place of investment. For the effective tax rate which capital income is subject to not only depends on the tax rate alone but also on the prevailing rate of inflation, on depreciation allowances, governmental measures directed towards promoting the modernization of the capital stock (such as investment tax credits, reductions in the interest rate and other subsidies), etc.[1] Depending upon the structure of the tax system, the effective rate of

---

[1]   In case of a tax rate of u the project under consideration must not only earn at least the interest rate of the next best alternative (i), economic depreciation (a) and the rate of inflation (q), but also a gross return (p) which compensates for taxation (which is higher by the factor $(1 - u)$) for offering a competitive return. However, at the same time the required gross rate of return is decreased by the present value of tax deductable depreciation allowances according to the tax rate prevailing, minus eventual obligations (uz). If investment allowances (k) are granted, they decrease the necessary rate of return directly. Thus, the required gross rate of return is increased by taxation to $p = (i + a + q)(1 - k -$

taxation can, therefore, be lower or higher than the statutory corporate income tax rate. Moreover, it is the marginal effective rate of taxation rather than any average rate which is relevant for the incentive to invest.

An investment only offers a competitive rate of return, if the expected gross rate of return is high enough as to make up for the effective rate of taxation. Thus, the taxation of corporate income drives a wedge c_{St} between the necessary gross rate of return of an investment before taxation p and the rate of return i of an investment after taxation took place:

$$(44)\ c_{st} = p - i$$

The effective rate of taxation t_{eff}, marginal investment is subject to can be calculated by relating the tax wedge to the rate of return on investment after accounting for taxation:

$$(45)\ t_{eff} = (p - i)/i$$

Hence, everything else held constant, countries with a higher effective rate of taxation will be less attractive for investors.

Quantifying the effective rate of taxation on marginal investment, however, is a difficult task since the size of the tax wedge depends on a vast amount of specific tax regulations including personal aspects, the repercussions of which can hardly be estimated. The effective marginal rate of taxation can differ widely according to the kind of investment undertaken, the nature of the investor, the financing, the maturity structure and the specific location within a country.

In the studies undertaken so far, estimates of the effective marginal rate of taxation focus, therefore, mostly on country-wide averages or they consider only part of the relevant regulations. However, since the structure of taxation within a country and the distortions in the allocation of capital induced thereby also influence the prosperity as well as the attractivity of a country for mobile resources, calculations which focus on investment in general can offer only crude evidence for the actual marginal rate of effective taxation. In addition, many critical assumptions have to be made, for instance, about the economic depreciation of the capital stock, the expected rate of inflation, the discount factor applied, the kind of

---

$uz)/(1 - u)$. For a detailed formal treatment of the effective rate of taxation see, for instance, Sievert et al. 1989, Vol. I, p. 113, or Bovenberg et al. 1990. On the consequences of deductable depreciation allowances for the cost of capital see the classic articles of Samuelson 1964 and Hall and Jorgenson 1967. White and White 1981 provide an overview of the discussion. The methodological problems faced in calculating effective tax rates are discussed by Sievert et al. 1989, Vol. II, pp. 131-8. See also Bradford and Fullerton 1981, Fullerton 1984 and Bradford and Stuart 1986.

investment undertaken, the capital structure, etc., all of which influence the results substantially.

Table 4.5:   *Effective rates of taxation t_{eff} according to calculations of King and Fullerton in per cent: Germany, United Kingdom and United States 1980[1]*

Assumption	Germany	United Kingdom	United States
Assets			
– Machinery	63.4	-57.5	26.4
– Buildings	59.9	56.4	54.1
– Inventories	70.4	45.9	54.5
Industry			
– Manufacturing	65.0	10.7	61.2
– Other industry	69.5	12.0	24.4
– Commerce	61.3	55.0	48.8
Source of finance			
– Debt	-17.9	n.a.	-72.5
– New share issues	73.2	-1.8	81.8
– Retained earnings	85.4	48.2	66.5
Owner			
– Households	82.4	104.6	73.4
– Tax-exempt institut.	26.5	-34.5	-21.3
– Insurance companies	9.1	14.5	22.4
Overall	64.8	30.0	49.9

Source: King and Fullerton 1984, p. 272.

Most of the international comparisons of effective taxation try to calculate the total marginal effective rate of taxation. Hence, in calculating the tax wedge due to capital income taxation, taxes paid at the corporate level as well as taxes paid by savers are taken into consideration.[2] According to the most far reaching study untertaken so far, capital

[1]   These calculations are based on the prevailing rate of inflation and the actual depreciation allowances. Moreover, King and Fullerton assume in their calculations that the structure of the balance sheet of the firms reflects the one of a representative firm in the respective country.

[2]   See King and Fullerton 1984, McKee, Visser and Saunders 1986, p. 91, Leibfritz 1986 and Sievert et al. 1989, Vol. 1, p. 462, for the period under consideration.

formation in Germany was relatively unattractive in the early 1980s.[1] Independent of the kind of investment and the sector of investment the effective rate of taxation t_{eff} calculated was higher than the one for the United States or the United Kingdom.

The only exception was a fully debt financed investment. In this case, Germany was in a much better position, since the deduction of interest payments in calculating the tax base mitigates the effective rate of taxation in case of a higher rate of taxation such as in Germany. However, a capital structure thus biased towards debt financing can hardly be found in reality since creditors would be exposed to a rather high risk without equity sharing in the risks. If at all, creditors will only shoulder that high a risk if they are offered a correspondingly high gross rate of return. Thus, although a higher debt-to-equity ratio might lower tax payments, it might well prove to be very costly by increasing overall capital costs. Since agency costs and risk premia due to shifts in the allocation of risks are left out of consideration in these studies, capital costs in the case of a debt-financed investment are clearly underestimated. Based on a uniform gross rate of return on investment, most of the studies undertaken more recently also come to the conclusion that the rate of effective taxation on capital formation in Germany is much higher than in other G7 countries.[2]

However, most of the studies focus on the rate of taxation on national capital formation only.[3] It is assumed that not only the creditor but also the debtor resides in the country under consideration. Naturally, these studies can only draw a rather rough picture of a country's locational quality and thus of the international attractiveness for mobile resources. For the consequences of taxation for international capital flows not only depend upon the total rate of taxation within a country. Another important point is whether capital income is taxed according to the source principle or according to the residence principle. And the net rate of return also depends on how both tax systems involved in international transactions fit into each

---

[1]   See King and Fullerton 1984. Calculations of the mid-1980s have shown similar results. See Leibfritz 1986 and McKee, Visser and Saunders 1986. More recent calculations can be found in Jorgenson and Yun 1991 as well as in the studies edited by Jorgenson and Landau 1993. The former focus primarily on the US, while the latter pull evidence from a variety of countries together. Poterba 1991 and Bovenberg et al. 1990 draw on Japan and the US.

[2]   Studies which show lower tax rates are normally directed towards estimating the average rate of taxation. The average rate, however, is only partially informative for evaluating how taxation affects investment activity. On this issue see also Fuest and Kroker 1989, pp. 8-10.

[3]   On this subject see also Bovenberg et al. 1990, p. 292, and for a detailed analysis Sinn 1987, pp. 193-6. The same considerations are raised by Boss 1988, p. 12. See also the calculations of the effective rate of taxation in case of foreign direct investments undertaken there. However, his study rests on the assumption that the gross rate of return is everywhere the same. If capital markets are open, however, the assumption of the net rate of return being the same everywhere is the more plausible one. Effective rates of taxation have thus to be added to derive the gross rate of return, even though this kind of procedure also has its problems. See on this point Sievert et al. 1989, Vol. I, pp. 172-83.

other, that is how international transactions are dealt with in terms of taxation in the country of investment and in the country where the saver resides.[1]

Yet, looking at the national side of the problem only and leaving any international aspects aside for a moment, the following consequences for locational quality can be derived. Any taxation of capital income at the corporate level according to the source principle raises the required gross rate of return. Thus, the higher the effective rate of taxation at the corporate level is, the less projects will offer a competitive rate of return. If this would be the only kind of taxation and with everything else being the same, increasing the effective rate of taxation either for instance by raising statutory tax rates or by lowering depreciation allowances will induce an outflow of capital.

If, instead, capital income is taxed according to the residence principle and if claims of foreigners are exempted from taxation, raising the effective rate of taxation can even induce an inflow of capital. For if taxation lowers the net rate of return which can be expected, national savings will probably shrink due to taxation, provided that the price effect is stronger than the income effect. Thus, capital will be more scarce than otherwise. If capital becomes more scarce due to the decline in national capital supply interest rates gross of taxation will show a tendency to increase. The pressure on interest rates might pull foreign capital into the country, provided that the rate of return on foreign capital is not also subject to taxation in the country of investment. If foreign capital is indeed attracted, taxation does not directly impair investment activity. Nevertheless, the inflow of mobile resources must not be taken as an indicator of high locational quality. For taxation impairs economic welfare, even if the national capital shortage should be mitigated by an influx of capital. Due to taxation current consumption is higher than in a situation where capital income is exempted from taxation.[2]

---

[1]   The theory of capital income taxation in an open economy and the institutional issues involved have attracted a great deal of attention in the late 1980s/early 1990s. See, for instance, Sinn 1987, Slemrod 1988, Giovannini 1989 and 1990, Bovenberg and Tanzi 1990, Salin 1990, Frenkel, Razin and Sadka 1991, Ihori 1991, Musgrave 1991, Spahn and Kaiser 1991, Dluhosch 1993, Gravelle 1994 and Feldstein 1994. Evaluations concerning the economic consequences, however, differ substantially. Whereas some see a case for harmonizing basic rules or even detailed measures, others do not.

[2]   If savers can escape taxation at home by moving their savings abroad, it might be possible that capital exports and capital imports increase at the same time. A case in point was the tax on interest income of 10 per cent introduced transitorily in Germany in 1989. Gross exports increased considerably. Net exports, although climbing too, increased by far less. Whether the balance on current account changes due to taxation depends in this case on the costs of transactions and on information costs as well as on individual preferences concerning the portfolio structure. An alternative route to escape taxation might be available if there are investment opportunities within the tax-imposing country which are

Moreoever, the direction of international capital flows also depends on how international capital flows are treated by the tax system. Even a country with a relatively low level of taxation of capital income can become unattractive for investors, if the country of residence imposes additional taxes on capital income earned abroad. Hence, the locational attractiveness not only depends on the effective tax rate on capital income within a country. Any additional taxes investors have to pay in their home country have to be considered as well.

International comparisons of effective rates of taxation which concentrate on international investment focus primarily on foreign direct investment, not on portfolio investment, although nowadays the latter is much bigger in volume. Moreover, calculations are most often based on the assumption of the parent company holding a hundred per cent of the stakes. Yet, in almost all studies undertaken, the effective rate of taxation depends very much on the capital structure of the subsidiary. The results of one of the most recent studies by the OECD (1991b) are only in line with the direction of international capital flows in the 1980s under special assumptions concerning the financing. Notably in the case of projects financed by retentions of the subsidiary, the descending order of tax wedges in the major industrialized countries matches approximately net capital flows.

As Figure 4.6 shows, proceeds claimed by foreigners are subject to a comparatively high rate of effective taxation in Germany, Italy and Japan if investment is financed solely by retentions of the subsidiary. In the United Kingdom, the United States and France, tax wedges are relatively moderate in comparison to the rest of the G7 countries. In Canada, the effective rate of taxation comes closest to the average. Although this seems to fit into the picture of international capital flows as observed in the recent past, the financing assumed is the exception rather than the rule. If, instead, it is supposed that investment is financed out of the cash flow, the assumption of a mixture of different sources should give a more realistic picture of the tax wedge foreign direct investment is subject to. Furthermore, retained profits are no option as far as new investment is concerned. For a business to get started a mixture of fresh equity and debt is necessary.

If marginal tax wedges are calculated under the assumption that all sources of financing are used alike[1] and specific tax treaties are considered, a different result emerges. In this case it is in Canada where foreigners face the highest effective rate of taxation on marginal investment. Japan and France mark a medium position. In the United States tax wedges are a bit lower than in France, Italy and Japan. However, this time, tax rates on

---

exempted from taxation, the result of which would be a distortion in the allocation of capital.

[1] That is by debt, new raised equity and retained profits.

proceeds from foreign direct investment are rather minor in Germany compared to international standards.

Figure 4.6:   *Average required transnational pre-tax rates of return when the subsidiary is financed through retained profits*

–   Source investment (investment from all other countries into named country).
–   Residence investment (investment from named country into all other countries).
–   Domestic investment.

G7 countries January 1991[1]

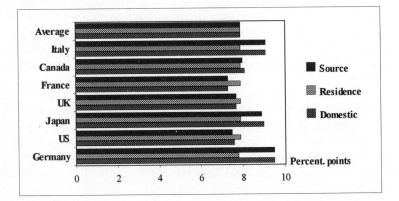

Source: OECD 1991b, p. 138.

Thus, everything else being the same, locational quality in Germany should rank among the highest, followed by the United Kingdom, the United States, France and Japan. However, from the other perspective, namely from the country in which the parent company resides, the incentive to go abroad should be quite low due to rather high tax wedges for Japanese firms, whereas investors residing in the United States or the United Kingdom face a smaller tax wedge in case of foreign direct investment.

Hence, all aspects taken together, Germany should be a quite attractive place to invest in case of a mixed financing since the tax wedges foreigners are subject to in Germany are comparatively low and the incentive for German firms to move abroad is not that strong.[2] In Japan, tax wedges are

---

[1]   These calculations are based on an inflation rate of 4.5 per cent p.a. The structure of assets reflects the average structure observed. Individual taxes are left out of consideration.

[2]   Other calculations which consider dividends out of international investment show a much more unfavourable position of Germany. See, for instance, Boss 1988, pp. 75-80.

substantially higher, but so are tax wedges for Japanese firms investing overseas. Marginal effective rates in the United States come close to those foreigners are liable to in Japan. US firms going abroad are taxed somewhat lighter than firms from Germany or Japan. Yet, it was the United States and neither Germany nor Japan which experienced a surge in net capital inflows during the 1980s. In the case of Germany not only the overall balance on capital account was in deficit, but so was the balance on foreign direct investment.

Figure 4.7: *Average required transnational pre-tax rates of return when the subsidiary is financed by one third loans from the parent, one third new equity from the parent, and one third retained profits*

– Source investment (investment from all other countries into named country).
– Residence investment (investment from named country into all other countries).
– Domestic investment.

G7 countries January 1991[1]

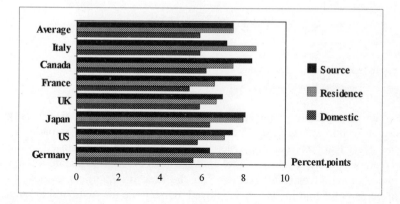

Source: OECD 1991b, p. 143.

However, particularly in the case of foreign direct investment, not only taxes enter the decision to go abroad or not. Protecting property rights on know-how from diffusing, agency costs and transaction costs also make for important aspects. And if acquiring the permissions necessary for undertaking an investment according to local law takes a considerable time,

---

[1] Based on rates of inflation of 4.5 per cent. The left side of the balance sheet is again referring to the average structure observable. Individual taxation is not included.

even a moderate tax-liability can become comparatively burdensome. The same applies to other factors complementary to investing locally.[1] If, for instance, as in the case of Germany concerning products of the mobile Schumpeter-type, unskilled labour is comparatively expensive, foreign direct investment becomes an attractive alternative. Cheaper labour can be used elsewhere without getting stripped of know-how.

Figure 4.8:   *Balance on foreign direct investment and balance on capital account* less foreign direct investment: Germany 1977-1993*

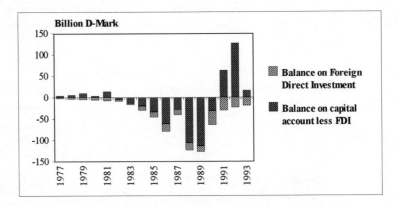

* including net errors and omissions, minus: Net capital export

Source: Deutsche Bundesbank (a), various issues.

Hence, especially in the case of foreign direct investment, taxation is one criterion amongst several concerning the decision to invest abroad. Thus, the fact that international capital movements do not closely reflect differences in taxation need not indicate that taxation is unimportant for international investment. Neither can the lack of empirical evidence be taken as proof that the theory employed, namely the intertemporal approach to the current account, is incorrect. For the differences in marginal effective tax rates on proceeds from foreign direct investment cannot be considered as an explanation for the overall balances on capital account as observed recently in the major industrial countries. Particularly since the 1970s, international capital flows between industrialized countries consisted for the most part not of foreign direct investment, but of portfolio investment.

---

[1]   For instance, in Germany property rights are much more attenuated by co-determination than in other countries. Thus, decisions can only be reversed by incurring relatively high costs, which means that adjusting to ever-changing circumstances becomes more difficult. On this subject see von Weizsäcker (1984).

Thus, calculations focusing on foreign direct investment are not necessarily representative concerning the question of whether taxation induced international capital flows and thus determines the balances on current account. The explanatory power of tax wedges referring to foreign direct investment is rather poor since portfolio investment is often treated somewhat differently from dividends on foreign direct investment by tax laws.

Yet, as we have already pointed out, most of the studies referring to portfolio investment focus primarily on national capital formation, without taking the sometimes rather complex international aspects of taxation into account. However, if taxation with regard to national capital formation is cut back and national investment is reacting more elastically than national savings, capital imports might well increase on balance due to tax policy. An increase in the effective rate of taxation might then induce a net outflow of capital. Thus, as far as we can consider the taxation of capital income within a country to be relevant for international capital flows, we can say that at least in the eigthies balances on current account were in line with differences in taxation.

To sum up, focusing on the amount and variety of taxation, there should be no doubt that taxation does influence the international allocation of capital. Taxation already implies a distortion in the allocation of capital because it is normally applied in a non-uniform way. The lack in transparency and the problem of interdependence, however, makes it difficult to evaluate quantitatively by how much taxation influences the international allocation of capital. The very same problems also make it difficult from a policy point of view to improve locational quality by a peace-meal engineering approach. For the interdependence of different tax regulations can lead to results which stand in stark contrast to what has been intended. An improvement in locational quality can thus most directly be achieved by reshaping the current tax system. In most countries tax systems are extremely complex and the rules are often inconsistent. Therefore, hardly anything can be said about who is effectively taxed and who is favoured. What needs to be done is to broaden the tax base while at the same time lowering tax rates significantly. Eventually, what even has to be considered is to exempt investment from taxation altogether. As far as taxes can be earmarked, a user-cost of capital concept for government services would be more reasonable.

In a great many countries the restructuring of the tax system is already under way. All those which took a daring step forward into this direction have acquired a comparative advantage in the competition for mobile capital. In the long run, others can not refrain from following. However, only if the reform of taxation is carried forward without hesitating and only if it indeed offers a long term perspective, can locational quality truly improve, since what is important for investment is the expected course economic policy will take.

E. Public Demand for Capital

The balance on current account is not only shaped by saving and investment decisions of the private sector. For as far as the public sector demands or supplies capital in addition to the private sector, budget policy also influences interest rates. By affecting national capital scarcity budget policy might well contribute to the volume and direction of international capital flows.

a) The budget constraint of the publics: an intertemporal perspective

As we are concerned with the evaluation of balances on current account we will first focus on the intertemporal issues of fiscal policy: does the public sector in the same manner as the private sector operate under an intertemporal budget constraint? What are the main differences between both? Are they of importance when it comes to evaluating balances on current account? It seems quite obvious that governments also face a budget constraint, although usually not exactly in the same way as the private sector.[1] Governmental expenditures have to match revenues, just as for any single individual. Likewise, the intertemporal stream of governmental expenditures need not be the same as the one provided by tax revenues. Governmental expenditures and tax revenues need not be balanced in each single period, but in the long run. Solvency requires that the present discounted value of governmental expenditures must be met by the present discounted value of tax revenues. If there is already a debt outstanding in the period under consideration the budget constraint has to be modified, since the serving of the already accumulated debt absorbs some of the revenues of the future.[2]

By running deficits today, governmental expenditures are raised above current tax revenues, whereas in the case of accumulating wealth or reducing the stock of debt, governmental expenditures are smaller than tax revenues. Even though the latter is not that common,[3] national capital markets may be affected in both cases. However, as the time horizon of politicians is somewhat shaped by election periods, we can quite safely say that the public sector shows a bias towards deficit spending rather than the other way round. This applies at least as far as debt financing allows for shifting the burden of taxation intertemporally. Since politicians are not

---

[1]   On the issue of intertemporal budget constraints with special reference to the public sector see, for instance, Burda/Wyplosz 1993, chapter 3 and 5.

[2]   On the arithmetics see Cohen 1991, pp. 21-27.

[3]   However, there are exceptions, one of which was Germany in the 1950s accumulating the so-called 'Juliusturm'.

necessarily in charge anymore when the debt is to be served, they will tend to prefer debt financing instead of tax financing.

Yet, as far as private savings increase in line with deficit spending, that is in case the Ricardian equivalence principle holds, national capital scarcity need not be shaped by budgetary policy.[1] While the Ricardian equivalence principle might be theoretically appealing, we will see in short that reality looks different. Moreover, the theorem rests on assumptions which are rather stringent. For in case of nobody being sure who will pay for the debt everybody may speculate on the possibility of somebody else but not him, who pays. If prospective tax payers do so they do not take the discounted value of future tax payments or cuts in non-interest expenditures for serving the public debt fully into account in their intertemporal considerations. The same applies if there is an opportunity to escape taxation, for instance by mobility.[2] Thus, budget policy has to be considered as an important element which adds to either local capital demand or supply.

What makes for the difference between the private and the public sector with regard to the budget constraint is that the government can try to increase revenues either by raising tax rates or broadening the tax base. Another way of trying to ease the intertemporal budget constraint (actually, the most common) would be monetary policy.[3] For if money supply is increased in an unexpected way it might well be possible (at least transitorily) to reduce claims on the already outstanding government debt in real terms, thereby reducing real government expenditures. In short: since the state has the power to redistribute resources from the private sector towards the public sector the budget constraint is not as well defined as in the case of the private sector.

For sure, the constraint holds by definition, even in the case of not serving the debt which has to be considered as a special kind of tax, namely a confiscatory one. Thus, in principle, running deficits today must be paid for by higher taxes later on. In this sense, the same intertemporal considerations come into place as in the private sector. It is rather in the budget itself that the ambiguity arises. For the volume of the budget is limited by the power to tax and significantly dependent on the so-called 'Ordnungspolitik' applied. Yet, the usual equations of textbook economics trying to capture the economic consequences of fiscal policy give no

---

[1]   See Ricardo 1819 as well as the reformulation by Barro 1974 and the overview by Bernheim 1987.

[2]   See, for instance, Brennan and Buchanan 1987. As Rowley 1987 points out, Ricardo himself was rather sceptical about the equivalence of tax financed and deficit financed public spending. Barro compared Ricardian equivalence to the Modigliani/Miller theorem which is 'literally incorrect' but 'forces theoretical and empirical analyses into a disciplined, productive mode' (Barro 1989, p. 52).

[3]   On the fiscal consequences of monetary policy see, for instance, Siegel 1979, Eisner 1986, Tanzi, Blejer and Teijeiro 1987 as well as Blejer and Cheasty 1991.

information about the latter. However, the fact that the public sector does not operate under the same clear cut budget constraint as the private sector does not mean that the government can escape its intertemporal budget constraint. Nor does it allow for the conclusion that fiscal policy is of minor importance concerning the balance on current account and its evaluation.

As far as the budget constraint of the government is relaxed via redistributing resources from the private sector to the public sector, everything else staying the same, the easing occurs at the expense of the private sector which has less room to manoeuvre. Focusing on aggregates, there can be no doubt that resources are limited in supply, thus making for a budget constraint. Whether the intertemporal shape of the government budget is the outcome of any optimizing approach comparable to the one assumed in the case of the private sector, is a different issue which shall therefore be left out of consideration for this moment.

Whereas the easing of the intertemporal budget constraint via increasing revenues (either in a direct way by increasing effective tax rates or broadening the tax base or in an indirect way as for instance by deregulating economic activity) is pretty much a matter of practical fiscal policy, there is also a more theoretical case to be mentioned, the Ponzi scheme,[1] in which the intertemporal budget constraint is not that binding. The point in case is the theoretical possibility of servicing any already accumulated debt by simply issuing new bonds. And in contrast to the former, the debt arithmetics underlying are the same, independent of whether we focus on an individual, a firm, the private sector, or the public sector.

For if a Ponzi scheme[2] like this would be in reach, the kind of intertemporal budget constraint which calls for raising taxes or curbing non-interest expenditure later on in case of deficit spending seems to vanish. According to some simple arithmetics based on aggregate revenue and expenditure streams in time, a policy like this should be available whenever the average real interest rate to be paid on the already outstanding stock of public debt is smaller than the real growth rate of the economy.[3]

The latter becomes evident by looking at the law of motion of deficit spending and interest payments for serving any outstanding stock of public

---

[1]   Yet, the Ponzi scheme which will be discussed below has more far reaching implications than theory might at first glance suggest. For if the decisions of investors of whether to buy government bonds or not are guided by growth prospects of the overall economy, the public sector's room for manoeuvre (that is budget constraint) will depend on how public policy affects the growth rate. Since the currency risks as well as the country risks of government bonds vary considerably with growth prospects, the Ponzi-scheme is closely linked to the balance on current account. However, from this perspective growth rates are not exogenous anymore.

[2]   On Ponzi games in general see Kindleberger 1989 and with special reference to the public sector von Weizsäcker 1979, O'Connel and Zeldes 1988 and Dluhosch 1994.

[3]   In addition, primary deficits, i.e. deficits excluding interest payments, must not be too high. For details see Dluhosch 1993, pp. 159-66.

debt.[1] Although the limits of deficit spending usually are reached well in advance, the very extreme to which deficit spending can be theoretically pushed is the case in which all annual savings of the private sector are absorbed by the public sector.[2] Proceeding from an initial level of debt D_0, government debt (D) can in the long run at most climb according to the growth rate of the capital market. The volume of the latter in turn is driven by the growth rate of the economy (g). By and large, this applies also in an open economy setting as we will see below. Thus, the theoretical ceiling of deficit spending can be described by the following equation:

$$(46) \left(\frac{dD}{dt}\right) = gD_0 e^{gt} \qquad\qquad \forall\, t = 1...\infty$$

With interest i on government bonds the nominal burden interest payments (IP) of the already accumulated debt make for are given by

$$(47)\ IP = iD_0 e^{it} \qquad\qquad \forall\, t = 1...\infty$$

Now suppose, fiscal policy tries to cover any liabilities arising out of the intial debt of D_0 by simply issuing new bonds. What are the necessary conditions for a policy like this being sustainable? If the government operates a Ponzi scheme like this, the theoretical margin left is the difference between the maximum growth path of deficit spending according to the growth rate of the capital market and the nominal burden due to interest payments (cash flow, CF):

$$(48)\ CF_t = gD_0 e^{gt} - iD_0 e^{it} \qquad\qquad \forall\, t = 1...\infty$$

Aggregated over time,[3] the leeway provided by the growth of the capital market can be written as:

$$(49)\ C_t = D_0 + \int_1^\infty (gD_0 e^{gt} - iD_0 e^{it})dt$$

with $C_0 = D_0$

---

[1]   See Niehans 1985 and Blanchard et al. 1990, pp. 10-2, for the intertemporal arithmetics of deficit spending. Although the presentation to be found in Blanchard et al. is somewhat different from the one chosen in this book, their framework is basically the same.

[2]   What has to be kept in mind, for instance, is that savings of the private sector are by no means independent of the fiscal policy applied.

[3]   Although neither individuals nor politicians have a time horizon of infinity, the economy itself is to be modelled that way.

$$(50) \quad C_t = D_0 + \left[D_0 \, e^{gt}\right]_0^\infty - \left[D_0 \, e^{it}\right]_0^\infty \quad \forall \, t = 0 \ldots \infty.$$

Looking at the last equation, it becomes obvious that there is no intertemporal budget constraint in case the growth rate should be continuously higher than interest rates. Obligations can be simply rolled over. The depth of the capital market is growing even after taking account of interest payments. As the interest rate on government bonds approaches the growth rate of the economy, the government has permanently funds of D_0 at hand. The possibility remaining is obviously a situation in which the real interest rate to be paid is higher than the real growth rate. Facing a situation like this, a policy of running deficits and simply rolling over any interest payments due is not sustainable in the long run, but must be compensated for later on by running a corresponding sequence of budget surpluses.

$$(51) \quad \lim_{t \to \infty} C_t = +\infty \; (g > i); \quad \lim_{t \to \infty} C_t = D_0 \; (g = i); \quad \lim_{t \to \infty} C_t = -\infty \; (g < i)$$

Yet, in case of $(g > i)$, it seems possible to serve the outstanding debt by running new deficits in the amount necessary for covering any claims in interest payments. According to this logic, deficit spending need neither imply an increase in tax revenues nor a cutting back of other expenditures. However, nowadays in most of the G7 countries, real interest rates on government bonds are considerably higher than the rate of economic growth. Real interest rates climbed substantially in recent times, especially since international capital movements had been deregulated and monetary policy had switched towards a more stability-orientated course. Actually, any attempt to play Ponzi will prove to be unsuccessful in the long run. Notwithstanding the fact that some governments currently do run a budget policy which is not sustainable in the long run, for the time being we can well put the availability of a Ponzi scheme as a theoretical issue aside. Moreover, economic limits of government debt can be reached well before any theoretical limit of government debt is in sight. Or to put it in somewhat different words: not every kind of fiscal policy which is feasible according to mathematics is actually sustainable. Consequently, we can well assume that something similar to an intertemporal budget constraint has to be obeyed.

Thus, economic policy operates under an intertemporal budget constraint which together with the budget constraint of the private sector (firms and households) adds up to the overall budget constraint of the economy.[1] The

---

[1]   The issue of individual and overall budget constraints is well presented by Cohen 1991 and, although in a static manner, by Burda and Wyplosz 1993. In principle, the central bank has to be added, an issue on which we will dwell later on.

fact that public policy shows a bias towards deficit spending does not alter the arithmetics. Since any budget policy has an intertemporal component, fiscal issues have to be considered in any explanation of the current account based on the intertemporal approach. However, for examining their consequences for the balance on current account we first have to focus on a single period in time. We will slightly touch upon the issue of the intertemporal budget constraint of the public sector and the bias towards deficit funding again when we look at the expenditure side of the budget and the economic limits of deficit spending in an open economy.

b) National absorption and production: an intratemporal perspective
National capital demand and supply are not only affected by the budget balance. For there can be no doubt that besides balances, it is also the allocation of public expenditures which makes for a factor of importance with regard to capital scarcity and locational quality. If, for instance, the government does offer services complementary to private investment, local private investment activity and capital demand can be shaped by fiscal policy even in case of the government posting a balanced budget. The same applies for the revenue side, since revenue can be raised in a more or less resource consuming way. Needless to say not every kind of governmental expenditure makes for an increase in the rate of return private investors can expect. Notwithstanding these additional channels of influence, let us also put the allocative issue for a moment aside, thus focusing on aggregates only. Both, the optimization aspect and the expenditure side, will re-enter the picture later on.

Referring again to the basic intratemporal equation of national accounting,[1] we see that the current account is shaped by the savings and investment decisions of the private sector (first term on the right hand side of the equation) and deficit spending of the public sector (second term on the right hand side of the equation):

$$(21') \ CA = (Ex - Im) = (S - I) + (T - G)$$

with: CA: current account = exports (Ex) minus imports (Im)

As opposed to a closed economy, national absorption need not be constrained by national production if international capital movements and international trade are possible. Instead of crowding out private demand for capital within the economy, governments posting a deficit can contribute to an inflow of capital. If national capital scarcity is mitigated by an inflow of capital which implies a real transfer in the same direction, it is the serving

---

[1] In this case, a broad concept of international trade is applied, including not only trade in goods but also in services, thus referring to the current account rather than the trade balance.

of the debt which calls for a retransfer later on. In contrast, by reducing the pressure on national capital markets curbing deficit spending can stimulate capital exports as savers look for a higher rate of return elsewhere.

c) Deficit spending and the current account: empirical evidence
Especially in recent times international capital flows and therefore also balances on current account seemed indeed to be shaped significantly by budgetary policy. However, a linkage between the current account and deficit spending thus strong cannot be taken for granted. Even balances on current account which mirror deficit spending do not prove that it was primarily budget policy which was responsible for the direction and size of international capital flows.[1]

The most outstanding example of 'twin deficits' often referred to in the recent past are the United States in the 1980s. For in the early 1980s deficit spending in the United States soared in the course of reshaping the tax system and lowering the effective rate of taxation on corporate income earned. Expenditures, however, had not been curbed at the same pace as revenues plummeted, instead, they had even been increased. In the same period, the United States became the world's greatest debtor nation. Since the early 1980s, the United States have been sucking up capital from the rest of the world for more than US$ 800 bn. Complementarily, the current account slipped into deficit, which climbed steadily between 1982, the first year in deficit, and 1987 to almost US$ 170 bn. Subsequently, the balance on current account turned around again, closing with a slight surplus in 1991 just for entering another swing into deficit thereafter (see chapter 5.I).

In 1990/91, it was Germany which posted huge budget deficits and experienced a deficit on current account for the first time since 1981. Budget deficits on the federal, state and local level (including social security funds) climbed in the course of German unification from 9.0 bn D-Marks in 1989 to approximately 107.5 bn D-Marks in 1991 (1992: 117.0 bn, 1993: 129.5 bn D-Marks). The overall budget deficit of the public sector (including railways, post office, Treuhand, and all the funds implemented for smoothing the process of unification) was even considerably higher. And it was exactly in 1990/91 that the German balance on current account made a swing of more than 140 bn D-Marks, turning from a hitherto large

---

[1]   See also the discussion in Viñals 1986. There are also statistical problems involved (Eisner 1986, Kotlikoff 1992) since from an economic point of view the implict deficit (such as the one posted by the pay-as-you-go system of social security and other future obligations of the public sector) should be included in any figure of public debt for evaluating locational quality. An overall account like this, however, is not common. Thus, official figures include only part of the public debt. Any relation which focuses on the official data only, can therefore be severly misleading.

surplus of 108.1 bn D-Marks (1989) into a deficit of 33.1 bn D-Marks (1991).[1]

Figure 4.9:   *Budget deficits (overall government), balance on current account and GDP deflator: United States 1973-1993*

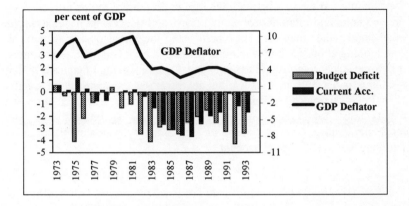

Source: Council of Economic Advisers 1995.

Although in the two examples mentioned deficit spending added significantly to capital demand, thus attracting foreign capital, it was not only the public sector which increased its capital demand. This applies especially for the US, but also (at least for the early 1990s) for Germany. As the respective case studies show, private investment increasing by more than private savings also contributed to capital scarcity. Therefore, one has to be careful when talking about 'causation' while focusing on deficit spending and the current account. It is capital scarcity in general which attracts capital and consequently implies a transfer of resources which shows up in the balance on current account.

Hence, a balance on current account moving in line with deficit spending need neither indicate that there is a direct causality underlying nor that there is an automatism running from budget deficits to balances on current account. To be sure, intertemporal as well as international comparisons are loaded with measurement problems.[2] The accounting is merely guided by

---

[1]   For the figures see Deutsche Bundesbank (a). Numbers of the Bundesbank usually differ from those of national accounts. Yet, the movement is basically the same.

[2]   On measurement problems see Blejer and Cheasty 1991. See also the discussion on international comparisons of deficits corrected for differences in inflation in Dluhosch 1993, pp. 144-57. Measurement problems are also one of the reasons why the prospects of

conventions rather than economics, and conventions also vary both nationally and internationally. Implicit deficits such as those of social security are usually not included in the figures, neither are a number of other future claims on government. An in depth analysis of public policy and locational quality should therefore actually focus on overall figures. Unfortunately, no such accounting has been undertaken until yet since obtaining the information necessary is a difficult task indeed.[1] Thus we will focus mainly on the link between the capital demand of the public sector on the one hand and international capital flows and the current account on the other hand rather than on public policy and locational quality in general. Yet, looking at budget policy in other periods of time and in other countries, it becomes clear that even in case of capital markets being liberalized deficit spending can result in a crowding out of private investment or capital shunning away instead of being drawn into the country. Yet, even attracting capital must not to be mixed up with signalling a comparatively high locational quality. A much closer look is in order for evaluating balances on current account and capital account.

Figure 4.10:   *Budget deficits (overall government), balance on current account and GDP deflator: Germany 1978-1993*

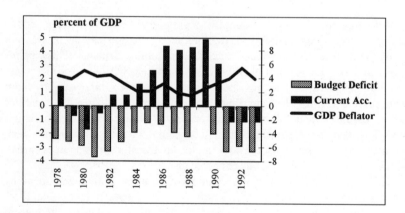

Source: OECD 1994c.

Focusing on the 1970s, no such close relationship can be identified in the G7 countries although budget deficits posted in this period were all but

---

[1]   attempts to curb deficit spending via caps laid down in the constituiton or elsewhere are hardly promising.
But see Kotlikoff 1992 who tries to get at an estimate for the US.

minor. In relation to GDP, they often exceeded those of the 1980s by far. However, this does not imply that budget policy is not that relevant in explaining balances on current account. For international capital markets were much more strangulated by governmental regulations in the 1970s than in the 1980s. Differences in scarcity could therefore not be as easily ironed out by international capital flows as in the 1980s. Moreover, the 1970s were a period of time in which monetary policy in most of the industrialized countries was eased, whereas the 1980s saw a decline in inflation rates. If monetary policy is eased as budget deficits are on the rise the increase in nominal and real interest rates can be somewhat retarded due to liquifying markets. Transitorily, capital outflows rather than inflows might be stimulated and balances on current account can become active even though budget deficits are on the rise – at least as far as outflows are not curbed by controls on international capital flows. France and the United States are two examples in which budget deficits and balances on current account did not move in line in the 1970s, but in different directions. In both cases there is much evidence that it was primarily monetary policy which shaped the balance on current account in the period under consideration. Moreover, real deficits at these times had been much smaller because of monetary policy than shows up in nominal budget deficits. However, inflation could only be used to such an extent as a 'solution' to budgetary problems because capital markets were heavily regulated at that time.

A look at Italy and the United Kingdom in the 1980s shows that even in case of capital markets being liberalized budget deficits need not come with deficits on current account and a curbing of deficit spending need not bring about a surplus on current account (OECD 1994c). In spite of running high budget deficits in real as well as in nominal terms, Italy showed an almost balanced current account between 1983 and 1988. Even though capital markets have recently been somewhat deregulated, Italy ran a surplus on current account for the first time since 1986 while fiscal policy has not substantially changed course. The United Kingdom showed a substantial deficit on current account in 1988 and 1989, although public budgets were in surplus.

d) Limits of sovereign debt: economic policy, reputation and credibility

A clear cut relationship between fiscal policy and the balance on current account can only be expected if two conditions prevail, a necessary and a sufficient one. The condition necessary for international capital flows reflecting scarcities due to budgetary policy is pretty obvious: a change in deficit spending only shows an impact on the balance on current account if the consequences of a switch in budgetary policy are not dominated by other disturbances. If, for instance, investment activity of the private sector slows down as budgetary deficits increase, it might well be the case that the balance on current account remains unchanged, although demand for capital by the public sector picks up. Only to the extent that total capital demand changes in line with the demand of the public sector, comparatively high budget deficits might show up in a deficit on current account and relatively low budget deficits in surpluses on current account – provided that the situation prevailing on world markets stays the same and provided that savings behaviour remains unchanged.

However, there is another condition to be fulfilled. The credibility of the debtor must be high enough to induce investors to grant loans. This presupposes that the government enjoys credit. The confidence that the government is able to serve the debt and is willing to do so is important. This becomes all the more clear by looking at Latin America where some of the countries (especially Brazil) are running comparatively high budget deficits which do not show up in deficits on current account.[1]

In principle, public borrowing could be viewed like private borrowing. Efficient capital markets should be expected to make sure that capital borrowed by states is used as efficiently as capital borrowed by private investors. Thus, they should also curb the bias of politics towards deficit spending. Yet, as far as public finance is concerned, markets do not work that smoothly as in the case of private indebtedness. One reason might be the expectation of a bail-out by international organizations or the like. However, the main reason is the redistribution issue (power to tax) already mentioned.

The risk of sovereign borrowing for an investor lies not so much with the probability that a whole economy becomes insolvent. Rather it lies with the governmental ability to pay (which is limited by the power to tax) and – even more important – willingness to pay. The country's pure ability to pay can be preserved by fluctuations in the exchange rate, provided they are allowed to take place. Therefore, the transfer of interest payments and principal need not fail even if demand for goods of the debtor country should prove to be rather low or if demand for imports should be quite inelastic at the current exchange rate.[2] For in this case the currency of the debtor country would face severe pressure. The depreciation is the stronger, the lower the propensity in the previous creditor nation to spend interest and principal for buying products of the former debtor country and the less inclined people are over there to refrain from buying products of the creditor country. The exchange rate changes until the flow of goods and services is steered into the direction of international capital flows.[3]

---

[1]   In this case, monetary policy might again be of importance. For it is often monetary policy which is considered a 'solution' for budgetary policy facing difficulties (via inflation).

[2]   To be sure, the real transfer burden differs depending on elasticity.

[3]   Indicators which aim at measuring the ability to pay of the country indebted by looking at the export performance at some point in time are therefore, although common, not convincing when it comes to evaluating sovereign borrowing and its sustainability. At best, they offer something like a criterion in a regime of fixed exchange rates.

As long as the rate of return on investment in the debtor nation is comparatively high and economic growth is well ahead of interest rates, the risk of an unwillingness to pay should be relatively low. For maintaining the contract is beneficial, both from the perspective of the creditor as well as from the perspective of the debtor. Both can increase their real income thereby.[1] If, however, loans are not allocated in a growth enhancing way, servicing the debt implies not only a smaller increase in real income, but probably even a lower disposable income in real terms later on. If the debt is high, there may be stiff opposition to service the debt from those struck with the burden which can express their dissent either by the voice mechanism or by mobility.[2]

As far as the G7 countries and their current indebtedness is concerned, the possibility of countries refusing to service their debt explicitly might be considered as being minor.[3] However, in times of high capital outflows even these countries imposed capital controls, deposit requirements and other regulations which lowered the rate of return to be expected by foreign investors. Moreover, as far as claims of foreigners are denominated in the currency of the debtor nation, it has to be expected that monetary policy is eased following the pressure of fiscal problems, under the alleged assumption that budgetary problems could be solved thereby. Instead of using the inflation tax, effective tax rates might be increased directly. This would also lower the rate of return which can be expected by foreign investors.

If it is recognized by investors that loans are on a large scale not used for investment purposes, but consumption, they will take the risk of a depreciation of their claims into account and will therefore demand a higher risk premium. The risk premium will rise with the debt-to-GNP ratio before foreign investors refrain from a financial engagement altogether since the interest rate can no longer offer a compensation for the risk shouldered.[4] A capital scarcity which is solely due to the government running deficits which are not matched by productive investment will in the long run deteriorate the confidence of international investors. This does not necessarily mean that the very project financed by issuing debt or even governmental outlays in general show directly a pay-off sufficient to cover interest payments (which is hard to account for in the case of the public sector) but overall economic prospects should make servicing the debt not too hard (which for sure is no precise indicator either). Since, normally,

---

[1]   For a cash-flow-based analysis see Niehans 1985.

[2]   On exit and voice see Hirschman 1970. For the importance of the relationship between the rate of economic growth in the debtor nation and the interest rate for budgetary policy see von Weizsäcker 1979 and Niehans 1985.

[3]   For an empirical evaluation focusing on OECD countries see Alesina et al. 1992 and the comments by Obstfeld 1992.

[4]   See Stiglitz and Weiss 1981.

there is no such thing as a collateral in case of sovereign borrowing, economic prospects and therefore credibility of economic policy (which shapes economic prospects significantly) makes for a substitute. Economic prospects will even gain in importance the more mobile potential tax payers become since the uncertainty of servicing the debt climbs with mobility in case of a pay-off smaller than the interest rate. Thus, it might well be that although capital is relatively scarce due to budgetary policy, capital flows out rather than in (as for instance in the case of Argentina in the 1980s[1]). Although far from perfectly, international capital flows do provide a check on the bias of politics to favour deficit spending (and interest groups in general) and to channel resources into consumption. Not so much that governments run into difficulties of funding which occurs usually at a very late stage indeed. Rather it is private investment which slows down in face of the required real rate of return being thus raised. Certainly, for some time governments can live on the reputation built up by servicing the debt in the past, thus running down the capital stock of good-will accumulated.[2] Furthermore, the restraints imposed on governments by investors are even weaker when the possibility of a bail-out exists.

Thus, the reputation issue and the power to tax makes the competition for mobile resources amongst governments a very imperfect one. Consequently, attracting capital due to deficit spending need not indicate high locational quality. As long as the promise of a good return on investment is judged as being credible, capital will be attracted even if allocated in an inefficient manner or used for increasing consumption.

However, once the capital stock is used up, it is hard to regain goodwill. Markets will be much more reluctant if it comes to granting loans. Even if economic policy in the prospective debtor nation is making progress towards a framework in which the economy can flourish, it requires much more an effort to attract private capital. Yet, if successful, there will be a hard landing if there should arise the slightest doubt about the future course of economic policy which can be rather painful. This is an experience recently made by Spain and to an even larger degree by Mexico. Whereas the EU lends stability to Spain, in Mexico the issue at stake is even bigger. In spite of NAFTA, the Mexican economy is not that cushioned by political and economic integration.

The reputation issue is also the reason why in case of the United States the probability of a hard landing in the mid-1980s as deficits sky-rocketed was not as high as expected by some analysts (Marris 1985). Besides the fact that investment activity was also on the rise, the United States could

---

[1]   For details about the case of Argentina see Mastroberardino 1994.

[2]   For sure, the disciplining mechanism does not work smoothly in case of uncertainty. This is because of the actual fulfilment of obligations of the contracting parties taking place at different times. Therefore, there will be agency costs, especially if governments are involved.

lean on its goodwill as a reliable contracting party accumulated in the past. For sure, the latter applies neither for all time (since the capital stock is limited in size) nor do markets 'forgive' *any* kind of economic policy.

One more point is to be mentioned concerning the evaluation of budget deficits and balances on current account there. For it makes a difference whether the inflow of resources in the course of deficit spending is financed by an inflow of private capital or by running down the accumulated stock of foreign reserves. A case in point is the German balance on current account in the late 1970s. For budget deficits climbed rather continuously in the years between 1977 and 1981, namely from 31.7 bn D-Marks to 69.6 bn D-Marks, as the sign of the balance on the German current account turned.[1] In 1979, it showed for the first time since 1962 a deficit (9.9 bn D-Marks). This trend continued in 1980 even stronger (25.1 bn D-Marks). With the curbing of deficit spending in the years following, the German balance on current account turned again into surplus. However, deficits on current account from 1979 to 1981 were neither solely the outcome of budgetary policy, nor were they the result of a comparatively high locational quality. That they did not indicate an improvement in locational quality can be seen by focusing on investment activity. Whereas gross investment increased in 1979 by some 7 per cent in real terms, in 1980 the increase was already moderate, approximately 2 per cent. In 1981, gross investment even decreased in real and in nominal terms. Since savings were on the rise at the same time, the private sector in general showed a positive balance on financial flows. Nevertheless, the deficit on current account cannot be traced back to the public sector attracting capital from abroad. For it was not capital imports on the rise, but foreign reserves of the Bundesbank declining which brought about the swing in the balance on current account. The main factor which allowed German absorption to increase above production was therefore primarily the Bundesbank financing the excess in imports.[2]

To sum up: according to the intertemporal approach to the balance of payments, governmental activity should make for an important issue in explaining and evaluating balances on current account since fiscal policy also involves intertemporal considerations. By borrowing against future revenues, government can add to national capital demand, thereby increasing capital scarcity locally. However, deficit spending on the rise need not imply that national capital scarcity is increased. For as far as the Ricardian equivalence principle holds, private savings rise in line with deficit spending since individuals are anticipating that tax revenues have to be increased or non-interest expenditures be curbed for servicing the debt. The intertemporal stream of disposible income then calls for an

---

[1] For the figures see Sachverständigenrat 1994/95, statistical annex, and OECD 1994c.

[2] On the change in foreign reserves see Deutsche Bundesbank (b).

intertemporal shift of consumption, thereby smoothing the decline of consumption possibilities ahead. Although empirical evidence on the Ricardian equivalence principle is rather weak and theoretical shortcomings raise doubts about the validity of the theorem, capital scarcity need not increase even in case of deficit spending on the rise. For despite capital being internationally mobile national investment can be crowded out by running an unsound fiscal policy. Whether the decline in investment activity (or its growth rate in a dynamic setting) mitigates national capital scarcity, remains an open question. For it might well be that either private savings decline as economic prospects are getting gloomy or savers are looking elsewhere for an opportunity which pays. Thus, international capital mobility does by no means imply that deficit spending automatically translates into deficits on current account.

However, at least as far as the last fifteen years are concerned, there is a huge body of empirical evidence that deficit spending contributed significantly to the shape of the current account balances in the G7 countries. Although (at least temporarily) private investment also rose, budget deficits posted by the US government and the German government contributed to national capital demand and thereby induced surges in capital inflows. Thus, balances on current account have at least partially to be traced back to deficit spending as the intertemporal approach would suggest.

Sucking up foreign capital by government spending has to be evaluated differently from an investment induced inflow of capital. Due to the power to tax and the difficulty of evaluating the efficiency of non-marketable public services, governments do not face the same stiff competition which ensures an efficient allocation of capital in the private sphere. Once having built up a reputation of being a reliable debtor, capital can even be attracted when governments are running an unsound fiscal policy. For sure, once the goodwill is used up, it is difficult to regain. But until this point is reached, one has to remember that current account balances can be due to public deficit spending or private investment. So, they have to be judged quite differently. As it is difficult to calculate any rate of return from government activity, overall economic prospects and private investment activity have to be added to the picture.

5. Four Case Studies

After having analysed the two competing approaches of the balance of payments in a theoretical framework, we now discuss them in four case studies, namely the United States, Japan, Germany and Spain. All of them illustrate very well different adjustment processes to different policy changes. Moreover, they commonly show that the balance of payments cannot be interpreted meaningfully without taking intertemporal utility considerations of individuals into account.

Yet, they deviate from one another. The US have exhibited persistent deficits on the current account since the beginning of the 1980s. The Japanese current account, on the other hand, has been in surplus since then. Many observers, especially proponents of the competitiveness approach, see a stringent linkage between alleged Japanese protectiosm and the trade balances in the two countries. This has to be questioned. The third case is Germany which current account has switched from surplus to deficit during the unification. These three countries can be seen in a framework of more or less flexible exchange rate regimes.[1] Spain, in contrast, has to be analysed in a fixed exchange rate framework. The adjustment process of the balance of payments after Spain became a member of the European Community, therefore, differs from the former ones.

I. The United States: persistent deficits

A. US Performance in the 1980s: a Matter of Exchange Rate Crowding out?

In the early 1980s, US price and cost competitiveness deteriorated sharply. At the same time, US imports soared. Within five years time, the dollar appreciated by almost 50 per cent, making it obviously increasingly difficult for US firms to sell abroad while improving the ability to sell of foreign firms in the US substantially. No matter which indicator of price and cost competitiveness is chosen, all show pretty much the same picture. By and large, international price and cost competitiveness deteriorated in line with the nominal rise of the dollar.

Whereas the US currency appreciated by some 46 per cent between 1980 and 1985, relative normalized unit labour costs rose by 42 per cent. Drawing on relative value added deflators, the decline in competitiveness was even slightly stronger, namely 43 per cent, and even if we focus primarily on traded goods, US firms did not do any better. Only when based

---

[1]   Germany as a member of the EMS is partly integrated in a fixed exchange regime. Nevertheless, with the D-Mark as an anchor for other currencies, the German central bank has a high degree of montary autonomy.

on relative consumer prices, competitiveness declined by less. However, the difference is hardly worth mentioning. Moreover, as far as external competitiveness is concerned, US consumer baskets might be less informative anyway. At that high a price many US firms were outperformed by their foreign competitors. Whereas US production of tradeables faced a tough stand as the exchange rate climbed ever higher, it was particularly German and Japanese firms which gained in market share.

Figure 5.1:   Balance on current account and international price and cost competitiveness: United States 1977-1994

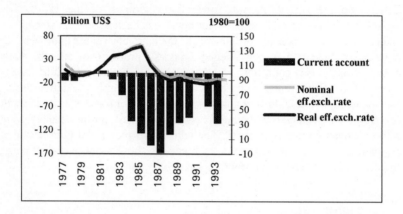

+: Surplus

Source: IMF (a), February 1995.

Consequently, on balance, US exports declined substantially. From 1982, the very first year in deficit, the balance on current account climbed well above US\$ 100 bn reaching a first peak in 1987 with almost US\$ 170 bn (3.7 per cent of GDP), while plunging shortly thereafter to less than US\$ 7 bn in 1991 (0.1 per cent of GDP). Imports picked up again quite strongly in the early 1990s, thus giving rise to another swing into deficit which reached approximately US\$ 104 bn in 1993 (1.6 per cent of GDP).[1]

As US competitiveness deteriorated sharply in the first half of the 1980s, central bank officials and finance ministers decided in September 1985 to reinforce the decline of the dollar which was already under way for getting the deficit down (Louvre Accord). Their main goal was to avoid the triggering of a major trade war which loomed as US deficits grew in size.

---

[1]   Figures of the International Monetary Fund database differ somewhat from those published by the Council of Economic Advisers 1995

Yet, as the figures show, deficits proved to be quite persistent staying with the US for another two years. The stickiness of the deficits casts again doubts on the notion of the exchange rate as being an exogenous variable at the disposal of politicians.

It was (and still is to a substantial amount) particularly the bilateral deficit *vis-à-vis* Japan, which was traced back to US competitiveness sliding.[1] Yet, not all of the poor performance was attributed to exchange rate crowding out.[2] As deficits proved to be persistent despite the dollar declining again in the late 1980s it was more and more European and Japanese trade policy which was claimed as being unfair. With trade policy being blamed, protectionist pressures to support US industries or to urge Japan to curb its exports and open its markets for American goods became even stronger. For, once markets should get lost, it was argued, they would be hard to regain due to hysteresis effects thus having a negative impact on US competitiveness even in the long run. Trade policy is, therefore, an issue on which we will put our special focus in the case study on Japan, showing that US interest groups claiming support by US trade policy have no basis, neither in economic theory nor in Japanese trade policy.

In the US case study we will rather concentrate on the issue of whether the US deficits of the 1980s can indeed be traced back to international price and cost competitiveness declining. As we will show, the poor performance of American industry in terms of price and cost competitiveness has to be considered as part of the adjustment process to capital flows switching direction rather than being itself the cause of the 'American disease'. By turning from Keynesian fine tuning to a much more micro-orientated concept, US economic policy led to a surge in net capital imports. Concentrating on the strengthening of the supply-side rather than effective demand pushed investment acitivity in the US while at the same time giving

---

[1]   The number of studies dwelling on the international competitiveness of the US is enormous. To name just a few: Lenz 1991, Dollar and Wolff 1993, Hilke and Nelson 1987 and 1988, Krugman 1994, Magaziner and Reich 1982, Nelson and Wright 1992 and Tyson 1992. See also the annual report of the Competitiveness Policy Council 1994, especially set up for focusing on US competitiveness. Opinions concerning the usefulness of the concept and the performance of the US, however, differ widely.

[2]   Time and again, the Council of Economic Advisers has put the issue of US price and cost competitiveness on his agenda. Exchange rate crowding out (1984, pp. 43-7), was considered as one important factor for the rising deficit on current account, besides a decline in exports to heavily indebted developing countries and faster economic growth in the US. In the council's 1985 report (1985, pp. 102-06), the movement in the balance on current account was also explicitly put into the context of fiscal policy, especially tax policy and capital imports. In 1987 (1987, pp. 113-22), the Council called for policy coordination to reduce 'imbalances' (p. 120). Another explanation of the deficit drawing basically on the competitiveness approach, this time, however, from the demand side, had been put forward by Lawrence 1990. According to his study, the gap can be traced back to an import elasticity substantially greater than that of exports. The notion of differences in demand giving rise to trade 'imbalances', however, can be criticized as being based on a partial equilibrium analysis.

rise to the so-called 'twin deficits' as particularly federal government posted ever higher deficits in the course of reshaping the tax system.[1]

In addition, we will touch upon the issue of international macroeconomic linkages due to changes in the balance on current account. We will examine whether the sucking up of imports by the US promoted economic activity in the world economy. As US exports and imports are not a negligible factor on the international scale, it is worthwhile to have a look at whether balances on current account matter with regard to the transmission of economic activity.

But, let us first take a look at the US itself for examining the price and cost competitiveness story before turning to the question of whether the US provided an engine for the world economy giving rise to export led growth elsewhere. Yet, a closer look at US price and cost competitiveness reveals that all of the indicators signalled a deterioration much sooner than trade flows. For it was already in 1979 as the dollar began to appreciate, at the time that US monetary policy switched course from trying to steer US-interest rates to a pragmatic quantity-orientated concept. In line with the change in monetary policy nominal and real interest rates rose substantially, the consequences of which appeared not to to be confined to the US as all of the major industrialized countries experienced a rise in interest rates. Thus, it seems a likely supposition that it was primarily monetary policy being responsible for the rise in interest rates as well as the dollar and not so much a disease of American industry suffering from a major crisis.

B. The Ups and Downs of Monetary Policy, Interest Rates and the Dollar: all but a Macro-Issue?

Problems of calculating real interest rates aside, there is no doubt that in principle changes in interest rates as well as in exchange rates, either nominal or real, can be due to monetary policy. So it was in the United States. In 1979, US monetary policy switched from its interest rate focus to a more quantity-orientated line. Although not following a strict stability-orientated path, the policy of disinflation proved to be quite successful in bringing the rate of inflation down from 13.5 per cent in 1980 to 3.0 per cent in 1985. There can be no doubt that the steep appreciation and the law of one price facilitated the task of monetary authorities. Yet, as a matter of fact, monetary policy was substantially less expansive than in the 1970s. As priorities in monetary policy changed interest rates rose steeply, both in nominal and in real terms. Although volatility increased too as monetary policy stepped back and forth, interest rates remained comparatively high.

---

[1]   See also Scheid 1987, who provides an excellent study on the subject. A more recent study focusing on the twin deficits is provide by Blecker (1992).

Figure 5.2:   *Nominal interest rates (government bonds) and GDP deflator: United States 1977-1993*

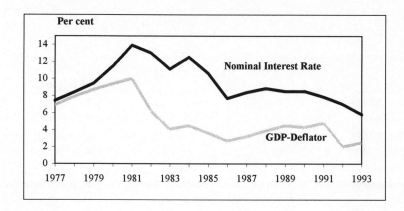

Source: IMF (b), edition 1994.

But, in 1981/82, the peak in nominal interest rates was reached. Subsequently, short term nominal interest rates plummeted again. In case of long term interest rates, it took somewhat longer for getting down. However, as nominal interest rates kept only slowly in pace with the decline in inflation, real interest rates climbed even further before they went down as well.

Anyway, there is good reason to assume that the hike in nominal and real interest rates was mainly due to expectations concerning the future rate of inflation being rather static. For in case of adaptive expectations they were still shaped by the high inflation experience of the 1970s though monetary policy switched course in the early 1980s to a much more stability-orientated line. Yet, even though interest rates came down somewhat again as expectations were updated, interest rates remained substantially higher than in the 1970s.[1]

As rates of inflation had been rather low for a couple of years the trend towards higher rates cannot be explained any more with expectations lagging behind. As only the hike, but not the trend in real interest rates can be traced back to monetary policy, we must look for other factors giving rise to higher interest rates. Although the US cannot be considered as the only cause for interest rates rising worldwide as capital in general became more scarce in the 1980s, it was also the US which no doubt on balance

---

[1]   See Scheid 1987 for a detailed analysis of monetary policy, interest rates and the current account in the early 1980s.

added to capital demand. However, as we will see later on, there was a time in which monetary policy again played an important role.

Table 5.1:   *Real interest rates on government bonds 1977-1993*

	United States	Japan	France	Germany	United Kingdom
1977	0,5	0,9	0,3	2,5	-1,2
1978	0,5	1,1	-1,1	1,6	0,9
1979	0,7	5,0	-0,6	3,5	-1,4
1980	2,1	4,6	1,6	3,6	-5,7
1981	3,9	5,0	4,4	6,3	3,3
1982	6,8	6,4	4,0	4,6	5,3
1983	7,0	6,0	3,9	4,5	5,6
1984	8,0	4,5	5,0	5,7	6,1
1985	7,0	4,7	5,1	4,7	4,9
1986	5,0	3,1	3,4	2,6	6,6
1987	5,2	4,2	6,4	3,9	4,5
1988	5,0	3,9	6,3	4,6	3,4
1989	4,0	3,2	5,8	4,5	2,5
1990	4,3	5,2	6,9	5,1	4,7
1991	3,1	4,3	6,0	4,0	3,4
1992	5,0	3,4	6,3	3,4	4,8
1993	3,3		4,6	3,4	4,7

Source: IMF (b), edition 1994, own calculations.

C. The driving Forces of US Price and Cost Competitiveness I: US Capital Supply on the Decline

The most striking thing about US savings rates is that they are rather small compared to international standards.[1] US gross national savings rates were well below those of Germany, one of the main capital export countries of the 1980s. If compared to Japan with its outstanding savings ratio the US performed even more poorly, reaching only half of the savings to GDP ratio of Japan by the early 1990s. Even the OECD average was substantially higher in 1992, namely by some 5 percentage points. Yet, the emergence of

---

[1]   There are quite a number of studies trying to figure out why the US saving rate is that low. See, for instance, Bosworth, Burtless and Sabelhaus 1991.

balances is not so much a matter of whether levels differ. Instead, we must focus primarily on changes. Although ups and downs follow a cyclical pattern, the US savings behaviour is distinct from those of other major industrialized countries as it shows a clear trend downwards. From more than 20 per cent of GDP in 1979 savings ratios headed downwards throughout the 1980s to 14.5 per cent in 1992. In Japan, however, no such clear trend can be observed as the savings ratio hovers around 30 per cent. In Germany savings ratios proved to be quite stable as well. Rather than declining they picked up slightly in the second half of the 1980s. While Germany's savings ratio was approximately 2 percentage points higher than the one of the US at the start of the 1980s, the gap widened to more than 9 percentage points in 1989/90. As far as the OECD average or capital supply in general is concerned, the savings ratio was flirting with the 20 per cent mark, showing a slight decline in the first half of the 1980s, though it has to be kept in mind that the US has its weight in the OECD ratio. Anyway, US savings behaviour proved to be substantially different from the one in other countries, giving *ceteris paribus* rise to a shortage in capital supply. What makes for another difference is that the cyclical pattern seemed to be somewhat more pronounced in the US than elsewhere. This applies at least for the downswing in the early 1980s with US savings heading down well below their long-term trend.

Figure 5.3:   *Gross national savings: Japan, Germany, OECD and the United States 1977-1993*

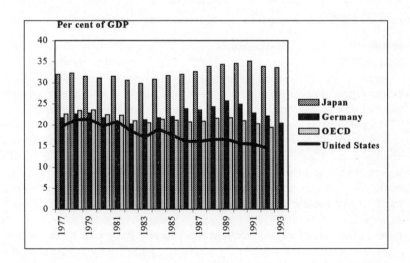

Source: OECD 1994c.

Private savings contributed significantly to the decline. Although competing with Scandinavian countries and the Netherlands for being last in line, US-savings in terms of diposible income are desperately small compared to international standards. Even though savings picked up somewhat in 1984, the rise proved to be transitory in nature, more due to the economic upswing than signalling a reversal of the trend. Shortly thereafter, savings rates headed downwards again. While already low by the turn of the decade, they were even cut in half in percentage points of disposible income during the 1980s, reaching a poor 4 per cent in 1993/94.

Figure 5.4:   Household savings rates: Japan, Germany and the United States 1977-1995

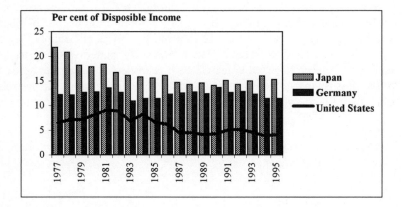

1994/95: OECD-estimates and projections.

Source: OECD 1994c.

Japanese savings, on the contrary, proved to be more than 10 percentage points higher throughout the 1980s, with the band even widening towards the 1990s. German households, as well, saved much more, namely some 12–13 per cent of disposible income, showing only a slight decline in the period from 1982 to 1984 as the economy picked up and precautionary savings went down again. Many analysts attributed the decline in US savings to a real income effect as share prices were on the rise. Yet, one might raise serious doubts of whether the decline in US savings is indeed due to a real income effect. Whereas share prices showed ups and downs, savings did not. Anyway, with regard to capital scarcity, we must focus on flows rather than stocks. Concerning the former there can be no doubt that, relative to income, US capital supply changed significantly in size since the early 1980s. However, as one side of a pair of scissors is not enough for cutting the paper, we will have to take a look at the movement of sectoral balances in US capital supply and demand in the 1980s.

D. The Driving Forces of US Price and Cost Competitiveness II: US Capital Demand on the Rise

a) The 'Twin Deficits': too short a story
Focusing on the current account in the 1980s, budget policy in the United States is one of the most often mentioned factors which contributed to capital demand, thus giving rise to the surge in capital imports.[1]

Table 5.2:   Gross Savings by sector: United States 1977-1994

	Gross National Saving bn US$	Gross Personal Saving bn US$	Gross Business Saving bn US$	Overall Government Deficit (NIPA) bn US$	Gross Private Domestic Investment bn US$	Net Foreign Investment bn US$
1977	354.9	87.9	267.1	-16.8	358.3	9.2
1978	412.8	107.8	305.0	2.9	434.0	10.7
1979	457.8	123.3	334.5	9.4	480.2	-2.0
1980	499.5	153.8	345.7	-35.3	467.6	-11.5
1981	585.9	191.8	394.1	-30.3	558.0	-9.5
1982	617.0	199.5	417.5	-108.6	503.4	2.5
1983	641.4	168.7	472.7	-139.8	546.7	35.0
1984	742.7	222.0	520.7	-108.8	718.9	94.0
1985	735.7	189.3	546.4	-125.3	714.5	118.1
1986	721.4	187.5	533.9	-146.8	717.6	141.7
1987	730.7	142.0	588.7	-111.7	746.3	155.1
1988	802.3	155.7	646.6	-98.3	793.6	118.0
1989	813.3	152.1	667.3	-77.5	832.3	89.3
1990	861.2	170.0	691.2	-138.4	808.9	78.5
1991	937.3	211.6	725.7	-185.9	744.8	-8.1
1992	980.7	247.9	732.8	-257.8	788.3	56.6
1993	1002.5	192.6	809.9	-215.0	882.0	92.3
1994		204.2			1037.5	

+: Capital Import;   -: Budget Deficit
Source: Council of Economic Advisers 1995, own calculations.

---

[1]   See, for instance, Feldstein 1986 and Penner 1987.

Starting in 1981, federal deficits almost quadrupled over the next five years. The main swing in budget balances took place between 1981 and 1982 as deficits climbed by more than US$ 76 bn. Although state and local government budgets showed a substantial surplus which even grew in size between 1982 and 1984, state and local surpluses have not kept pace with deficit spending on the federal level. Thus, on balance, deficits exploded in the first half of the 1980s, rising from a mere US$ 30 bn in 1981 to almost US$ 150 bn in 1986. Even though state and local government balances showed a surplus, in total, deficits jumped nevertheless already in 1981/82 from US$ 30 bn to almost 109 bn and kept on ballooning between 1983 and 1986. With deficits peaking in 1986, fiscal policy proved to be somewhat less expansionary thereafter. By 1989, deficits had declined to US$ 78 bn. However, while 1986 marked the peak in deficit spending as far as the 1980s are concerned, 1992 should put even the deficits of the 1980s in the shade, both in absolute and relative terms.

In terms of GDP, deficits increased by far the most in 1983, reaching 4.1 per cent. While hovering around 3 per cent in the years ahead, deficits declined transitorily in 1989 just for another boost in the early 1990s. In 1992, with economic activity still lingering, the deficit to GDP ratio even broke the record of the 1980s. Yet, the deficit to GDP ratio loses somewhat its informative character as the volume of the capital market does not grow in line with GDP as in case of the US in the 1980s.

Figure 5.5:   Federal and overall budget deficits: United States 1977-1993

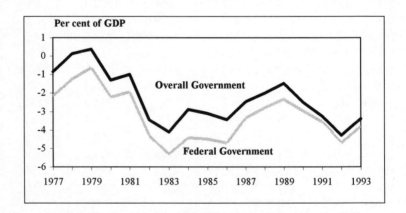

Source: Council of Economic Advisers 1995, own calculations.

Hence, the US version of supply side economics[1] aiming at strengthening private incentives by curbing taxation failed at least to achieve the auto-consolidation hoped for. As part of the supply-side concept, depreciation allowances were extended well ahead of economic depreciation in the early 1980s by the Economic Recovery Tax Act (ERTA), thus lowering the effective rate of taxation on capital income substantially. As the rate of taxation was lowered, tax revenues plummeted. Yet, while economic activity indeed speeded up as the tax system was shifted towards a more consumption-orientated concept, tax revenues climbed not as expected. As government expenditures were even expanded instead of being cut, deficits boosted with no major swing in sight. Although depreciation allowances were again somewhat reduced shortly after they came into effect (Tax Equity and Fiscal Responsibility Act), deficits proved to be persistent. Several deficit control acts trying to check deficit spending failed to do so. By and large, the rise in capital demand was not compensated for by an equivalent increase in savings.

As the notion of Ricardian equivalence also proved not to be valid, deficits took an ever higher share of private savings. While in the case of a cyclical deficit savings need not increase for the Ricardian equivalence principle to hold, with savings still on the decline as deficits proved to be structural in nature, capital demand of the public sector provided a major drain on the US capital market. Thus, government took indeed an ever larger bite of national capital supply.

With private savings for several years on the decline, the increase in deficit spending looks even more dramatic if contrasted to gross private savings. While 1979 it was still in surplus, the deficit to savings ratio switched sign in 1980, reaching a ratio of 7.1 per cent. In the years following, public capital demand took an increasing share of private savings which amounted to almost 22 per cent in 1983. In 1984/85, the bite taken by the deficit was somewhat lower, while heading towards another 20 per cent in 1986. The highest ratio however, was again posted in 1992 with 26 per cent of total domestic savings.[2] With capital scarcity being on the rise US interest rates remained high in nominal as well as in real terms,[3] although the updating of expectations concerning inflation worked into the opposite direction.

---

[1] Although the term got popular, studies offering a consistent analytical foundation are rather rare. For the main pillars of US-supply side policy in the 1980s see, for instance, the studies in Canto, Joines and Laffer 1983 or Hailstones 1982. For a more historical sketch see Boskin 1987, an analytical approach can be found, for instance, in Lucas 1990.

[2] For a recent evaluation of US fiscal policy see Auerbach 1994.

[3] However, this notion was strongly criticized by Evans 1985. The rise in interest rates was transitorily even reinforced by monetary policy switching course towards a more stable money supply.

Figure 5.6:   *Gross national savings, overall budget deficits and deficit to savings ratio: United States 1977-1993*

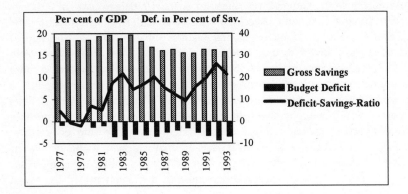

Source: Council of Economic Advisers 1995.

Table 5.3:   *Overall government financial balances: various countries (including social security) in per cent of GDP*

	1979	1980	1981	1982	1983	1984	1985	1986
United States	0,4	-1,3	-1,0	-3,4	-4,1	-2,9	-3,1	-3,4
Germany	-2,6	-2,9	-3,7	-3,3	-2,6	-1,9	-1,2	-1,3
Japan	-4,7	-4,4	-3,8	-3,6	-3,6	-2,1	-0,8	-0,9
G7 Countries	-2,1	-2,7	-2,8	-4,0	-4,3	-3,5	-3,3	-3,3
	1987	1988	1989	1990	1991	1992	1993	1994*
United States	-2,5	-2,0	-1,5	-2,5	-3,2	-4,3	-3,4	-2,0
Germany	-1,9	-2,2	0,1	-2,0	-3,3	-2,9	-3,3	-2,7
Japan	0,5	1,5	2,5	2,9	3,0	1,8	-0,2	-2,0
G7 Countries	-2,4	-1,8	-1,1	-2,0	-2,7	-3,6	-3,9	-3,5

+: Deficit
*: Estimate
Source: OECD 1994c.

In Germany, the United Kingdom and Japan, on the contrary, budget deficits were on the decline in the course of the 1980s. The mere fact that deficit spending was curbed in other major industrialized countries seems to indicate that the successful strive for consolidating government finances there has added to the attractiveness of the United States for international capital. For countries which headed towards lowering budget deficits (either automatically via the cyclical upswing or because of actively cutting deficit spending) experienced a decline in interest rates and became the primary capital suppliers of the world, whereas the United States turned from a creditor nation into a debtor nation.

However, while moving more or less in line in the 1980s, the US balance on current account and US budgetary policy diverged in 1991. Whereas the balance on current account declined substantially, budgetary deficits sky rocketed in absolute as well as in relative terms.[1] At the same time, the economy lost in dynamics. The consequence of which was that a higher part of the public deficit could be financed out of national capital supply. In addition, the Federal Reserve Bank tried to decrease interest rates for stimulating private investment activity. In other countries, however (especially Germany), interest rates climbed in real and in nominal terms, thus making investment more attractive over there. The change in local scarcity induced a corresponding change in the direction of international capital flows, in the course of which the balance on current account in Germany first deteriorated while the US balance became more favourable.

Although interest rates in the mid-1980s declined well below those of 1979-81, the fact that real interest rates were relatively high compared to the 1970s promoted the notion that the US capital import proved to be detrimental to economic activity in other parts of the world. While strengthening the US economy, a net capital import of that high a scale would, it was argued, provide a major drain on the economies losing capital. Moreover, as foreign indebtedness of the US would be due to public deficits on the rise, a crash landing of the dollar was predicted by many analysts[2] as liabilities of the US increase and investors become more reluctant to keep on supplying their capital. Anyway, with US capital demand thus raised compared to other countries, current account balances followed suit, although with the exception of 1987/88 with a slight lag. Even though in terms of GDP balances on current account were not that dramatic, they became quite a policy issue.

However, the fact that balances on current account moved basically in line with deficit spending does not yet prove that it was fiscal expansion alone being responsible for the surge in capital imports and the decline in US cost and price competitiveness. Hence, we should be rather careful in

---

[1] See Council of Economic Advisers 1992, tables B-26 and B-100.

[2] See, for instance, Marris 1985.

drawing conclusions before having had a broader look at the macro-data. Focusing on the different sectoral balances is slightly more informative as the public and the private sector both compete for the capital supplied. What matters for capital scarcity given supply is changes in capital demand of the public and the private sector, although a reservation also applies in case of the latter as crowding out is neglected. On an ex-ante-basis, private capital demand might have grown stronger as figures suggest.

Figure 5.7: *Current account balances and overall deficits of the public sector: United States 1977-1993*

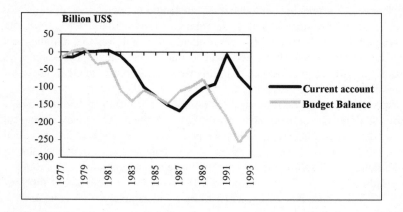

+: Surplus

Source: Council of Economic Advisers 1995 and IMF (a), February 1995.

b) More of the story: the ups and downs of private investment activity
Anyway, time and again, it was the private sector which increased its demand by even more than the public sector. The change in capital demand of the public sector was stronger only in the case of 1982, 1985/86 and the recession of 1990-92. In these years, the pressure on the capital market was mitigated by the fact that capital demand of the private sector declined, thus indicating a countercyclical budget policy. However, in the years remaining and especially as far as the first half of the 1980s is concerned, the US experienced quite an investment boom. Reshaping the tax system towards a more consumption based system gave the business sector much more room for new investment. Although frequently criticized as being detrimental from a national welfare economic point of view since, it was argued, projects would be promoted, the social rate of return of which was

negative,[1] investment activity was clearly on the rise. As cash flows grew due to the expansion of depreciation allowances, the business sector could increase investment substantially even without taking recourse to the capital market. Yet, in 1984, the increase in cash flow even fell short of capital demand by the business sector. Hence, by raising capital on the market, the business sector even added on balance to capital demand. Consequently, gross business savings proved not to be enough to cover both the rising deficit of the public sector as well as the additional investment not to mention the decline in savings by private households, the gap being filled by net capital imports. Whereas gross investment increased between 1982 and 1985 from US$ 503.4 bn to 714.5 bn, gross savings increased only by half of that, namely from US$ 616.9 bn to 735.7 bn. Hence, on balance, it was also the private sector which contributed significantly to the US capital shortage. The improvement in the investment climate contributed to the rise in US interest rates. In other words: in the US, high capital demand of the public sector coincided with an increase in capital demand of the business sector in the 1980s, the combination of which gave rise to the surge in net capital imports. The balance on capital account in the 1980s does therefore only partially reflect differences in national fiscal policy.

Figure 5.8:   *Gross private savings, gross investment and investment–*
savings ratio: United States 1977-1993

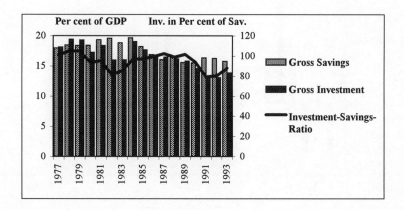

Source: Council of Economic Advisers 1995.

---

[1]   US tax policy was strongly critized as being detrimental to national economic welfare by Sinn 1984. However, welfare economics fails to recognize the benefits of tax competition; see Dluhosch 1993. On the pros and cons of a more consumption based tax system see, for instance, the Meade Report of the Institute for Fiscal Studies 1978 and Bradford 1986.

Thus, in spite of budget policy moving in line with balances on current account in major industrialized countries in the 1980s, balances on current account can only partly be traced back to budgetary policy. Capital flows from Germany and Japan and, time and again, also from the United Kingdom to the United States, reflected not solely differences in budgetary policy. Whether the latter itself might have given rise to capital flows of similar size has to remain an open question since a capital scarcity which is solely due to deficit spending tends more to promote capital exports rather than imports. By putting capital off, fiscal policy would have weakened the dollar rather than strengthening the US currency. But, as the power to attract foreign capital is shaped by the capital stock of debt policy built up in the past, and the power to tax as well as expectations about the willingness to pay, time and again, capital imports might even rise in case of private investment lingering. However, at least as far as the early 1980s are concerned, private investment rather boomed.

Figure 5.9:   Annual real change in gross investment: United States versus rest of the OECD 1979-1995

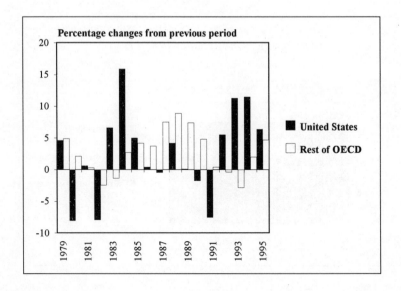

Source: OECD 1994c.

That budget policy was not the sole cause for international capital flows switching direction becomes also visible when investment activity is compared internationally. Whereas investment activity in the United States picked up after the recession of the early 1980s and even speeded up from 1983 to 1985, gross investment in the major surplus countries, that is Germany and Japan, increased only sightly. Obviously, US economic policy switching from macroeconomic fine tuning to promoting micro-incentives, while already under way under the Carter administration, showed their major impact in the early 1980s as the US was not only the first in line but also coming more strongly out of the worldwide recession.

Taking recourse to the international capital market proved to be not much of a concern as long as investment activity was strong, no matter whether foreign investment was actually flowing into government bonds or private investment. As long as interest payments can be paid out of an increase in productivity, international capital flows prove to be beneficial from a worldwide as well as from a national perspective. Although at first glance implying a drain for capital export countries, in the aggregate, individuals will also get their pay-off from the intertemporal division of labour being widened.[1] The more expectations about the future course of the economy are well founded, the less likely a crash-landing of the capital-import currency becomes. If capital imports can indeed be traced back to economic prospects being enhanced, the ups and downs in the value of the currency are more due to Marshallian elasticities rather than to capital flows becoming erratic. Balances on current account in Germany, Japan and the United States must thus be put into the context of improving economic prospects in the US, both by turning away from Keynesian interventionism and the regulation of specific markets.

As far as the second half of the 1980s is concerned, the latter does not apply as well as growth rates in private investment flattened out. Budget deficits, however, at the very start a clear outcome of tax policy aiming at improving private investment incentives, became persistent. Yet, the increase in capital supply of the private sector due to sectoral capital demand lingering lagged far behind the continuously strong deficit spending of the public sector. The difference in movement of sectoral balances is a clear sign that in the very period under consideration budget policy was the primary driving force when it comes to explaining and evaluating balances on current account. Moreover, what contributes to differences in evaluation concerning both periods is that net imports in goods and services were significantly financed by central banks becoming much more active in the second part of the 1980s. Monetary policy switched course in 1985, with regard to internal matters as well as external matters as both are linked together for monetary policy showing an impact on nominal exchange rates. In the long run, however, a constellation like this would be a rather shaky foundation for a steadily high transfer of capital. Foreign investors,

---

[1]   Distributional issues and different pay-offs of vested interests aside.

however, proved to be patient, rating the United States at least in the second half of the 1980s still high.

E. A More Consistent Explanation of US Price and Cost Competitiveness

The swing in US international price and cost competitiveness during the 1980s completes the picture. While the intertemporal approach to the balance of payments can both provide an answer to the decline in US price and cost competitiveness as well as its subsequent improvement with balances persisting, the competitiveness approach fails to do so. Instead, according to the competitiveness approach, the improvement in US price and cost competitiveness must have shown up in an improvement of the balance on current account. Not so in the US.

The attempt to talk down the dollar is basically in line with the notion of balances on current account (either overall, sectoral or regional) reflecting national differences in competitiveness. However, that the constant effort to do so proved to be quite unsuccessful in bringing about a change in trade flows underpins the fact that balances on current account must be traced back to international capital flows thus reflecting by and large differences in locational quality rather than in the national ability to sell.

As far as central banks refrained from dirty floating, the balance on current account reflected capital scarcities with exchange rates adjusting endogenously instead of being the ultimate cause of the 'American disease'. With price and cost competitiveness increasing by more than the market can bear, the dollar would have tended weak instead of strong. Hence, the fact that nominal as well as real unit labour costs in Germany or Japan climbed between 1980 and 1985[1] by less than those of the United States does not prove that the US ran deficits since its overall ability to sell abroad declined. No doubt, real unit labour costs expressed in national currency increased by some 27.5 per cent in the United States, whereas in Germany they climbed by some 15 per cent and in Japan by 10.2 per cent. However, if differences in unit labour costs would have been the reason for American products losing their competitiveness on international markets and thus allowing German and Japanese firms to catch up on world markets, the D-Mark as well as the yen should have experienced an appreciation, whereas the dollar should have depreciated. The international competitiveness of US products would have been preserved. The swing in the current account of the United States would have hardly taken place.

For the exchange rate not compensating for differences in the movement of unit labour costs between 1980 and 1985, but even reinforcing them, indicates that the high investment activity in the United States combined with rather low savings of the private as well as the public sector was the

---

[1]   This is the period in which balances on current account were built up.

major driving force behind the current account. As trade flows did not react elastically to the change in the structure in demand due to the international shift in purchasing power the real transfer necessary had to be brought about by a major swing in nominal and real exchange rates. Hence, in the course of the US attracting capital, the dollar appreciated substantially in the first half of the 1980s *vis-à-vis* the German mark and the yen, both in nominal as well as in real terms.[1]

The real appreciation of the dollar enforced a shift in production from tradeables to non-tradeables within the United States (and the other way round in the major capital export countries). The prices of the latter by and large climbed in relative terms due to the higher demand in the course of the capital inflow, while the rise of the dollar impaired the ability to sell in the case of tradeables. Consequently, the supply-side of the US switched to non-tradeables whereas US demand headed the other way. With the supply- and demand-structure shifting in opposite directions, net imports increased while the dollar went down again. Hence, the exchange rate crowding out proves to be part of the adjustment process, being a consequence of the deficit on current account rather than its source. The latter holds as long as the exchange rate of the American currency was not supported by central banks intervening[2] – and the latter was not the case until the second half of the 1980s. The Marshallian dynamics in the intertemporal approach also reveals why deficits proved to be persistent despite all indicators of price and cost competitiveness improving.

F. The US in Deficit: How Much of an Engine for the World Economy?

Now, what about the international repercussions of the US in deficit? Did they matter not only in the sense of shaping the structure of capital export countries, but also in the sense of stimulating economic activity in general as exports were on the rise? The latter was at least the prevailing view in the US in the mid-1980s as the US administration urged its main trading partners to share in the burden by easing monetary policy and shifting towards a more expansionary policy. Doubts remain.[3] To be sure, the US added to the intertemporal division of labour. However, the notion of balances on current account having a stimulating impact is much different from that.

Recalling again our discussion about the national accounting identity and its supply-side interpretation reveals that the notion of an international transmission of economic activity via balances on current account does not

---

[1]   See also Hoffman and Homburg 1990 for a more formal treatment.

[2]   In this case, it would have been the central bank financing the deficit on current account. See chapter 2.II.

[3]   See chapter 2.II as well as the discussion in Bhandari and Putnam 1985 and Scheid 1987, pp. 159-211.

hold under the circumstances prevailing, neither nowadays nor in the 1980s. The assumption of the US as having been an engine for the rest of the world exactly draws on the competitiveness interpretation of the national accounting identity proven to be rather shaky a foundation in case of flexible exchange rates.

In a purely Keynesian setting with money supply driven by demand and effective demand lacking on a worldwide scale, the world-wide impact of the rise in the deficit on current account would be probably more clear: by absorbing the surplus in savings, the US would have transformed what would otherwise be a leakage in effective demand for imports, thus pulling its main trading partners towards more economic activity. This was also the kind of logic providing the basis for the so-called 'locomotive theory', which already failed in the 1970s. Yet, with a Keynesian setting not given and monetary supply by and large not being endogenous, the balance on current account was basically a matter of structural change.

Hence, the call for a more expansionary policy in Europe and Japan in the mid-1980s would have certainly failed to achieve its goal, namely bringing down the US deficit on current account. Instead, by stimulating capital exports, an easing of monetary policy in Europe and Japan would have even increased the US deficit on current account. Concerning policy lessons, we have therefore to focus on structures rather than aggregates. If there is a lesson to be taken from the US price and cost competitiveness issue, it is that economic policy can facilitate structural change thus lowering adjustment costs by promoting the openness of markets.

II. Japan: persistent surpluses

A. Overview

'Oddly, the Japanese fondness for novelty is all but unknown overseas. The general image of the Japanese is exactly the opposite: a band of xenophobic nationalists who refuse to use anything made outside of their country' (Ohmae 1990).

This statement instantly highlights the extensive discussions not only about trade related questions and capital flows, but also about the Japanese attitude towards its international partners in the western hemisphere in general. Many observers, both Americans and Europeans, are deeply convinced that Japan is something special.[1] Indeed, Japan is said to be locked against foreign goods as well as alien ideas. This point of view, of course, is not widely accepted in Japan itself. Moreover, Japanese imports were rather booming during the last years.

---

[1]   See for instance Altman 1994. For the opposite view see Bhagwati 1994.

One of the most important factors behind this controversy is the Japanese balance of payments, which in the last decade has been characterized by huge surpluses in the current account, especially in the trade balance, and by enormous deficits in the capital account. Particularly, the trade balance *vis-à-vis* the US is in a high surplus. Moreover, the structure of exports and imports is mainly inter-industrial, whereas the US and the European Union are marked by a very high share of intra-industrial trade.

In accordance with the developments concerning liberalization, technical progress and the flexibilization of currencies since 1973, the Japanese balance of payments, like other industrialized countries' balances of payments, has been subject to change. Whereas during the fixed exchange rates era and the time of capital controls there was no clear cut connection between net trade and net capital flows, this has become different since the international liberalization of capital flows has emerged. The current account mirrors the capital account. Moreover, the magnitude of net flows has increased in the course of the liberalization.

Up to 1980, it is impossible to identify a trend in the Japanese balance of payments. Since then, it is characterized by significant surpluses in the current account and high deficits in the capital account. In relation to GNP, the net flows reached their peak in 1985 (capital account) and in 1986 (current account) respectively. Until 1990, net balances declined; since then, they have grown again. During the times when the net positions shrinked, the yen depreciated in real terms, and it appreciated while the net positions enlarged. At times, the authorities intervened heavily in the foreign exchange markets. This is reflected in large variations of the currency reserves.

The surplus in the trade balance exceeds the current account surplus since the Japanese balance of services is traditionally in deficit. However, since the Japanese net foreign assets have risen due to the persistent net capital outflows, the earnings on those assets have grown steadily, causing the deficit in services to diminish in the 1990s. In addition, Japan shows a net outflow of transfers. Thus, the surplus in the current account is beneath the net exports (OECD 1994a, p. 29). The latest appreciation of the yen has caused the volume of exports to shrink in 1993 and 1994, whereas the dollar value has grown again. This phenomenon is not new: during the appreciation of the yen after February 1985, the export volume fell whereas the dollar value increased (Corker 1989).

This chapter provides a closer look at the factors behind the developments of the balance of payments. From a theoretical point of view, we can distinguish two main hypotheses. The first claims that the Japanese firms are more competitive than their rivals. The competitive advantage is at least partly traced back to unfair trade. This hypothesis is based on the competitiveness approach which focuses on the de jure trade regime, the de facto trade behaviour and the currency regime in Japan in order to analyse the roots of the alleged Japanese superiority. This is meant to answer the question whether the Japanese advantages are natural or artificial. The second hypothesis traces the imbalances back to differences in international capital supply and demand; it is based on the intertemporal approach. Here we mainly focus on the high Japanese private savings rate which distinctly exceeds the industrialized world's average savings rate, the investment behaviour and the governmental budget.

One cannot analyse the Japanese balance of payment without looking at the rest of the world since the national economies have become more interdependent during the last twenty-five years due to the liberalization of trade and capital flows and due to the rise of advanced communication technologies. To give an example, it is doubtful whether the Japanese capital outflow would have been that high and persistent without the US large governmental deficits throughout the 1980s.

B. Japan's Competitiveness and the Structure of Trade

a) Introduction

In this section, we try to trace back the surpluses on the high competitiveness of the firms in Japan. Many claim that the latter is raised artificially by means of protectionism.[1] Following conventional wisdom, these do not only include ordinary state interventions such as tariffs and some non-tariff trade barriers, but also the public procurement and the special Japanese form of industrial organization, the keiretsu (Lawrence 1993).

In order to evaluate the importance of trade policy for the high surpluses in the current account, especially in the trade balance, it is convenient to take into account the RCA index as a measure of competitiveness[2] and the Grubel–Lloyd coefficient.[3] The figures are to be compared with the structure of protection, for Japan, the US, and Germany respectively. Thus, it is possible to analyse whether protectionist measures have a significant influence on the structure of trade flows and the balance of payments. Therefore, we now turn to the Japanese trade regime.

b) Trade policy in Japan: an evaluation

In general, the Japanese trade regime has become more free-trade-oriented in the past few years. Average import tariffs are very low, at least compared with the United States and the European Union.[4] Tariff escalation, however, can be observed (GATT 1992, Vol. I, p. 60). The agricultural sector is

---

[1] See for instance Lawrence 1987 and Lincoln 1990.
[2] This has been done in chapter 3.II.
[3] Instead of the Grubel–Lloyd coefficient, one could concentrate on export–import ratios (Goto 1991, pp. 11-3). The message of both indicators is similar.
[4] For details see the annex in GATT 1992 Vol. I, Table AV.8.

protected by the highest average tariffs. Within the industrial sector the tariffs on Heckscher–Ohlin goods are the highest ones. The tariff protection in Japan is in accordance with the tariff structure of industrialized countries. It can be explained very well by the political economy of protection.[1] Industries with comparative disadvantages are more likely to be protected than others when international competition becomes stiffer. By and large, the tariff structure thus does not provide empirical evidence in favour of the hypothesis that Japan is different from other industrialized countries (Heitger and Stehn 1988).

However, since import tariffs have lost their importance due to several GATT rounds it is not adequate to focus on them only. As the political economy of protection suggests, a tariff reduction does not mean a reduction in overall protection. Instead, there have been created many substitutes for tariffs which are more or less compatible to the GATT rules. Traditionally, the most important non-tariff trade barriers (NTTB) are import quotas, voluntary export restraints (VER), export subsidies and anti-dumping measures. In addition, some protectionist measures have gained attraction in the last few years, among which technical standards, government procurement behaviour and bilateral negotiation on trade results (managed trade) are relevant, especially when looking at Japan.

Import quotas in Japan are maintained on agricultural products, on some chemicals and on some other industrial products. These quotas are not directed toward one single country, in general. Some of them are to be removed and substituted for tariffs in accordance to the results of the Uruguay Round. Japan does not apply the Multi Fibre Agreement (MFA) to developing countries. Instead, it is the only industrialized country that is subject to import quotas imposed on its textile and clothing exports by the United States. Export promotion also is not pursued very extensively. The Japanese government rather concentrates on export restraints in order to balance the Japanese trade.[2] Japan also abstains from VERs and from countervailing duties. Only one anti-dumping measure is reported by the GATT (1992, Vol. I, p.98).

Concerning the setting of technical standards, there always has been great concern about Japanese behaviour. This, among others, has led the Japanese government to massive efforts in order to harmonize and adjust its standards and other technical requirements to international practice. Another sensible issue in Japan's international relations is the public procurement procedure. Since the end of the Tokyo round, Japan has formally opened the public demand to foreign suppliers. Following the

---

[1] For a survey on the political economy of the tariff structure of industrialized countries see Anderson and Baldwin 1981 and Freytag 1995a, pp. 106-14.

[2] We will judge this measure later when discussing the chances of using trade policy in order to balance the current account.

GATT Trade Policy Review Mechanism, this opening was welcomed by US officals (GATT 1992, Vol. II, p. 146). What still makes the US representatives feel uneasy is the fact that import promotion in Japan does not prove a successful measure in order to diminish the Japanese–American trade imbalance (ibid). Import promotion belongs to the bilateral trade related measures which are especially negotiated between the United States and Japan. Other examples for this kind of policy are the market-oriented sector-specific talks (MOSS) and the Semiconductor Trade Agreement (STA).[1] These examples show that not mainly Japan, but the United States impose trade restrictions on their partners.

Nevertheless, the critics of Japanese trade policy still argue that the Japanese success (which in their eyes includes the huge trade surpluses) is not alone driven by productivity of market oriented firms. No critic ever fails to mention the almighty MITI as one of the driving forces behind the enormous growth of the Japanese economy. It has concentrated throughout the years on so-called 'sunrise industries' which probably would have been successful anyway (Lawrence 1993, pp. 4-6). This helped Japanese firms to conquer new markets and to gain markets shares, the critics argue. Moreover, it is called to be of strategic importance to be the first to produce and sell new goods. Even if there exists a first mover advantage, the role of the MITI is overemphasized and misinterpreted: instead of predicting the future extremely precisely, the MITI seems to have supported the development of 'sunrise industries' after their sun had risen.

The complaints also are not limited to state interventions. They also focus on state failures, namely the omission of a proper antitrust legislation. The Japanese economy is highly interconnected through the system of keiretsu which links Japanese firms in three ways (Lawrence 1993, pp. 11-5). First, a keiretsu can be a horizontally linked group of firms. Banks are said to play a crucial rule in the horizontal concentration, for they can provide credits at preferential interest rates which gives the borrower a cost advantage compared with his competitors. Second, the link between the firms can be vertical. Third, the firms have organized a very tight distribution system.[2] It is argued that by all three forms of keiretsu barriers to trade are erected, making it very difficult for foreign firms to enter the Japanese markets. Empirical evidence is not unambiguous. Lawrence (1991, pp. 318-20) calculates the effects of keiretsu on Japanese imports. His results suggest that keiretsu have a negative impact on imports. Their effect on exports is not clear, on the other hand. The third form of keiretsu, the distribution networks, induce high price markups, compared with retail

---

[1]   For a detailed evaluation of these measures see Bergsten and Noland 1993.

[2]   It is also possible to distinguish only two forms of the keiretsu, the horizontal and the vertical one. The latter can be distinguished further in production and distribution concentration.

prices in Germany and the US, at least for brand name products (ibid, p. 328). Therefore, Lawrence concludes that the Japanese markets are more closed than those of other industrialized countries. Other observers are not convinced that keiretsu affect the trade balance, that is exports and imports, significantly. First of all, Saxonhouse (1993, pp. 26-7) argues that it is all but easy to calculate the impacts of informal, or organizational barriers on the trade structure and the trade balance at all. When analysing Japan's trade structure, Petri (1991, pp. 62-76) comes to the conclusion that producer's concentration correlates positively with import penetration. This result contradicts the findings of Lawrence (1991). As becomes clear in Saxonhouse (1993, pp. 35-9), the results obtained depend heavily on the applied methods. Therefore, it seems not warranted to conclude that Japan's economy is more closed than the one of other countries just because of the existence of horizontal or vertical conglomeration.

Moreover, another reservation about the keiretsu's influence on trade flows is at hand. The main bank system, indeed, was successful in at least two respects. First, it improved information and credit evaluation via monitoring the firms. Therefore, the loan risk premia could have been reduced. Second, it helped to avoid bankruptcy (Patrick 1994). Since the system was not created, but developed in an evolutionary process, it can be justified economically. It cannot be judged as a barrier to trade. Moreover, Japanese firms often change their main bank affiliation (Saxonhouse 1993, p. 38) which is in contrast to the belief that the horizontal integration of Japanese firms (including banks) gives all of them the opportunity to get loans at preferential interest rates. Obviously, it is not that easy to receive preferential treatment for those firms which have been changing the main bank. During the 1970s and 1980s, the debt–equity ratio which used to be very high in Japan as a consequence of low cost of capital fell. This is seen as an effect of the diminishing reliance on the system of main banks (Frankel, 1991, pp. 230-2). Thus, there is no advantage in capital costs for the economy as a whole although some enterprises may have such advantages. The same, however, can be true for some German firms which generally have a close affiliation with their main bank too. Nobody argues that the German markets are more closed than American markets only by quoting the German main bank system.[1]

To sum up, the empirical evidence cannot give support to the popular thesis that Japan's trade performance is to an overwhelming extend affected by formal or informal trade policy. This result has a very important implication. Since the Japanese trade policy regime does not differ too much from trade regimes in Europe and North America, we should be very careful when searching for the main determinants of the huge and persistent

---

[1]   On the contrary, others argue that these links are a barrier to entry for newcomers, in general, since they are not able to obtain the necessary loans (The Economist 1995).

surpluses in the Japanese trade balance. Nevertheless, trade policy is not harmless although not responsible for trade surpluses. Japan is still far from being a free trade oriented nation. As a recent study by Sazanami, Urata and Kawai (1994) shows, Japanese trade policy costs their consumers between US$ 57 bn and US$ 110 bn. Therefore, Japan should be interested in dismantling protectionism for pure self-interest.

c) Regional trade flows

Japan is one of the biggest trading nations in the world. The world market share of Japanese exporters is about 10 per cent which is third behind exports from the US and from Germany. In 1992, Japan exported 9 per cent of its GDP. The ratio of imports to GDP was nearly 7 per cent.

The regional structure of trade has been changing in the last ten years. These changes, naturally, have not taken place abruptly, still they are remarkable. The biggest market for Japanese exports in the 1980s was North America where almost 40 per cent of Japanese exports were sold in 1984. In 1993 the share of sales to North America was 31 per cent. This is even less than the South East Asian markets absorb. Their share of sales rose from some 20 per cent in the mid-1980s to more than 30 per cent in the1990s. The third huge Japanese export market is the European Community whose share has been varying between 15 and 20 per cent in the last 10 years.

Japanese imports show a more stable structure. The share of North American exporters remained constant. It is about 25 per cent; the same amount is sold by producers from South East Asia. Both shares have somewhat fluctuated, but a stable trend in one or the other direction cannot be identified. The same holds for the European Union. Its exporters provide some 15 per cent of Japanese imports. The fourth important supplier of Japanese imports is the OPEC. Its share has risen in the last 10 years: from 4 per cent to 8 per cent. Since the demand for oil is rather inelastic in the industrialized world, the OPEC's share will vary with the oil prices. Therefore, it is convenient not to see a trend in the recent development of Japanese imports from the OPEC countries.

d) Inter-industrial vs. intra-industrial trade

Apart from the regional disaggregation of trade flows, the analysis of the sectoral trade structure is important. Normally, the structure of trade flows is determined by comparative advantages which are, following neoclassical reasoning, set by the country's factor endowment. In chapter 3 we already computed some measures of sectoral competitiveness, one of them being the RCA index. The Japanese trade structure, in general, fits neoclassical international trade theory; Japan has comparative advantages in the production of most Schumpeter goods analysed in Table 3.3, except inorganic chemicals and chemical materials.

The Japanese trade structure is different from the one which can be observed in other industrialized nations. The international division of labour in the last decades has advanced towards a growing intra-industrial trade. Nearly all OECD member countries have moved into this direction (OECD 1994c, p. 41). Intra-industry trade is complete when an industry's exports exactly match its imports (usually expressed in terms of value). If, on the contrary, certain products are only exported or only imported, the inter-industrial trade in this product is complete. For instance, it could be expected that an industrialized country having only poor natural resources like oil, coal, etc. is only importing these resources. Therefore, one often observes total inter-industry trade in Ricardo goods. On the other hand, industrialized countries are expected to have a similar product range. The goods they offer, nevertheless, are not homogenous so that, due to different preferences of the countries' inhabitants and due to economies of scale in production, both exports and imports take place (Grubel and Lloyd 1975).

In order to measure the level of intra-industrial trade a nation has reached, an index, the Grubel–Lloyd coefficient, is computed (Grubel and Lloyd 1975, pp. 19-24). This coefficient can be calculated for single industries as well as for an economy as a whole. It is the value of total trade minus the value of the (absolute) difference of exports and imports in per cent of the value of total trade, calculated for the respective industry.

$$(52) \quad B_i = \frac{(Ex_i + Im_I) - |Ex_i - Im_i|}{(Ex_i + Im_I)} * 100$$

with i = industry

If $B = 100$, we observe complete intra-industrial trade, whereas $B = 0$ indicates complete inter-industrial trade. Sometimes it is convenient to calculate the index for any industry concerning only one trading partner, for instance the index B_i of the Japanese producers of road vehicles with respect to the United States. Moreover, the index is estimated for the economy as a whole by adding up all industries in order to gain one figure which is used for international or intertemporal comparisons. The formula then is:

$$(53) \quad B = \frac{\sum_i (Ex_i + Im_i) - \sum_i |Ex_i - Im_i|}{\sum_i (Ex_i + Im_i)} * 100$$

International comparisons are carried out in order to gain information, if there exists something like a 'normal' structure of trade for industrialized countries. A country's deviation of the so-called normal structure can give some information about its factor endowment, about the competitive behaviour of its firms and about its trade policy. We discuss the value of such information in the digression following next.

Table 5.4:   *Intra-industrial trade in Japan, the US and Germany 1992, 25 industries, Grubel–Lloyd index, two-digit level SITC*

	Japan	USA	Germany
Ricardo goods			
SITC 01 Meat and Preparations	0,57	82,14	57,29
SITC 03 Fish and Preparations	11,10	72,22	41,14
SITC 05 Vegetables and Fruits	5,48	92,96	24,51
SITC 11 Beverages	8,09	34,44	66,97
SITC 12 Tobacco and Manufactures	17,79	36,37	92,07
SITC 32 Coal, Coke and Briquettes	8,65	19,95	88,53
SITC 33 Petroleum and Products	6,91	20,00	25,18
Heckscher-Ohlin goods			
SITC 61 Leather	99,88	98,17	95,67
SITC 65 Textile Yarns, Fabrics, etc.	74,13	82,40	94,44
SITC 67 Iron and Steel	43,94	54,60	93,08
SITC 84 Clothing and Accessories	10,78	22,10	50,05
SITC 88 Photo Equipment, Optical Glasses, etc.	39,91	65,69	98,55
Immobile Schumpeter goods			
SITC 71 Power Generating Equipment	29,46	94,88	77,82
SITC 72 Machines for Special Industries	27,32	84,82	54,21
SITC 73 Metalworking Machinery	28,25	96,31	62,20
SITC 74 General Industry Machinery	30,56	92,97	65,50
SITC 78 Road Vehicles	15,49	64,43	72,52
SITC 87 Precision Instruments	65,32	70,18	75,56
Mobile Schumpeter goods			
SITC 51 Organic Chemicals	82,81	93,77	84,74
SITC 52 Inorganic Chemicals	61,29	92,92	86,41
SITC 58 Plastic Materials, etc.	42,57	82,05	77,93
SITC 59 Chemical Materials	99,73	60,01	71,45
SITC 75 Office Machines, ADP Equipment	33,41	84,26	69,78
SITC 76 Television Receivers	19,63	59,78	85,58
SITC 77 Electric Machinery	35,51	88,27	84,23

Source: OECD 1993, 1994a and 1994b, own calculations.

An international comparison is carried out by OECD (1994c, p. 41) where it computed the Grubel–Lloyd coefficient of major industrialized countries. As mentioned above, Japan shows the lowest Grubel–Lloyd coefficient of all G-7 countries. We calculated the Grubel–Lloyd coefficient for Japan, the United States and Germany. In contrast to the OECD, when calculating the economy-wide index, we included not only trade in manufactured products, but all exports and imports. Our figure for Japan exceeds the figure computed by the OECD by nearly 10 percentage points, whereas the figure for Germany in our calculation equals the OECD figure. Table 5.4 shows the significance of Japan's inter-industry trade, compared with the figures for the US and Germany.

Digression: inter-industrial versus intra-industrial trade: what is the normal trade structure?

We now turn to the question of whether there is a normal trade structure for industrialized countries. Since all industrialized countries with the exception of Japan show a high degree of intra-industrial trade, it is usually taken for granted that this is the 'regular' structure. Hence, following this view, there is something special about the Japanese trade structure.

In order to explain the structure of trade and the deviations from normality two hypotheses, contradicting each other, can be identified: the first claims that an 'unnaturally' low coefficient follows a high level of protection; in other words: Japan's low intra-industrial division of labour is due to high trade barriers towards foreign competitors. Lawrence (1987), as Lincoln (1990) does, argues that Japan's low share in intra-industrial trade indicates a high level of protection. They both come to the conclusion that Japan's markets are more closed than the markets of other developed countries. Having the evaluation of Japanese trade policy in mind, the validity of this judgement is doubtful.

The second hypothesis claims the opposite: the higher sectoral protection is, the higher is the share of intra-industrial trade in this sector due to the fact that trade barriers raise the price of imports relative to the price of exports; in addition, it is possible to lower export prices selectively by export subsidies. Provided, the price elasticity is larger than unity, sectoral imports will be lower, and sectoral exports will increase in the course of protection. Since, normally, protection is given to those industries without comparative advantages ($Ex < Im$) the summand ($Ex - Im$) in absolute terms will decrease. This leads to an increasing coefficient. If, however, industries with comparative advantages ($Ex > Im$) are protected, the coefficient will be cut down. For the summand ($Ex - Im$) in absolute terms will increase due to protection leading to a decreasing coefficient.[1] Therefore, one has to be extremely careful with the results obtained by testing the hypotheses.

---

[1] The application of this line of argument to the whole economy instead of selected sectors is problematic. If all imports are discriminated, the currency will appreciate and exports will be reduced as well.

Of course, these extreme positions are not the only explanations one can think of. The truth may be half of both or none of both. Goto (1991, p. 7) works out two propositions about the causes of a certain level of intra-industrial trade.

(1)   Given the country's relative size, its intra-industrial trade is the smaller, the more its factor endowment differs from the world average.

(2)   Given the country's relative factor endowment, its intra-industrial trade is the smaller, the larger is the country.

The more the factor endowment of two countries differs from one another, the more complementary division of labour takes place, hence, the higher is their inter-industrial trade. The reason for this trade structure is that both countries have comparative advantages in different products. Therefore their range of goods differs very much as well. On the other hand, a similar factor endowment causes a similar product range with some differentiation. The European countries are proper examples for proposition 1 (in the reversed sense).

Proposition 2 can be interpreted in the following way: a large country is more varied than a smaller one. Thus, less trade with foreigners takes place at all. Moreover, it is plausible that international trade is due to complementary specialization. The US provide a powerful example. In addition, Goto explains the higher share of intra-industrial trade in Korea, compared with Japan, in this way.

He therefore points out that both propositions hold for Japan, especially if compared with Korea (Goto 1991, pp. 8-9). Moreover, by using a slightly changed regression equation with the same sample of data as Lawrence, he obtained rather different results which resolve Japan from suspicion of being closed.

Before introducing and discussing our empirical findings, it is necessary to show the limits for interpretation of the Grubel–Lloyd coefficient. Normally, the coefficient will become smaller the higher a country's overall trade imbalances are, since *ceteris paribus* the sectoral value of exports minus imports grows. Saxonhouse (1993, p. 25) computed the Grubel–Lloyd coefficients for five countries and the EC-12. In a second step he adjusted the figures for trade imbalances. The coefficients for all countries grew; the Japanese figure, however, grew the most, both in relative and absolute terms. Two explanations for low intra-industrial spezialization which again are traced back to the competing hypotheses can be thought of in this case. If, as the competitiveness approach suggests, the trade imbalances are caused by trade policy, the Grubel–Lloyd coefficient is low due to trade policy, too. The meaningfulness of the indicator remains high. If, however, the trade imbalances are caused by international differences in savings and investment, that is capital supply and capital demand, the story is different. In this case, part of the low intra-industrial trade can be explained by such differences in international savings and investments. We have to keep this reservation in mind until we have drawn a conclusion about which approach, the competitiveness approach or the intertemporal approach, better fits the Japanese data. The second reservation about the indicator is a statistical one. The more the trade flows are disaggregated, that is the higher the chosen SITC level is, the smaller the coefficient will become. For differentiated products are not accounted in the same industry, but in different industries (Bhagwati 1991, p. 36). Hence, choosing a higher SITC level is likely to erase the existence of intra-industrial trade. Eventually, international differences in the structure of trade flows with regard to inter- and intra-industrial trade can be wiped out that way.

In order to test both of the hypotheses mentioned above, we draw a comparison of the US, Germany and Japan concerning the correlation between the level of sectoral protection and the Grubel–Lloyd index. We use a rather rough method to test the hypotheses. First, we calculate the Grubel–Lloyd coefficient of 25 industries on the SITC two-digit level for Japan, the US and Germany. The results are shown in Table 5.4. Second, we evaluate the degree of protection by industry using the GATT Trade Policy Review Mechanism (TPRM) for these three countries.[1] Confining on the TPRM ensures that the data are comparable. We express the degree of protection in an ordered ranking by taking into account all tariffs and non-tariff barriers the countries impose on their imports. Thus, we obtain three classes for a) little or no protection, b) medium level of protection, and c) high or very high protection, '1' corresponding to a low and '3' corresponding to a high degree of protection. Third, we match the degree of protection and the coefficient for every single industry. Following the first, conventional, hypothesis, the coefficient should be the lower the stronger the industry is protected. In contrast, following the second hypothesis, a high coefficient is correlated to high industrial protection.

The results are surprising since in none of the industries does the first hypothesis prove to be valid for either of the three countries. Instead, in eleven industries higher sectoral protection corresponds to a higher sectoral share of intra-industrial trade. The office machinery industry provides a very illustrative example. It is protected in both the US and Germany and not protected in Japan. The Japanese Grubel–Lloyd coefficient as regards this industry is by far the lowest of the three countries. German and American trade and industrial policies in favour of office machinery seem to have shrinked imports and stimulated exports; both of which are suitable to increase intra-industrial trade. At first glance, the same holds for automobiles. High intra-industrial trade with cars in the US and Germany is

---

[1]   In the case of Germany, we used the TPRM for the EC. Since the EC trade policy regime is harmonized there should be no reservation.

linked with higher protection of road vehicles. However, it is appropriate to suppose that comparative advantages exist in all of the three countries. Therefore, one can argue that in the German case the intra-industrial trade in automobiles would even be higher without protection for (*Ex - Im*) would have been smaller, if no trade barriers existed.

Table 5.5:   *Protection and intra-industrial trade in Japan, the US and Germany 1992, 25 industries, Grubel-Lloyd index, two-digit level SITC*

	Japan		USA		Germany	
	P	GL	P	GL	P	GL
Ricardo goods						
SITC 01 Meat and Preparations	2	1	3	82	3	57
SITC 03 Fish and Preparations	2	11	2	72	2	41
SITC 05 Vegetables and Fruits	2	5	2	93	3	25
SITC 11 Beverages	3	8	2	34	3	67
SITC 12 Tobacco and Manufactures	3	18	3	36	3	92
SITC 32 Coal, Coke and Briquettes	2	9	2	20	3	89
SITC 33 Petroleum and Products	1	7	1	20	1	25
Heckscher-Ohlin goods						
SITC 61 Leather	3	100	2	98	2	96
SITC 65 Textile Yarns, Fabrics, etc.	3	74	3	82	3	94
SITC 67 Iron and Steel	2	44	3	55	3	93
SITC 84 Clothing and Accessories	3	11	3	22	3	50
SITC 88 Photo Eqp., Opt. Glasses, etc.	1	40	2	66	1	99
Immobile Schumpeter goods						
SITC 71 Power Generating Eqp.	1	29	2	95	2	78
SITC 72 Machines for Special Ind.	1	27	2	85	1	54
SITC 73 Metalworking Machinery	1	28	2	96	1	62
SITC 74 Gen. Industry Machinery	1	31	2	93	1	66
SITC 78 Road Vehicles	1	15	2	64	2	73
SITC 87 Precision Instruments	1	65	1	70	1	76
Mobile Schumpeter goods						
SITC 51 Organic Chemicals	2	83	2	94	2	85
SITC 52 Inorganic Chemicals	2	61	2	93	2	86
SITC 58 Plastic Materials, etc.	2	43	2	82	2	78
SITC 59 Chemical Materials	2	100	2	60	2	71
SITC 75 Office Machines, ADP Eqp.	1	33	3	84	3	70
SITC 76 Television Receivers	1	20	3	60	3	86
SITC 77 Electric Machinery	1	36	1	88	1	84

P = level of protection;   GL = Grubel–Lloyd coefficient

Source: OECD 1993, 1994a and 1994b, GATT 1992, 1993 and 1994, own calculations.

The other industries are either protected to the same amount so that international differences in the intra-industrial division of labour cannot be traced back to differences in the level of protection, or neither hypothesis can be rejected, that is the results are intransitive: an example is the industry 'photo apparatus, optical goods, watches and clocks' (SITC 88) which is protected in the US and nearly not in Japan and Germany. The share of intra-industrial trade is the highest in Germany, followed by the US, third is Japan.

Figure 5.10:   Intra-industrial trade and protection: another perspective

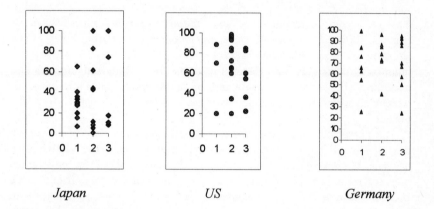

Japan   US   Germany

Source: See Table 5.5

In Figure 5.10, we plotted the sectoral level of protection with the sectoral Grubel–Lloyd index. Following hypothesis one, high protection is negatively correlated with high intra-industrial trade. The plots, therefore, should fall from the left top of the graph to the right bottom. The second hypothesis predicts the opposite: high protection is positively correlated with high intra-industrial trade. Consequently the plots should be concentrated on a line from the left bottom to the right top. None of which is the case (although the results fit a little better the second hypothesis). The correlation coefficient is near zero.

To draw a conclusion, it is rather difficult and by no means convincing to trace back international differences in the share of intra-industrial trade to differences in trade policies of the countries in question. As the results suggest, neither a country's inter-industrial bias nor its intra-industrial bias is due to closed markets. Whether the Japanese trade structure instead can be explained by 'closed minds', as Lawrence (1987, p. 547) asks, is subject to an emotional discussion which we do not want to enter.[1] Nevertheless,

---

[1]   A fine-drawn judgement on this debate can be found in Bhagwati 1991, pp. 24-44.

the results should be handled with extreme care having in mind the fact that we use such a crude method. Anyhow, we would rather like to follow the two propositions made by Goto (1991) if anything.

e) High surpluses in the light of the strong yen
During the last twenty years, in real effective terms the yen oscillated very much, no matter which index to measure its external value is used. Three significant appreciations and two perceptible depreciations can be observed. This volatility was not easy to handle for Japanese entrepreneurs. Naturally, changes in the real external value cause adjustment processes on a nation's supply-side, as the example of the United States unambiguously makes clear.[1] Currency revaluations influence the international competitiveness of firms in different sectors. A real appreciation *ceteris paribus* worsens the situation of firms offering tradeables, since their price-competitiveness diminishes which is likely to let exports fall. Moreover, imports are becoming cheaper to the inhabitants of the country. Some producers of tradeables will lose their competitiveness and have to disappear from the market.

The situation of the sector of non-tradeables *ceteris paribus* improves, on the other hand, in the course of a real appreciation. Since the relative price of tradeables has fallen in the course of the real appreciation, on average incomes earned there will fall too. A reallocation of factors will take place because the relatively high incomes in the sector of non-tradeables are an incentive for capital owners to invest there and for people to head for jobs. The economy as a whole is subject to structural change. The more volatile the real exchange rate is, the higher the pressure for structural change can become.

Nevertheless, one should not omit to mention that exchange rate volatility is not exogenous. Instead, it is a reflection of supply and demand on the exchange rate market. Therefore, a simple analysis of the effect of a parity change can fail to provide the correct explanation and, furthermore and even worse, can lead to the wrong policy recommendation.

Having this in mind, the analysis can lead to exactly the opposite diagnosis and interpretation: the competitiveness of the Japanese sector of tradeables was so high that they were able to sell much more than they could produce. Demand exceeded supply which forced prices upwards. As a result, the yen appreciated. Following this interpretation, the Japanese international sector caused the appreciation instead of being hurt by it.

The latter interpretation is not shared by many observers. Instead, the exchange rate is viewed as an exogenous variable. As regards the balance of payments, it has often been argued that a long-term phase of a stronger yen

---

[1]   Keeping in mind, however, that this does not suggest that the change in the exchange rate is the ultimate cause of structural shifts in competitive positions.

would cause the high trade surpluses to diminish (Lawrence 1987). To put it the other way round, without the strong yen during 1985 to 1987 the Japanese surplus would have been even higher (Corker 1989, pp. 482-7). Corker supports his argument by estimating an export demand function, an export price function and an import demand function in order to explain the determinants of trade surpluses and in order to simulate the implications of a weaker yen. The problem with this kind of analysis in the tradition of the elasticity approach is that it neglects the identity:

$$(54)\ Ex - Im = S - I$$

in an open economy. Surely, it is possible to estimate the volume and direction of trade flows by using price elasticities of demand for exports and imports. Nevertheless, one should not forget to include a capital account constraint. Therefore, it is not convincing to conclude that Japan's surpluses would have been even higher without capturing the appreciation's implications on savings and investments. Moreover, it is rather speculative to make any suggestions about the impact of any realignments on the current account.

C. Can Trade Policy Determine the Current Account?

It has become clear that the persistent and huge Japanese trade surplus is not caused by special trade and industrial policies in favour of certain industries. The Japanese protectionism does not differ too much from German or American protectionism, neither concerning the instruments used nor concerning the level. On the contrary, the severe attacks the Japanese government was subject to in the last decade seem to have induced it to tear down trade barriers and to open markets for foreign competitors. Today, the state interventions are not unusually high by international standards.[1] If, however, it was right that the Japanese trade surplus was caused by trade policy, one should have expected the surplus to be reduced, as trade barriers were declining. Similarly, a majority of developed as well as developing countries ought to have a trade surplus, because protectionist tendencies can be identified all over the world. Since this is simply impossible, we have to look for other determinants of the Japanese persistent and high trade imbalances.

The results presented here notwithstanding, many urge either the western governments to impose protectionist measures on Japanese firms or the Japanese government to promote imports, for instance by Voluntary Import Expansion (VIE). Besides the distorting effects of protectionism for the

---

[1] Whether there are barriers to entry caused by oligopolistic structures and a high Japanese preference for home made products, can hardly be measured.

imposing country itself,[1] it is doubtful whether interventions and corrections of relative prices really diminish trade imbalances.

From an economic point of view, it is small wonder that the bilateral and even sector-specific agreements of the past did not show the desired results (if they were really desired at all!). Notwithstanding those agreements, the Japanese surplus and the US deficit in bilateral as well in multilateral trade did not disappear. The reason for that inertia is quite simple: if an agreement is made in order to enforce successful import promotion in Japan, demand for dollar will *ceteris paribus* increase and the dollar will appreciate. This, of course, is likely to increase the prices of American commodities for Japanese customers expressed in yen. The rising prices supress demand for US commodities and increase demand for Japanese goods so that the trade balance will not change. The Japanese VIE, therefore, artificially increase the volume of international trade and promote structural change in the United States. Yet, it is rather doubtful whether such a structural change will improve American factor allocation and welfare if it is based on political negotiations.

Another example for the misconception of the role of trade policy in handling the trade imbalance is the STA. The US administration and the Japanese government agreed on a worldwide price increase for Japanese semiconductors in order to raise the chances for US suppliers especially on their home market. The prices for DRAMs indeed went up. Moreover, because of the MITI's urge to cut down production in Japan the Japanese sales into the United States fell (Tyson 1992, pp. 113-24). In addition, the price increases for semiconductors proved to be a problem for the American producers of computers. Their competitiveness naturally fell. This example shows that selective protection in favour of one industry meant to cut down a deficit in the trade balance, in general, hurts other industries, especially downstream industries. The diminishing sectoral trade deficit in semiconductors *ceteris paribus* causes a growing deficit or a decreasing surplus in other industries.

D. Japan's Capital Account 1983-1994

Following the intertemporal approach, savings and investments play a crucial role for the existence of current account imbalances. For the difference of savings and domestic investment equals the difference of exports and imports (given changes in foreign reserves are zero). The Japanese gross savings rate has been very high compared with the OECD average. Only Luxembourg has had a (much) higher gross savings rate, and Switzerland almost reaches the Japanese rate. Consequently, private savings, when expressed as a percentage of the disposable household

---

[1]   See, for instance, Corden 1971 and 1974.

income, are also considerably high,[1] especially in comparison with the countries with high deficits in the current account.

The determinants of Japan's high savings rate are analysed by Horioka (1986, 1994). As the most important reason for the high savings he identifies the age structure. The share of Japanese middle-aged people – potential high earners and high savers between 40 and 64 years of age – has grown considerably in the period from 1980 to 1993: from 28.7 per cent of the population in 1980 to 35 per cent in 1993. This trend has increased aggregate savings. Another determinant of high private savings is the old-age security system which does not provide a complete old-age income like, for example, the German security system does (Holzmann 1990). This forces the people to save in order to keep their previous living standard after retirement. A third cause for the Japanese savings is seen in bequest motivations. 'Japan's saving rate has been high because the Japanese desire to accumulate wealth in order for their children to live as well as Americans do' (Hayashi 1986, p. 199). Whereas the first two determinants are in accordance with the life-cycle hypothesis in its simplest form, the latter can be applied to a modified form of the life-cycle theory: utility maximization includes the utility of the following generation or even of more than one subsequent generation. In this respect, Horioka (1994) asks whether the current Japanese generation has been able to fully collect all the benefits of the high growth rates Japan has achieved in the past decades. For the Japanese have consumed less than most citizens in OECD countries. Yet, there can be no doubt that these high savings take place voluntarily. Therefore, one has to conclude that the utility of less consumption and more savings compared with other people was the highest possible Japanese citizens could derive out of their income.

The Japanese investments have also been noteworthily high when compared with the US, Germany and Europe as a whole. On average, investment exceeded 10 per cent of net national product (NNP) which is not the case in the other countries (Bosworth 1993, p. 22). This finding is in accordance with the Feldstein–Horioka hypothesis which claims that a country's savings and investments move by and large in line to one another (Feldstein and Horioka, 1980, Feldstein 1994). Nevertheless, the difference between savings and investment has been considerable high and has been growing lately. This development is due to the private sector as well as the governmental budget. The private sector's savings exceeded its investments for many years. Moreover, the Japanese government budget has been in surplus from 1985 to 1992. In 1993, the government balance turned into deficit. According to a forecast by the OECD (1994c), this deficit is going to last.

---

[1]   In the OECD, only Belgium, Italy and Portugal show higher rates.

This situation – deficit on capital account and surplus on current account – is not likely to last indefinitely. It may be supposed that the capital account deficit will diminish.

First of all, there may be some structural reasons. A major reason for structural changes in the Japanese balance of payments may be the aging population in Japan as well as in other industrialized countries. The share of people older than 64 has been continuously rising for more than a decade: from 9.1 per cent to 13.6 per cent in 1993. According to the life-cycle hypothesis, an aging people will reduce its national savings rate. In a fully funded system, dissaving of pensioners increases, whereas in a pay-as-you-go system pensions financed through public expenditure will rise. This causes net capital outflows to decline (OECD 1989/90).

Moreover, it may be possible that the attitude towards consumption will become more positive in Japan so that the savings rate will decrease in the future. Given such a change in behaviour, net capital outflows will decline.

Besides the long-term determinants of decreasing net capital and commodity flows, there are a number of factors which may affect these balances in the near future. The Japanese government has implemented four economic packages, starting in 1992, which are costly. They include public investment, loans at preferential interest rates, improvements on the housing market, subsidies for small and medium-sized firms and personal income tax cuts up to 20 per cent (OECD 1994a, pp. 46-52). Second, the recession in Japan seems to be successfully combatted. Therefore, private investment probably will be stimulated. Third, it is possible that savings will decrease in the course of the Kobe earthquake since private firms, households and insurance companies may be forced to sell assets in order to rebuild the city. Both components of the right-hand side of the modified accounting identity:

$$(21') \; Ex - Im = (S - I) + (T - G)$$

may decrease as a result of this scenario. This leads to diminishing net capital exports, causing the yen to appreciate further. Therefore and since their purchasing power contracts, foreigners may be induced to buy less Japanese products. As a consequence, the surplus in the trade balance may diminish as well.

E. Settlement: Japan as Main Capital Supplier for the World

In this case study, we took a closer look at the Japanese balance of payments and its determinants. Again, we distinguished two competing hypotheses about the reasons for the high surplus in the current account, that is the competitiveness approach and the intertemporal approach.

After all, we cannot support the competitiveness approach while analysing some peculiarities of the Japanese international trade relations. First, when we took a closer look on the trade regime, we noticed that trade barriers erected by the government are not unusually high. Rather the opposite is the case: compared with the US and the EU, there are less non-tariff trade barriers in use. Whether there exist many informal barriers, be it because of irrationality of Japanese consumers, be it because of oligopolistic structures, we would not decide. To us there was no overwhelming evidence supporting the thesis of Japan being special in terms of international trade relations. Second, after matching sectoral protection with the shares of sectoral intra-industrial trade, there is no evidence supporting the popular hypothesis that Japan's low share of intra-industrial division of labour is due to its closeness. On the contrary, there rather seems to be evidence for the opposing hypothesis that the western countries' high share of intra-industrial trade is – at least partly – due to their selective protectionism.

Therefore, the results presented here do not support conventional wisdom. The huge and persistent surpluses on current account the Japanese economy accumulated in the last years are not caused by state-driven or by informal protectionism. Moreover, it simply cannot be due to Japan having comparative advantages in so many industries. If there was an absolute advantage in all industries, the yen would appreciate insofar that industries having only a small absolute advantage would face comparative disadvantages after the change in prices. The real exchange rate always separates industries with and without comparative advantages from each other.

Keeping this result in mind, we extended the analysis by the capital account. Not only has Japan high surpluses on current account, but also there exist huge net capital flows. Both savings and investments in Japan are very high by OECD-standards. Nevertheless, the difference between domestic savings and domestic investments has been considerably high as well. A big part of the difference has been due to governmental budget surpluses. Consequently, there has been a net capital outflow, showing the peculiarity that, up to 1990, there were net short-term capital inflows mirrored by net long-term capital outflows which amounted roughly to the sum of the short-term capital surplus and the current account surplus. In 1990, the situation changed as described above. The capital account and the current account have proved to move as two sides of a coin throughout the 1980s and the 1990s.

This leads to the conclusion that Japan cannot be blamed for showing the huge and persistent surpluses. Instead, one has to think very positively of Japan as the world's leading capital supplier. Capital demand has risen in the last decade and will probably increase more due to the growing population and the industrialization process in many developing countries.

Therefore, any suggestions to repress Japanese savings (Haynes, Hutchison and Mikesell 1986, p. 14) have to be rejected. Quite the opposite, it has to be feared that the Japanese savings – like those of other industrialized countries – will decline since the population in these countries is aging. In this aging process, it is plausible that people will save less and consume more than before. To sum up, it is fairly safe to assume a growing capital demand and a shrinking capital supply. The correct policy recommendation, therefore, is to encourage private and public saving, not only in Japan.

III. German unification: from surpluses to deficits

A. German Unification and its Consequences for the Balance of Payments

Over years, even decades, the German balance of payments was known to be characterized by persistent surpluses on current account.[1] In the second half of the 1980s the surplus on current account reached a historical peak by climbing to even more than 4 per cent of GNP. However, right after German unification, the balance of payments underwent a dramatic change. For in 1990 the balance on current account deteriorated sharply: in the first quarter of 1990 the current account still showed a surplus of 29.2 bn D-Marks. Soon thereafter, the surplus went down to 8.3 bn D-Marks (last quarter of 1990). Since 1991 the current account was in deficit in almost every month. With the German current account slipping into deficit, the discussion about the balance on current account and its determinants has been fuelled anew.

B. The Arguments Put Forward: the Competitiveness Approach and the
   Intertemporal Approach Revisited

The most recent development of the German balance on current account is frequently traced back to the demand for goods in the eastern part of Germany. Under the circumstances prevailing in the late 1980s, an additional demand for western products on such a scale would have to translate, it was argued, into an import surge. In 1989/90, as German unification took place, capacities for production in West Germany were almost fully employed. Demand for German exports, however, petered out due to the cyclical downswing the rest of the world experienced. With imports increasing at the same time as exports slowed down, current account surpluses obviously had to decline. Consequently, most of the analysts expected that the German balance on current account would swing

---

[1]   Giersch, Paqué and Schmieding 1992 provide a good historical sketch of the overall economic development of Germany since the late 1940s.

back into surplus again as soon as the demand for western products in the eastern part of Germany was satisfied and economic acitivity in the world economy picked up again.[1]

Figure 5.11:   The German balance on current account 1989-1994

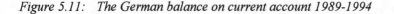
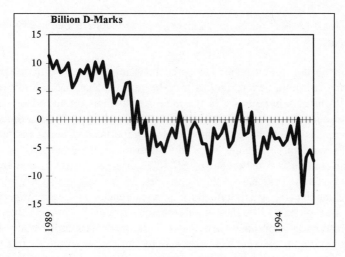

+: Surplus
Source: Deutsche Bundesbank (a),)b), various issues.

Yet, there were also analysts who saw capital scarcity in Germany as one of the main reasons for the overall economy showing a smaller surplus on current account.[2] For one thing, the capital stock in the eastern part was in a bad condition, therefore the marginal return for investors was considered to be rather high. In addition, deficit spending by the German government (all levels of government including social security funds) for smoothing the process of transformation of the centrally planned economy into a market led economy jumped from 9 bn D-Marks (1989) to 107.5 bn D-Marks (1991).[3] It is argued that both the increase in deficit spending as well as the

---

[1]   For the surge in imports argument see, for instance, Arbeitsgemeinschaft deutscher wirtschaftswissenschaftlicher Forschungsinstitute e.V. 1991, p. 9, and Walter 1991, pp. 176-7, as well as Institut der deutschen Wirtschaft 1991 p. 3. Similar arguments have been brought forward by the German Council of Economic Experts (Sachverständigenrat 1991, paragraph 112-3), although also seeing the capital-scarcity element.

[2]   See Börsenzeitung 1991, p. 10, and Dluhosch 1991.

[3]   In this figure, deficits posted by the German railway, the Bundespost and the Treuhand, the German privatization agency, are not yet included. The 'Fonds der deutschen Einheit',

poor condition of the capital stock, contributed to a capital shortage, thus putting pressure on German interest rates and sucking up savings from Germany as well as from other parts of the world. At least as far as 1990/91 is concerned, the complementary transfer of resources from the rest of the world took place very smoothly because of the prevailing cyclical situation in the rest of the world, showing up in a rapid decline of the German surplus on current account.

C. A Closer Look at the Swing: Current Account Deficits due to a Surge in Imports?

Having the discussion about the competitiveness versus the intertemporal approach in mind, severe doubts may be raised about the validity of the surge-in-imports hypothesis as the main explanation for the swing in the German balance on current account. For if everything else stays the same, gross exports should have to adjust to gross imports. This applies at least as long as nominal exchange rates are allowed to fluctuate. To be sure, German unification mattered. So, nobody can argue seriously that by and large everything else stayed the same. Yet, as we will see in a while, the substantial changes which took place on a macroeconomic scale fit perfectly into the picture of the intertemporal approach rather than the competitiveness approach. Anyway, if it were primarily trade flows changing course, the exchange rate should work as an equilibrating factor for the two sides of the balance on current account. Let us therefore have a closer look at the mechanism at work in Germany.

If the German current account is disaggregated into its different components, it becomes visible that the trade surplus went down sharply since the second quarter of 1990. Hence, a first glance at the statistics seems to confirm the notion that the eagerness for western products was the main driving force behind the recent swing of the German balance on current account. Arguments based on international trade flows can claim plausibility: with productive capacities almost fully utilized imports boosted. Because of the slack in demand in the rest of the world, foreign goods were quite elastic in supply thus making it easy for Germans to switch towards imports. Yet, for the very same reason, exports flattened out. According to this logic, both the surge in imports and the rather sluggish demand for exports implied that the current account balance went down in so short a time. Thus, one cheer for the surge-in-imports-theory. However, it is again the competitiveness approach which provides the basis for this kind of argument.

---

however, as well as the ERP Fund and the Fund for the settlement of loans is already contained therein. See Deutsche Bundesbank (a).

Figure 5.12:   German exports and imports 1990-1994 (seasonally adjusted)

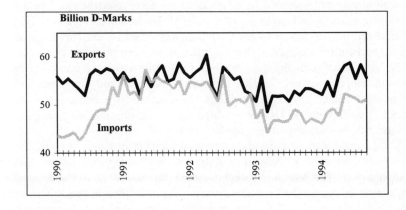

Source: Deutsche Bundesbank (a), various issues.

While convincing at first glance, we find by recalling our basic results of chapter 2.II that imports will only translate into a decline of the surplus on current account if at the very same time more capital is flowing into Germany than before. With income staying more or less the same, the latter might theoretically be the case if either the savings behaviour of market participants (individuals, firms, government, central bank) is undergoing a change, or in the case of market participants investing more in the country in which the import propensity has increased. If, instead, market participants aim at buying more imports without on balance more capital being attracted or savings becoming smaller, imports cannot be paid for at the current exchange rate.[1]

If neither income nor savings behaviour changes noticeably,[2] market participants can only increase their expenditures on imports while at the

---

[1]   For the necessary and sufficient conditions that an increase in the propensity to import shows up in the current account see chapter 2.II. Moreover, see Willgerodt 1981, p. 193.

[2]   The quarterly data on the savings(-to-disposable income) ratio (SR) for the unified Germany show a relatively stable savings behaviour of private households, even during the period of unification:

Year	1988				1989			
Quarter	I	II	III	IV	I	II	III	IV
SR	15.6	11.4	11.3	15.8	16.0	11.5	11.1	15.2

Year	1990				1991			
Quarter	I	II	III	IV	I	II	III	IV
SR	16.8	13.2	12.8	16.3	16.7	13.7	12.1	15.9

same time decreasing their expenditures on other goods. The reason why this applies for a country is pretty much the same as the reason why an individual cannot increase his expenditure with income and savings remaining constant – even if he wants to do so. Thus referring again to the economic situation of Germany in the early 1990s we have to start our line of argument as follows: whereas East Germans asked for their own goods before unification took place, they switched to western products thereafter, at the same time reducing their demand for locally produced goods. With demand slowing down, locally produced goods should have become relatively cheaper as goods produced elsewhere, hence becoming more attractive to foreigners. Thus, everything else remaining the same, imports can increase – when exports are on the rise as well.

If foreigners step in easily thus replacing German demand, not only the former current account balance will be left unchanged, but so will the exchange rate. The reason is straightforward: on the one hand the demand for foreign exchange climbs as Germans ask for more foreign goods. On the other hand the supply of foreign exchange widens also as foreigners ask exactly for the goods which Germans refrained from buying.[1] Hence, the volume of goods traded internationally increases whereas the balance on current account stays the same.

For sure, the case that foreigners ask exactly for the goods being suddenly in excess supply is, even under normal circumstances, not very likely. This applies even more for the New Länder of Germany right after unification, the firms of which often produced goods which were neither on a national nor on an international scale competitive. Many of the goods produced by firms in the eastern part of Germany were not marketable at prices covering costs of production and wages were sticky. Whether this was mainly due to the fact that the goods supplied did not meet the preferences of foreigners and Germans, or due to the fact that income as well as consumption declined in the rest of the world as the recession set in, is of minor importance so far.

If, for instance, goods not being marketable any more do not match the preferences of foreigners either, it indeed looks as though the higher propensity to import shows up in a smaller surplus on current account. However, even in this case, imports cannot increase in value by more than exports. So, if Germans should have asked for more foreign goods than they were exporting at the current exchange rate, the demand for foreign exchange should have gone up. If the exchange rate would have been

---

Source: Deutsche Bundesbank (a). On the savings behaviour of the private sector in the former East Germany which also proved to be quite stable; especially see Sinn and Sinn 1991, p. 65.

[1]   If products of the New Länder only become competitive if their prices are lowered, this process can be accompanied by a depreciation of the D-Mark. If, however, investors do not change their behaviour, the balance on current account will lack movement.

allowed to fluctuate, the German currency should have depreciated in nominal as well as in real terms, the result of which would have been that international goods become more expensive for Germans whereas German products become relatively more attractive to foreigners. Thus, the demand for imports in Germany would have been mitigated, while at the same time exports should have been stimulated. Compared to the point of departure, namely before the import propensity rose, the flow of foreign goods into Germany would have been probably bigger in size thereafter. At the same time, however, foreigners would have also imported more German goods than before. To sum up: in case of exchange rates being flexible, Germans can only increase their demand for imports to the extent that foreigners ask for more goods of German origin and therefore supply foreign exchange. Thus, if market participants in the rest of the world are not inclined to invest in Germany and if Germans do not change their savings behaviour, the supply of foreign exchange necessary for a surge in imports can only be earned by increasing exports of goods and services – if the possibility of running down foreign reserves is for a moment left out of consideration.

To sum up: higher imports must be paid. Hence, everything else staying the same, the value of goods and services flowing into Germany can only increase if exports climb as well. Yet, under these circumstances, the balance on current account should have remained basically the same, despite demand switching. In a regime of flexible exchange rates only gross exports and imports and therefore the level and structure of international trade can change in response to an increase in demand for foreign goods and a devaluation of the domestic currency.

The situation becomes a different one if the German central bank intervenes by buying D-Marks while at the same time selling foreign exchange thus trying to avoid the nominal devaluation.[1] For in this case import values and export values are disconnected even if capital market transactions of private market participants should remain the same. As far as the Bundesbank supplies foreign exchange by running down the stock of reserves accumulated in the past, demand for foreign goods and services can be increased without exports of goods and services climbing as well. Part of the demand for foreign goods is then financed by the Bundesbank. Looked upon from a macroeconomic perspective, the economy is running down its wealth if claims on foreign GNP accumulated in former times are mobilized. Yet, even via this mechanism, net imports can only be increased transitorily.[2] But in the short run, a higher propensity to import could have indeed been responsible for the melting down of the German surplus on

---

[1] For the conditions under which this applies and on the details of the adjustment process following see chapter 2.II.

[2] Since the stock of foreign exchange is limited in size, this will only be temporarily possible. In the long run and everything else staying the same, imports can even in this case only be increased if exports rise too.

current account since 1990 – if at the time of the swing the Bundesbank had sold foreign reserves. Yet, although the Bundesbank became active in supplying foreign reserves, it did so only for a very brief period of time, namely in the first half of 1991 as the German mark considerably lost in value in real as well as in nominal terms *vis-à-vis* most of the currencies of Germany's main trading partners.

Figure 5.13:   Real and nominal effective exchange rate of the D-Mark 1989-1994

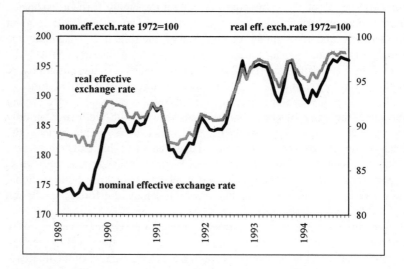

Source: Deutsche Bundesbank (a), various issues.

In March as well as in April 1991, the Bundesbank tried to stabilize the exchange rate of the German mark by selling 8.5 bn D-Marks in foreign exchange.[1] With foreign exchange supplies increased by intervention, not only gross imports but also net imports could increase. Germany's absorption could even climb above production, although at least in March 1991 Germany was still a net capital export country. *Ceteris paribus*, the increase of consumption and investment above aggregate income would not have been possible had the Bundesbank not supported the German currency.

However, March and April 1991 were not the first time that the surplus on current account went down. Even half a year before it decreased substantially. Yet, in this period neither the German currency lost in value

---

[1]   See Deutsche Bundsbank (a).

vis-à-vis Germany's main trading partners (which would have been an indicator for a surge in imports) nor was there any significant change in the stock of foreign reserves. Instead of decreasing, foreign reserves increased slightly. But, a decline in the stock of foreign reserves would have been a necessary side effect of a current account deficit which is caused by an import surge. Hence, quite in contrast to common wisdom, only a rather small part of the fading surplus on current account can be ascribed to a higher propensity to import in the course of German unification, but by no means the whole slide which took place since the first half of 1990.

Figure 5.14: Change in the stock of foreign reserves of the Bundesbank 1990-1994

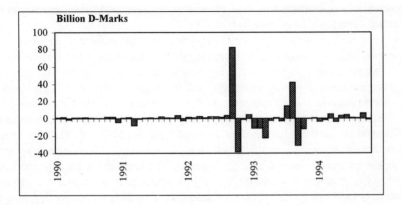

+: Increase

Source: Deutsche Bundesbank (a), various issues.

Moreover, a crude disaggregation of the current account reveals that even in the first quarter of 1991, in which the Bundesbank pumped a substantial amount of foreign reserves into the market, the trade balance as the main component of the current account still showed a surplus – even though the current account was in deficit since the beginning of 1991.[1] Thus, there must have been some additional factors contributing to the swing of the current account which do not show up in the trade balance. Hence, we must look for transactions which are recorded in other sub-balances of the current account. Whereas the balance on services also was in surplus, net public transfers showed an unusually high deficit in the first quarter of 1991.

---

[1]   See Deutsche Bundesbank (a), p. 2, for the data.

Yet, the increase in the deficit on transfers was due to a very special incident, namely the obligations Germany shouldered during the conflict in the Persian Gulf.[1] These transfers of the public sector have contributed to the swing in the current account since the beginning of 1991, because the Bundesbank was involved in the transaction providing the necessary foreign exchange. However, even public transfers cannot explain the whole swing. For the surplus on current account already went down in the second half of 1990. Hence, it still remains to be examined which forces drove the German balance on current account.

Seeing that the German surplus on current account went down since German monetary union, it seems quite obvious to assume, instead, that the swing in the current account has to be traced back to monetary problems in the course of the conversion of the East German currency. The rise in the rate of inflation shortly afterwards at least suggests the hypothesis that the increase in domestic prices had stimulated demand for foreign goods while at the same time dampening exports.

However, to escape the increase in prices by buying foreign goods is not an easy task – at least not in the aggregate. For in a pure regime of flexible exchange rates the demand for foreign exchange increases as market participants want to buy more imports[2] whereby the currency depreciates. Imports become more expensive, so that the demand for imports is curbed. The assumption that a currency losing in nominal value promotes an increase in net imports does therefore not apply – at least if exchange rates are free to move. More often than not, an expansionary monetary policy will even induce capital exports, whereby the balance on current account shows a tendency towards surplus. For if investors in the home country as well as foreign investors expect a devaluation in the time to come without nominal interest rates climbing by a similar amount, an investment abroad becomes relatively more attractive. As the monetary impulse continues, market participants will include the new rate of inflation into their contracts and nominal interest rates will move up.[3] With nominal interest rates on the rise, the incentive to invest abroad will again be tempered.[4]

As far as the higher rate of inflation impairs locational quality, the tendency towards net capital exports, and therefore towards a surplus on current account, will be lasting. That inflation is detrimental to locational quality can be taken for granted since the uncertainty about real returns on

---

[1]   See Deutsche Bundesbank (b), March 1991, p. 13.

[2]   Abroad it will be the other way round.

[3]   Whether nominal interest rates increase in line with the rise in the rate of inflation as creditors want them to, depends upon how well the future increase in the quantity of money is anticipated. If the increase of the quantity in circulation is fully anticipated, nominal interest rates might increase immediately.

[4]   On the international repercussions national monetary policy might have see Wohltmann 1991, pp. 223-45.

investment climbs as the rate of inflation is on the rise. For if inflation accelerates, fluctuations in the rate of inflation will become more pronounced. If market participants try to incorporate deviations of the actual rate of inflation from the one expected rate into their contracts in order to preserve the real rate of return, nominal interest rates also show substantial fluctuations. Thus, the uncertainty in calculating the real return will increase. Consequently, investors will be more reluctant, at least with regard to long term investments. Rather than curbing net capital exports, an inflationary policy will therefore reinforce net capital exports in a regime of flexible exchange rates and unrestricted capital flows. Yet, with net capital exports climbing, foreigners can increase their imports without increasing their exports. Hence, any surplus on current account in the country under consideration will even grow in size.

Once again, the balance on current account can only show a tendency towards deficit in times of inflation if the central bank supplies foreign exchange as monetary policy becomes more expansionary. With additional foreign exchange at hand net imports can be increased. Hence, inflationary tendencies could only have contributed to the decline of the surplus on current account in periods in which the Bundesbank was selling foreign exchange. However, what has to be stressed again is that the German surplus on current account already went down at a time when the Bundesbank was not intervening. Consequently, the swing must be traced back to the fact that since unification more capital has been attracted by Germany. Obviously, an investment in Germany is at least expected to earn a higher rate of return than elsewhere.

D. Capital Demand on the Rise

Compared to the rest of the world, interest rates in Germany rose substantially in nominal as well as in real terms at the turn of 1989/90. In early 1990, the rate of return on government bonds in Germany was for the first time for many years even higher than the one in the United States.

At the same time, capital inflows into the unified Germany were substantially stronger than in the previous two years. With capital inflows on the rise, the previously high net capital exports went down (1988: 127.5; 1989: 136.1; 1990: 94.4 bn D-Marks). For some months in 1991 the balance on capital account was even in surplus.

The coincidence of rising interest rates and net capital inflows suggests that capital demand increased strongly in this period. Indeed, when most of the industrialized countries slipped into recession in the late 1980s/early 1990s, nominal interest rates there showed a tendency towards decline. This tendency was even reinforced by monetary policy trying to reverse the cyclical downswing.[1] On the other hand, capital demand in Germany increased suddenly by a substantial amount, thus pulling German interest rates upwards in nominal as well as in real terms. Whereas in 1989 newly issued government bonds still offered on average a rate of return of 6.9 per cent, interest rates climbed to 8.7 per cent in 1990. By the turn of 1990/91 nominal interest rates on government bonds were even higher, namely 9 per cent.[2]

Figure 5.15:   Nominal interest rate differential* on government bonds: Germany versus the United States 1989-1994

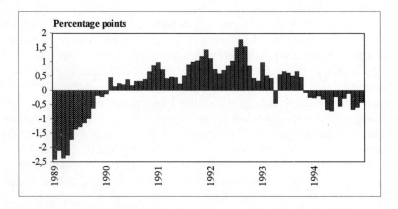

(*) German government bond rate minus US government bond rate.
Source: IMF (a), February 1995.

Being still exempted from the worldwide cyclical downswing was one reason for this high a capital demand. Compared to 1989, investment in the western part of Germany increased substantially compared to 1989, namely by some 60.5 bn D-Marks.[3] The main part of the increase in capital demand, however, was due to the significant rise in the public sector deficit. Whereas in 1989 the government was running a deficit of 25.8 bn D-Marks, the overall deficit (without even taking the substantial deficits of the Treuhand into account) posted in 1990 was some 123.6 bn D-Marks.[4] Thus,

---

[1]   On monetary policy in the rest of the major industrial countries see Arbeitsgemeinschaft wirtschaftswissenschaftlicher Forschungsinstitute 1991, p. 3 and p. 5.
[2]   See Deutsche Bundesbank (b), July 1991, p. 57*.
[3]   Based on data of the Deutsche Bundesbank (b), July 1991, p. 68*.
[4]   See the reference above and Deutsche Bundesbank (b), February 1991, in both cases: p. 65*. In this number deficits of the Treuhand are not included. But, even if the capital demand of the Treuhand is left out of consideration, in absolute terms there was never

the public sector was responsible for most of the additional demand. Instead of crowding out private capital demand by an equal amount, deficit spending came at the expense of net capital exports. Right after unification, foreigners switched from papers issued by the private sector to government bonds with a maturity of more than one year.[1] With the start of 1991, however, the supply of long term foreign capital went down significantly, instead, more short term capital was granted.

Figure 5.16: Net capital imports: Germany 1989-1994

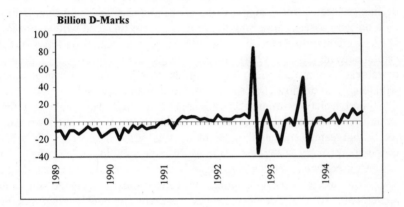

Including net errors and omissions.

+: Net capital import

Source: Deutsche Bundesbank (a), own calcucations.

Until yet, we have focused on the swing proper. But, what about the development thereafter? Does the intertemporal approach still hold? Two facts appear to be of special importance as it comes to the explanation of the movements taking place in 1992 and later on. First, the interest rate differential between Germany and the US twisted again as economic activity picked up sooner in the US. However, over the years, the German

---

before a public sector deficit like this in the Federal Republic of Germany. For an overview see the report 1990/91 of the German Council of Economic Experts, especially table 37* (Sachverständigenrat 1991). If the deficits posted by the Treuhand, the Bundesbahn, the Reichsbahn and the Bundespost are considered as well, the net deficit climbs even to 155 bn D-Marks. The only factor which mitigated the pressure on the budget was the pay-as-you-go system of social security which was in the year under consideration with approximately 11.5 bn D-Marks in surplus. For the data see Sachverständigenrat 1991, paragraph 198.

[1] For an overview see table 5g of the monthly report of July 1991 issued by the Deutsche Bundesbank.

balance of payments situation was quite robust, still showing a slight surplus on capital account. As nominal interest rates in the United States climbed, exchange rate expectations were obviously not static. Instead, investors expected the dollar to decline in value, so that on balance German interest rates remained attractive. Second, volatility of international capital flows increased substantially leading to ups and downs in the size as well as the structure while at the same time the D-Mark appreciated strongly in nominal as well as in real terms. The reasons for the latter were twofold.

First, volatility of gross flows increased significantly. A huge amount of capital flows was clearly driven by expectations concerning the future course of monetary policy and interest rates. Speculating on a further decline of interest rates capital flows concentrated much more than before on long-term assets. These long-term inflows were financed with short-term D-Mark credits, the latter showing up as short-term capital outflows in the capital account (Krüger 1995). However, as the expectations about a decline in interest rates turned out to be wrong, the former pattern of capital flows with long-term outflows and short-term inflows was resumed.

Second, volatility of net flows increased as well. For explaining this volatility of net capital flows as well as the strong appreciation we must recall that capital demand in Germany was still on the rise while the economic recovery in the rest of the world, especially in the US, was under way. Consequently, the supply of goods and services was not that elastic any more as it was right after unification thus leading to the real appreciation of the German currency *vis-à-vis* Germany's main trading partners. As the effective exchange rate headed towards the upper bound of the EMS it was speculation testing the credibility of a fixed exchange rate system, thereby shaping international capital flows much stronger than fundamentals. Hence, the very fact that the D-Mark appreciated has to be considered as an element of the adjustment process of the supply side to changes in the demand structure and can therefore well be explained by the intertemporal approach. Yet, the magnitude of the flows as well as their volatility must be seen in the context of the vulnerability of a fixed exchange rate system. For sure, the fact that some currencies were hit whereas others were not has to be traced back to local economic policy.[1]

Now, let us turn back to our basic question: what were the main factors leading to the swing in the German current account? How are they to be evaluated? A disaggregation of the balance of payments already showed that the swing was primarily driven by capital flows switching direction rather than trade flows. With net capital exports slowing down, Germans were able to increase their imports of goods and services. Rather than giving up consumption and investment of German goods, foreigners with

---

[1]   For a detailed evaluation of the EMS crisis, monetary policy and the adjustment issue see Krüger 1992 and 1995.

less purchasing power at hand refrained from buying locally produced goods. The result of this was that German imports rose whereas exports stayed basically the same. Thus the surplus on current account declined, although the Bundesbank kept from supplying foreign exchange. In principle, both the decline in net capital exports and the higher imports of goods and services are to be welcomed, since the capital scarcity in Germany is mitigated thereby. Public and private investment urgently needed for modernizing the capital stock in the New Länder becomes feasible without the need to cut consumption or investment in the western part of Germany by an equal magnitude.

However, so far, capital demand increased mainly through the public sector. Private investment, instead, is still lingering. Although growth rates are considerable by now, it has also to be kept in mind that they start from a rather low level. The portfolio adjustment of foreigners turning from long-term towards short-term assets can also be taken as an indicator for the fact that economic prospects of the New Länder are still assessed sceptically. The latter obviously applies also for German investors because net exports of long-term capital are still high. The reluctance to make a long-term commitment also shows up in foreign direct investment. Whereas in Germany right after unification foreign direct investment was of the same small amount as before unification, foreign direct investment outflows soared. Consequently, the German balance on foreign direct investment also showed a high net capital export in 1990. In 1991, the situation was pretty much the same.

Whether more long-term or more short-term capital is imported could be regarded as of minor importance – at first glance. For the pressure on the capital market seems in both cases to be eased by the inflow of capital. This appears even more to be the case since due to the transformation of the term structure there should be close linkages between the different segments of the capital market. If short-term interest rates rise, investors should shift from long-term towards short-term assets. Moreover, de jure short-term investments need not actually be short term in nature. If the rate of return at maturity still seems attractive compared to alternatives, investments could be prolonged even though de jure maturity has been reached.

Yet, although there has been a substantial inflow of short-term capital, the rise of net long-term capital exports can nevertheless be interpreted as a sign that locational quality is judged to be rather poor. Obviously, long-term investments are still considered to be too risky to be undertaken at a large scale.[1] With international investors remaining reluctant, it is also too early to draw any long term forecasts concerning the future development of the

---

[1] It has to be remembered, however, that a pattern of short-term inflows and long-term outflows can also be due to international intermediation. Therefore, it is not by itself a bad sign (chapter 4.II).

balance of payments. Whether the recent development makes for a trend which becomes stable over time or whether there will be another swing, depends on the allocation of government expenditure and on the rate of return investors expect from a private investment in the New Länder.

To be sure, the constantly high demand for capital by the public sector implies that real interest rates remain high for a longer period of time, whereby capital should be attracted. Although this can be the case, it need not be that way. If the funds mobilized by running public deficits are primarily spent on consumption,[1] debt service has to be financed either by increasing taxes or decreasing government spending.[2] Instead of attracting capital, a higher burden of taxes (alternatively: a decrease of government spending) or their anticipation by potential investors will make for an incentive to export capital,[3] since tax policy is an important instrument in the international competition on locational quality. A capital outflow, however, would impede the process of restructuring the eastern part of Germany. Yet, according to the Bundesbank, the rise of government debt in the course of German unification by some 105 bn D-Marks in 1991 was matched by gross public transfers into the New Länder climbing to some 170 bn D-Marks (net: 139 bn D-Marks).[4] The amount of transfers not used for investment is estimated by the Bundesbank of being some 85 bn D-Marks.[5]

If the funds were not mainly – as it was the case until yet – used for consumption, but for investment purposes, payment for interest as well as for settlement could be financed out of a higher GNP. In this case, the rate of return which can be expected by investors would not be exposed to the risk of higher taxes or smaller outlays on infrastructure. On balance, this would make an investment in Germany more attractive. If public investment is complementary to private investment rather than a substitute for it, the rate of return on private investments would increase, thus enhancing the incentive to invest in Germany.

---

[1]   Whereas the overall deficit (posted by all levels of government) in 1990 increased by some 56.5 bn D-Marks as compared to 1989, expenditure on investment for Germany on the whole increased only by 4.2 bn D-Marks. For the data see Sachverständigenrat 1991, tables 33* and 39*.

[2]   According to the joint report of the five leading German institutes for economic research consumption financed by deficits will deteriorate the reputation of Germany for locational quality, should they prevail. See Arbeitsgemeinschaft deutscher wirtschaftswissenschaftlicher Forschungsinstitute 1991, p. 23.

[3]   See also the assessment of Klodt 1992, p. 8.

[4]   Yet in this number services of governmental institutions, which are subsumed under the productive sector (Post Services, Railways and Treuhand), have not been included.

[5]   For 1992 the Bundesbank expected already at that time that there would be a further increase of gross transfers to 210 bn D-Marks (net: 180 bn D-Marks), but no decline in the ratio of transfer spend on consumption. See Deutsche Bundesbank 1992, p. 16 and p. 20.

E. The task Ahead: Removing Barriers to Investment

In 1990/91, numerous investment incentives were implemented for raising the rate of return on investment and improving the locational quality of the New Länder.[1] In March 1991, the already existing measures for promoting economic growth were supplemented by the 'Gemeinschaftswerk Aufschwung Ost'. Besides a prolongation of tax allowances the programme basically provided funds for restoring the infrastructure of the New Länder.[2]

In principle, the rate of return on private investment can be improved either via loans and guarantees or via tax allowances. The latter can be either in the form of investment allowances or special depreciation allowances, provided losses can be carried forward. Loans as well as guarantees lower the necessary rate of return for a promising investment, since they are offered at more favourable terms than those which the market asks for, especially if the specific risks of investments in the New Länder are taken into account. Should investors have trouble raising funds because of being short of collateral (for instance, because queries about property rights are still unsettled), government backed loans and guarantees can save investors from being rationed off the market and can thereby remove barriers to investment. In the same manner, capital costs can be lowered by special depreciation allowances or investment credits, since the postponing of tax payments has its own rate of return.[3]

Yet it must not be overlooked that measures with subsidy character such as, for instance, loans with an interest rate below the one prevailing at the market, provide for an additional burden elsewhere.[4] To be sure, in principle, they need not pose an additional dead weight loss as expenditures are shifted. Yet all too often the route taken is a different one, as in the case of Germany. Instead of curbing outlays elsewhere expenditures are financed by government debt, the demand for capital increases thus putting even more pressure on interest rates. Consequently, investment opportunities must earn a higher rate of return for being competitive. If tax financed, savings may decline, thereby lowering capital supply in the course of which interest rates rise as well. The latter applies especially if market participants expect that taxes are raised transitorily rather than permanently.[5] Those negatively affected will tend to stretch the loss of consumption possibilities

---

[1] See the compilation by the Deutsche Bundsbank (b), March 1991, p. 15-7. See also Brandt, Herrmann and Sabathil 1991.

[2] See Presse- und Informationsamt der Bundesregierung 1991, pp. 177-82.

[3] For the effects of tax allowances, special depreciation allowances, investment grants and interest deductions see Hall and Jorgenson 1967, pp. 391-414, and, more recently, Sievert et al. 1989.

[4] See Sachverständigenrat 1990, paragraph 347-9., and 1991, p. 21.

[5] This is expected by the Arbeitsgemeinschaft deutscher wirtschaftswissenschaftlicher Forschungsinstitute 1991, p. 17.

implied thereby over time. If they do so, they maintain their former level of consumption partly by saving less than previously planned. In theory, capital imports could fill the gap opened by the decline in gross national savings. Yet foreign capital is hardly ever that elastic in supply. Nearly always, foreign sources of financing are somewhat complementary to national sources in the same manner as debt and equity are due to agency costs when it comes to the capital structure of firms. Hence, with elasticity not being infinite, taxing the proceeds from savings implies investment forgone.[1] As both ways of financing, debt as well as taxes, raise the rate of return required, they both prove to be detrimental to investment incentives. If policy sticks to promoting investment via subsidizing capital in the New Länder, the curbing of other subsidies is to be preferred to the tapping of new sources of revenue or overdrawing those currently in place.

Moreover, the strategy of lowering capital costs artificially cannot develop fully its stimulating impact, if – as is still the case – there are other bottlenecks which impede investment.[2] If the real estate necessary for setting up production capacities or for collateral cannot be acquired the upturn in economic activity will fail to materialize – even though loans are granted and investments are backed by government guarantees. The latter applies also in case real estate can be acquired but risks or duties are to be taken over which are hard to estimate. In these cases lower prices for real estate and productive capacities already in place make only for a bad substitute. Should, for instance, investors have to pay for the ecological problems caused by the former state-owned enterprises in Eastern Germany, it might well be that projects already undertaken must be written off. Ex post considered they would turn out to be rather expensive. For a number of investors this will be too high a risk to be shouldered.[3]

Obstacles to investment prevail also on the labour market. With exchange rates fixed, investment activity depends also very much on local labour costs. Foremost detrimental to investment were the huge and across the board increases in real compensation which took place in the course of monetary union. The attempt to preserve employment by imposing firing constraints on investors proves equally costly (Sinn and Sinn 1991). For a strategy like this does not take into account that the East German economy has yet to undergo a substantial structural change in the transitional phase from a centrally planned economy to a market driven economy.

---

[1] For details on how taxation affects national investment see Dluhosch 1993. For a more optimistic view see Feldstein 1994.

[2] The stimulating effect, however, cannot be inferred from the demand for allowances, since those which flow into investments which would have been undertaken anyway cannot be seperated from the additional investment. See also Deutsches Institut für Wirtschaftsforschung and Institut für Weltwirtschaft 1991, p. 344.

[3] For an overview of the obstacles in the transitional phase see also Sachverständigenrat 1991.

As obstacles to investment still prove to be substantial, high wages are especially harmful to investment. Labour can only be employed if it claims wages that fit into the picture. Frequently, the latter means wages which are lower than those received by colleagues in the western part of Germany.[1] Losening the tight labour jurisdiction and allowing for the possibility of individual wage settlements, as recently suggested by the German Commission on Deregulation, would certainly prove to be beneficial for getting the economy started.[2] By curbing across the board increases in wages which do not reflect specific scarcities they increase the prospects of becoming employed while at the same time providing an incentive for investors to undertake a project in the New Länder. To be sure, it was not just labour market institutions responsible for private investment being rather sluggish. Public transfers added to the real wage persistence. Otherwise it would have been much more costly for those aiming at too high a wage to do so.

No doubt, removing obstacles to investment takes time. Many of the impediments are the outcome of several decades of socialistic mismanagement. Nonetheless, it is important to remove stumbling blocks as quickly as possible without creating new ones, thus improving the locational quality of the New Länder (as of Germany in general) and enhancing the attractiveness of Germany as a place for investment. Importing capital from the rest of the world makes it easier to build up a capital stock which is comparable to the one of industrialized countries of the western hemisphere. West Germany in the late 1940s, on the contrary, had to set up production capacities by referring basically to domestic savings.[3] If the only supply of capital would be German savings, the increase in capital demand had to adjust to the capital supplied in Germany. Interest rates would climb even further; German investment, however, could only increase as savings rise with interest rates. Hence, investment would be even lower as it actually is.

If, instead, capital markets are open and if projects in Germany promise a sufficiently high rate of return, foreign capital can be attracted. The demand for investment need not any longer adjust to the German supply of capital. If there is an inflow of capital because of capital being scarce, the pressure

---

[1]   For a detailed discussion of the problems prevailing on the labour market in the New Länder see Donges 1991, pp. 283-91, Wissenschaftlicher Beirat beim Bundesministerium für Wirtschaft 1991 and Willgerodt 1991, p. 189.

[2]   See Deregulierungskommission 1991, p. 149.

[3]   The volume of Marshall plan aid are often overestimated. Foreign aid including those of the Marshall plan figured up to (1945-1952) 17.4 bn D-Marks, or on average 2.2 bn D-Marks per annum. Gross investment, however, was well above. In 1950, for example, they ran up to 21.8 bn D-Mark. For the data on balance of payments see Bank deutscher Länder 1952, p. 75. For comparing figures the data expressed in US-Dollar were converted in D-Marks at the prevailing exchange rate of 4.20 D-Marks per dollar. For gross investment see Sachverständigenrat 1965, p. 215.

on interest rates is mitigated, more projects offer a competitive rate of return and are therefore carried out.[1] The capital intensity of production can be increased thereby. Since production is also increased, employment possibilities will climb even though capital intensity is raised. Correspondingly to the shift in purchasing power, international trade flows have to change their direction: whereas the surplus on current account in Germany becomes smaller, probably even turns into a deficit, the development abroad is just the opposite one. Yet a necessary condition for international capital being elastic in supply is an economic policy which improves the rate of return on private investment instead of channelling a great deal of resources into consumption. Otherwise, not only foreign investors will become reluctant to supply their capital to Germans as time goes by, but Germans will also increasingly prefer again to export their savings.

F. From a Creditor Nation to a Debtor Nation?

No doubt, the development of the German balance on current account since 1990 was to a substantial degree shaped by the German unification. Above all, it was the sudden increase in the demand for capital by the public sector in the course of integration – but also the rising private capital demand because of the unification boom – which induced investors to invest more of their savings in Germany. Thus capital imports increased substantially. The additional capital allowed Germans to import more goods and services than previously, leading to the swing in the current account.

For a movement like this to continue it is necessary that investors in Germany and abroad can expect a competitive rate of return on German projects. Only in this case, Germany can succeed in attracting capital for a longer period of time, instead of exporting capital. Currently, however, it is primarily the public sector which asks for capital to support consumption levels otherwise declining. If a situation like this prevails, the hitherto slight optimism of international investors could make place for a more pessimistic view. Hence, without a further improvement in locational quality the outflow of long-term capital will stay strong, perhaps even short-term capital will again be exported, thus making for another swing in the balance on current account, this time however, in the other direction (Watrin and Krüger 1995).

---

[1]   In 1989, total gross savings of OECD countries were approximately fifteenfold of German gross investments. For an overview see OECD 1991a, p. 17 and p. 51.

IV. Spain after joining the EC

In the second half of the 1980s, the Spanish economy experienced a strong expansion.[1] This development was characterized by above EC-average growth rates, an increase in employment and a virtual investment boom. The main factor contributing to this development was the EC entry in 1986 which was an important step towards liberalizing economic relations between Spain and the rest of the EC. At the same time it increased the readiness of foreign investors to export capital to Spain. Thus, EC membership not only opened up promising opportunities for Spanish and foreign producers, it also provided the capital to realize a high level of investment.

Figure 5.17: Exchange rates and the balance of payments: Spain 1980-1993

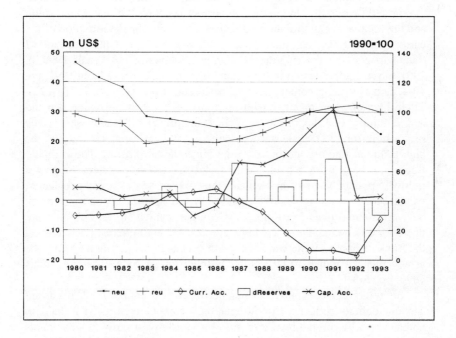

neu: nominal effective exchange rate; reu: real effective exchange rate.

Source: IMF (a), own calculations.

---

[1] This period is analysed in more detail in Dluhosch and Krüger 1991, Ortega, Salaverría and Viñals 1990 and Viñals 1992.

The subsequent development of the Spanish balance of payments can be used as evidence in favour of the intertemporal approach. It also highlights the differences of interpretation between the competitiveness approach and the intertemporal approach.

After joining the EC, Spain's current account surplus was quickly reduced. In 1987, the current account was nearly balanced and from 1988 onwards there was a deficit which peaked in 1992 reaching US$ 18.5 bn (see Figure 5.17). This deterioration of the current account was accompanied by a real appreciation and a considerable build-up of foreign reserves. The combination of increases in international reserves and rising current account deficits was made possible by net capital imports which outstripped the current account deficits by far. The turning point in this development was the year 1992 when the beginning of a severe recession and the EMS crisis hit the Spanish economy. In this year the net capital flow came to an abrupt standstill, foreign reserves drastically decreased and the peseta experienced a sharp real depreciation.

While the healthy development of real output and employment has been interpreted favourably, the deficit on current account, the real appreciation and the relatively high inflation rate raised concern. The deterioration of the current account has been interpreted as the direct effect of the reduction of trade barriers after entering the EC (Ortega, Salaverría and Viñals 1990, p. 190), the real appreciation in the second half of the 1980s (Alzola 1991, pp. 40-4) and the rising competitiveness of foreign firms (OECD 1988, p.22). Trade liberalization together with high growth rates of aggregate demand and a strong real appreciation fuelled import growth and were made responsible for the current account deficits. The real appreciation and the high inflation rate are attributed to the huge capital inflows. These capital flows are seen as a mixed blessing. Insofar as they reflect long-term inflows, especially direct investment, they are viewed as a positive factor, which enhances the productive capacity of the Spanish economy (Ortega, Salaverría and Viñals 1990, pp. 206-8). Other capital flows, however, are interpreted to be mainly speculative, attracted by high interest rates, forcing the Bank of Spain to intervene in foreign exchange markets and making the achievement of monetary targets impossible (Ortega, Salaverría and Viñals 1990, pp. 208-15).

This interpretation contains a number of critical points. First, if current account deficits reflect a low international competitiveness, it is hard to understand why foreign investors would want to invest fairly large amounts of capital in Spain. A decline in competitiveness should lead to a depreciation of the currency and capital outflows rather than inflows. Second, the relationship between capital flows and interest rate differentials is not unambiguous (Niehans 1994, Alonso and Linde 1993). It is by no means clear whether Spanish bonds were attractive because of high interest rates or interest rates were high because of investors' hesitance to buy

Spanish bonds. Since bond investment was subdued until late 1990 and since interest rate differentials came down only in 1991 the latter interpretation seems to be more plausible. Third, it is doubtful whether the current account and the capital account can be treated separately. Capital flows are equal to shifts in purchasing power and therefore influence the flow of goods and services.

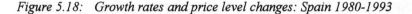

Figure 5.18:   Growth rates and price level changes: Spain 1980-1993

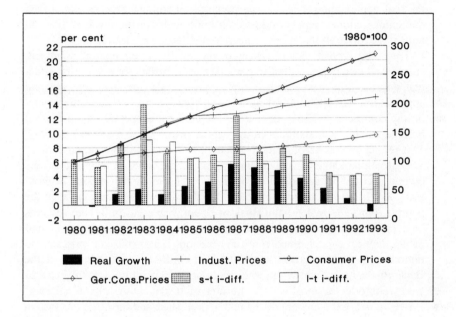

s-t i-diff, l-t i-diff: short-term and long-term interest rate differential between Spain and Germany.
Source: IMF (a), own calculations.

The intertemporal approach provides a unified explanation of the current account and the capital account.[1] The starting point is the EC entry which no doubt increased the locational quality of Spain. Spain had to liberalize foreign trade and investment and adopt to the institutional framework of the other EC countries. This reduced uncertainty about the future course of economic policy in Spain and increased the attractiveness of Spanish assets (Ortega, Salaverría and Viñals 1990, p. 217). Therefore, EC entry can be interpreted as a positive shock, which led to increased net capital imports.

---

[1]   See Dluhosch 1995. For an intertemporal analysis focusing on sustainability see Dolado and Viñals 1990.

These net capital imports increased the purchasing power of economic agents in Spain. Consequently, imports rose above exports.[1] The resulting current account deficit was simply a reflection of the capital imports. The real appreciation and the increase in international reserves indicate, however, that only a fraction of capital imports was used to pay for goods imports (or potential exports). Net capital inflows were larger than the deficit on current account. This put upward pressure on the exchange rate and forced the Bank of Spain to intervene in foreign exchange markets.[2] These interventions could contain the nominal appreciation – not however the real appreciation, because the purchase of foreign exchange increased the Spanish money supply and made it impossible for the Bank of Spain to reduce the inflation rate which remained well above EC average.[3]

Thus, the typical pattern, as predicted by the intertemporal approach, emerges. A rise in net capital imports causes a current account deficit and a real appreciation. The intertemporal approach also predicts that the real appreciation will be followed by a real depreciation even when the capital inflow continues. Whether or not this would have happened cannot be said because the EMS crisis reduced net capital inflows nearly to zero in 1992. This reduction was accompanied by a nominal and real depreciation.

Quite remarkable in the Spanish case is the slow adjustment of the current account to the capital account. In 1987, net capital imports of more than US$ 12 bn had to be completely bought off by the central bank. In the period from 1987 to 1991 the Bank of Spain increased its foreign reserves on average by more than US$ 9 bn per year. That amounts to about one half of the entire capital import in this period. This constant pressure to intervene in the foreign exchange markets conflicted with the aim of the Bank of Spain to reduce the rate of inflation. Therefore, capital controls were reintroduced, mostly with the aim of discouraging capital inflows.[4] However, since the amount of the real appreciation and the large increase in foreign reserves can be interpreted as an indicator of inflexibility in the real sector a better policy to shield monetary policy from capital account disturbances would be to liberalize the economy further. In an open

---

[1]   The reduction of trade barriers, on the other hand, can account for the increase in the volume of both exports and imports (between 1986 and 1992 imports more than doubled in nominal terms while exports rose by 60 per cent). Since trade liberalization favoured intra EC trade it also accounts for the observed shift in the pattern of trade.

[2]   Spain entered the EMS in 1989. In the years before, the Bank of Spain pursued a policy of 'DM shadowing' (The Economist 1990).

[3]   In accordance with the predictions of the intertemporal approach a broad price index such as the consumer price index which includes many prices for non tradeables rose stronger than the index for industrial producer prices which is a rough proxy for tradeables prices (see Figure 5.18).

[4]   In accordance with the rules for the single market, these capital controls were abolished in 1991. A detailed analysis of the capital controls and their effects is provided by Viñals 1990.

economy with a high degree of internal and external competition and a high degree of internal factor mobility (between sectors), it can be expected that changing capital flows will translate relatively easy into the necessary changes of the current account. Changes in reserves and real exchange rate changes would therefore be much smaller. Looked at from this point of view, the problem with Spain's deficit on current account was not that it was too large but that it was too small. In the light of the experience of Spain during the EMS crisis and the Mexican currency crisis this conclusion may be astonishing. It should not be overlooked, however, that a surplus on current account does not shield a country from a run on its currency.[1] Conversely, the position of the D-Mark since 1992 shows that international investors may regard a country as a 'safe haven' despite the fact that it runs a current account deficit. Furthermore, it has to be remembered that the Bank of Spain would have been able to reduce the inflation rate further, if the current account deficit had been larger. A lower inflation rate and consequently a lower real appreciation would have inspired more confidence in the peseta.

Another measure which has been proposed to ease the pressure on monetary policy is a more restrictive fiscal policy (Schadler 1993, p. 16). The public deficits remained high even during the boom in the second half of the 1980s and contributed to the strong capital demand. This proved fatal in the recession of 1993 when the deficit rose to 7.5 per cent of GDP. Furthermore, fiscal policy made it harder (if not impossible) for monetary policy to reduce inflation.[2] It is concluded, therefore, that a more restrictive fiscal policy would have been advisable to keep the current account deficit in check and to reduce the net capital inflow. Although a more prudent fiscal policy may have much to say in its favour, it is questionable, however, whether it should be used to achieve balance of payments targets (Dluhosch and Krüger 1991). In addition, it is not clear whether the desired results would have been achieved. After all, with a smaller public deficit foreign (and local) investors would have had less to worry about. The locational quality of Spain would have been judged even higher. Thus, much of the reduction in public capital demand would probably have been replaced by private capital demand.

To sum up, EC membership led to an opening of Spanish goods and capital markets. This raised expected returns on investment in Spain and lowered required risk premia. Therefore, net capital imports surged causing a deficit on current account and a substantial increase in foreign reserves. As predicted by the intertemporal approach, the rising capital inflows led to

---

[1]   Belgium, Denmark and Ireland all had current account surpluses in the years before the EMS crisis.

[2]   It is a well known result of the Mundell–Fleming model that fiscal policy is very powerful in a system of fixed exchange rates and free capital movements, whereas monetary policy has hardly any influence at all.

a real appreciation. In 1992, capital flows turned sharply and the peseta subsequently depreciated in nominal as well as in real terms. Provided that no additional shocks appear, part of this real depreciation should be reversed in the longer run.

6. Competitiveness and the Current Account: A Spurious Relationship

Since the early 1980s, when current account imbalances strongly increased, the causes and consequences of large current account imbalances have been discussed intensively. We have distinguished broadly two main interpretations of current account balances: the competitiveness approach and the intertemporal approach. The competitiveness approach interprets international competitiveness as ability to sell. Surpluses on current account are interpreted as an indicator of high and deficits as an indicator of low competitiveness. This theory, however, has been found wanting because it rests on two misleading assumptions. First, a country is treated like a single firm and, second, the volume of sales is used as an indicator of success instead of profits or income generated. If all firms of one country are treated just like one single firm, the interdependence of the competitive positions of various firms within a country is easily neglected. The most important of these interconnections is due to immobile factors of production. If certain factors of production are nationally mobile but internationally immobile, the competitive position of one firm is also affected by the competitiveness of other national firms. Concretely, if some local firms gain in competitiveness and push wages up, other local firms will be affected negatively because they also have to pay higher wages, whereas their foreign competitors do not. Thus, the loss of competitiveness of one sector must not necessarily be due to an increased competitiveness of foreign firms. Instead, the cause may well be an increase in competitiveness in other local sectors. Moreover, ability to sell focuses on sales. However, sales are not a good indicator of success, even on the level of the firm. For a firm profits are a better indicator of success and for an economy as a whole real income (or its growth rate) is much more meaningful. After all, people work, invest and take risks in order to earn a return.

The competitiveness approach not only provides a questionable definition of international competitiveness, it also proposes a stable link between competitiveness (defined as ability to sell) and current account balances which can be derived only under very special assumptions. Thus, a declining ability to sell (just like an increase in aggregate demand) only causes a deficit on current account in a system with fixed exchange rates and restricted capital movements. In a pure system of flexible exchange rates, there is no mechanism of automatic deficit financing via reductions in international reserves. Moreover, if capital is mobile, it is more likely that capital will flow out of the country whose competitiveness is declining. So, it would be more likely that a decline in competitiveness leads to a current account surplus – not a deficit.

The intertemporal approach, instead, focuses on savings and investment decisions in an international context. Whereas the competitiveness approach may have some explanatory power in the context of restricted capital mobility and fixed exchange rates (which both prevailed in the time between World War II and the 1970s), the intertemporal approach seems to be better suited to explain the balance of payments in a world of freely floating capital. Capital balances, and therefore current account balances, reflect supply and demand conditions in international capital markets. What is sometimes overlooked is that allocating capital strongly influences the allocation of goods. If the economic agents of one country are net borrowers of capital, they are necessarily also net borrowers of goods – not money. It is the decision about borrowing versus lending which determines the capital (current) account of an individual as well as of a country as a whole – not the decision between local and foreign goods. Thus, current account balances have to be traced back to capital account balances. Or, as Böhm-Bawerk (1914) put it: 'The capital account determines the current account' (our translation). This, in turn, has important consequences for the interpretation of current account deficits. First of all, a current account deficit (unless it is matched by a reduction in international reserves) implies that foreigners are willing to lend to a country or that local citizens are prepared to repatriate capital from abroad. Thus, on the side of international investors, it implies a certain amount of confidence with respect to rates of return and security of property rights. In addition, a current account deficit can either indicate good investment conditions or low savings. While low savings may give rise to concern, good investment conditions, for sure, are a sign of high locational quality. Thus, a current account deficit which is due to economic policy measures which enhance the marginal productivity of capital is a sign of high rather than low international competitiveness.

One important implication of the intertemporal approach is that a country's growth prospects are not restrained by a current account deficit. Rather, the opposite is true. A current account deficit increases the supply of real resources which can be used productively within an economy. Without a current account deficit, it would be impossible to raise investment above saving.

What is the role of the exchange rate in all of this? It is often claimed that exchange rates should serve to 'correct' current account imbalances. The fact that currencies have, at times, been appreciating (depreciating) despite of growing current account deficits (surpluses) or that current account deficits (surpluses) have persisted despite large depreciations (appreciations) has been worrying many observers. Such developments seem to prove that exchange rates are not directed by fundamentals and that trade flows do react only very sluggishly (if at all) to exchange rate changes. However, the intertemporal approach can provide an equilibrium explanation for the observed behaviour of exchange rates in the medium run. An intertemporal interpretation of the current account does not assign the task of balancing exports and imports to exchange rates. Rather, the exchange rate is assumed to equate the current account balance with the capital account balance. In our analysis of the adjustment process, it is shown how a capital inflow can generate an initial appreciation and a subsequent depreciation. Furthermore, the conditions under which changes in the capital account (current account) make larger or smaller exchange rate changes necessary are investigated. As has been shown, the amount of appreciation or depreciation depends on the share of non-traded goods demanded and the elasticity of supply, namely the time it requires to move resources from the tradeables to the non-tradeables sector and vice versa. So, if capital movements mostly affect the demand for tradeables and if the economies adjust smoothly and quickly, exchange rate changes can be quite small or even zero. If, on the other hand, a high proportion of demand is directed towards non-traded goods and if the real sectors adjust only sluggishly, the required exchange rate changes can be quite large – as, for instance, in the case of the dollar in the first half of the 1980s.

The theoretical analysis of the competitiveness approach is supplemented by an investigation of some of the most common indicators of competitiveness which are based on this approach: regional and sectoral trade balances, international trade in high tech products, revealed comparative advantage, market shares and real exchange rates. Each of these indicators proves to be problematic. Bilateral trade balances do not serve well as indicators of competitiveness because they do not take into account that firms of two countries also compete in the rest of the world. Therefore, they provide hardly any information on the competitive position of a country. Bilateral trade balances should not be interpreted as indicators of competitiveness but simply as a reflection of the welfare enhancing international division of labour. Sectoral balances, as well, are not very useful indicators of competitiveness. Rather, they show that countries differ with respect to factor endowments and economic development. Thus, sectoral balances may – at best – be used to analyse where an economy possesses comparative advantages and disadvantages. It has to be remembered, however, that even in this respect the informational content of sectoral balances is distorted by government intervention and that the situation in third markets is not taken into account.

Other indicators such as indicators of revealed comparative advantage, market shares or growth rates of exports do suffer from similar shortcomings. None of the indicators investigated provides information about state interventions – neither regulations which distort the working of internal markets nor measures regulating foreign trade. Thus, most of them give a biased picture of the competitiveness of the various sectors – overestimating the competitiveness of those sectors which are sheltered from foreign competition. Furthermore, local markets are usually neglected.

However, competitiveness has to be proven on a national scale as well. Focusing only on 'external' competitiveness may lead to serious misinterpretations. Other shortcomings of these indicators are that they are derived from past conditions and that they do not include the influence of capital flows on trade flows. Finally, many indicators focus on turnover instead of profits and income.

While most of these problems are avoided when the real exchange rate is used as an indicator of competitiveness, new problems of interpretation arise. Most important is the question whether the real exchange rate should be regarded as a determinant or as the consequence of competitiveness. For an analysis which is not committed to the very short run (say a few weeks or months) it is hardly warranted to view the real exchange rate as a variable which exogenously determines the competitiveness of an economy. Quite the contrary, it seems much more appropriate to interpret such phenomena as the strong real appreciation of the Japanese yen over the last ten years as the result of a strong increase in competitiveness. So, if the real exchange rate is used as an indicator of competitiveness it should at least not be interpreted in the way the competitiveness approach suggests. Moreover, it should be remembered that capital movements can cause temporary real appreciations or depreciations, which make it difficult to interpret real exchange rate changes in the medium or short run. As has been shown, it is possible that a capital inflow may cause an initial appreciation and a subsequent depreciation even if competitiveness constantly improves.

If the balance on current account is determined by intertemporal considerations, the explanation of current account balances requires a closer look at the determinants of capital supply and demand within a given country. The two large surplus countries of the 1980s, Germany and Japan, both saw their savings rate rise in the 1980s, while the largest deficit country, the United States, experienced a decline of the savings rate. The most important determinants of the savings rate are the age structure of the population and the organization of the pension system.

Capital demand, on the other hand, is mainly influenced by the relative endowment with capital (which coincides with the level of development) and the institutional framework. In a capital-rich country like the United States or Japan the marginal return on capital would be rather low in comparison to a developing country – provided there were no institutional differences. From this perspective, it could be expected that capital flows from capital-rich developed to capital-poor developing countries. However, political instability, lack of an appropriate 'Ordnungspolitik' and volatile inflation have made most developing countries unattractive for investors. Therefore, most capital flows take place between developed countries.

In order to explain net capital flows between developed countries from the capital demand side, a number of factors are analysed which are considered to be important for the local rate of return, such as labour costs, taxes and budget deficits. However, although the local rate of return would be the appropriate focus for pinning down locational quality in the most direct way, one has to keep in mind that such an approach faces a serious problem. What can only be measured are ex post returns. Hence, a careful interpretation is warranted. For, high ex post rates of return may signal high marginal productivity due to improved competitiveness. But they may also be due to sluggish investment and high capital exports. Therefore, an analysis of the relationship between rates of return and net capital flows provides only limited information. Thus, what would be ideally required are ex ante rate of return measures.

Similarly, it is hard to derive a relationship between labour costs on the one hand and the balance of payments on the other. The usual claim, that high nominal labour costs reduce the competitiveness of locally produced tradeables and therefore cause a deficit on current account is not convincing. To a certain degree the same is true for the opposite claim that high nominal costs of labour drive out capital and thus cause a surplus on current account. For as long as nominal labour costs are relatively high across-the-board, overall international competitiveness can be restored by a devaluation, if the nominal exchange rate is free to move. However, if real wage resistance exists or labour markets are distorted so that the structure of compensation does not reflect real scarcities, there will be unemployment and capital will be driven out of the country. So, contrary to the predictions of the competitiveness approach, there would be a surplus on current account. Only in a system with fixed exchange rates, it is possible that comparatively high nominal costs of labour temporarily lead to a deficit on current account.

Due to taxation there can be large international differences in the local costs of capital. There is no doubt that such differences in effective taxation do have a strong impact on international capital flows. However, such influences are hard to pin down quantitatively, as the tax systems not only differ in the various countries but are also highly complex. Although there have been many attempts to quantify the impact of taxation, it is nearly impossible to derive reliable figures of the effective tax burden which could be regressed on international capital flows. This is not only a problem for the academic analyst. It shows that changes of statutory tax rates may have unpredictable effects on the real rate of return and the volume of investment. Hence, the most important issue may be simplification of the tax system – not just changes in statutory tax rates. This would not only allow to make better comparisons between the real effective tax burden in various countries. It would also improve the national and international allocation of capital.

However, the current account is not only influenced by private savings and investments. The actions of the public sector can also become highly important. In fact, although international capital mobility does not imply that deficit spending automatically translates into deficits on current account, in the last fifteen years it seems to have contributed significantly to the shape of current account balances in the G7 countries. For instance, US and German government deficits strongly contributed to the surges in capital inflows of these two countries. Capital imports which are triggered by public deficits have to be evaluated somewhat differently than purely privately motivated capital imports. Due to the power to tax and the difficulty to evaluate non-marketable government services, governments have much more latitude in their spending decisions than the private sector. Hence, the market cannot always enforce an efficient allocation of funds in the same strict manner as in the case of private investors. Therefore, capital imports which primarily reflect high public deficits cannot be interpreted – like private capital inflows – as a sign of locational quality.

To put it in a nutshell: balances on current account are quite a poor indicator of the international competitiveness of an economy. There is no close link between the international competitiveness of local firms or locally produced goods and the balance on current account. Moreover, many indicators of competitiveness draw on a definition of international competitiveness as ability to sell. However, ability to sell is not a meaningful concept – neither for a country nor for a single firm. Explanations of the current account have to focus on the determinants of the capital account. This is not only true for individuals whose current account balances are explained in capital theory, it is also true for the economy as a whole. A current account deficit is due to the aggregate outcome of individual decisions about borrowing and lending. These decisions are primarily governed by interest rates – not by spot exchange rates, prices and quality of goods, trade restrictions, etc.

From this perspective, the US current account deficit simply means that, in the aggregate, Americans chose to become net borrowers and that the rest of the world was ready to lend to the US. Japan's current account surplus means that, in the aggregate, Japanese chose to lend and are prepared to invest abroad. It does not mean that Americans went on a spending spree because they liked Japanese goods so much – hoping that these purchases could be financed some way or another. It also does not mean that the Japanese current account surplus is due to open and hidden trade restrictions in Japan. Finally, it also does not mean that there is less demand for US goods because of the current account deficit. When Americans borrow abroad, they can buy more foreign goods without buying less American goods. Thus, the claim that the deficit is reducing demand for American goods and destroying jobs in America is without substance.

The development of the German balance of payments has also often been interpreted in a misleading way. The ability to sell was neither extraordinarily high during the 1980s, as the surplus on current account in that period might suggest, nor has it declined since then. Equally, the locational quality in Germany has not gained much ground during the first half of the 1990s, as the surplus on capital account seems to make believe. Rather, there seems to be no significant improvement in locational quality since the early 1980s – private agents still export capital on balance – the surge in capital inflow being mainly due to public borrowing.

The implications for economic policy are straightforward: trade and exchange rate policy are no suitable instruments to correct current account imbalances. Moreover, current account imbalances, even large and persistent ones, are not necessarily a problem. They may be simply a reflection of the efficient international allocation of capital. Still, at times, current account deficits or surpluses may signal problems elsewhere in the economy – for instance, when they are caused by large budget deficits or bad economic policy in general. However, in these cases, it is not the current account imbalance *per se* which merits action, but the underlying causes. If US government expenditure is used inefficiently then this is bad for US citizens – no matter what is the effect on the current account – and should therefore be reduced. But if these expenditures are used in a welfare enhancing manner, the US need not worry about the effect of the public deficit on the current account.

To conclude, a current account deficit or surplus by itself does not warrant political intervention. However, the following lessons for economic policy can be derived. Growing capital and current account balances clearly show that capital is more mobile than it used to be. This implies that economic policy itself comes under competitive pressures. Therefore, locational quality becomes an important issue on the political agenda. In order to enhance locational quality, a number of supply-side measures is suitable, such as tax reform, deregulation and the opening of markets. For even if trade balances are not a proof of trade barriers, the latter still exists, reducing the welfare of the very country which applies them. In a similar vein, exchange rate volatility is not a problem to be solved in international summits. Rather, it shows that factors within countries are not flexible enough. With a structure of production smoothly adapting to changes in relative prices, exchange rate volatility would be much lower. Therefore, once again we would propose supply-side measures as a remedy.

Bibliography

Aghion, P. and Howitt, P. (1992) 'A Model of Growth through Creative Destruction' *Econometrica*, 60, pp. 323-51.

Alesina, A. et al. (1992) 'Default Risk on Government Debt in OECD Countries' *Economic Policy*, 15, October, pp. 428-63.

Alexander, Sidney S. (1952) 'Effects of Devaluation on a Trade Balance' *IMF Staff Papers*, 2, pp. 263-78.

Aliber, R.Z. (1987) 'Exchange Rates' in Eatwell, J., Milgate, M. and Newman, P. (eds.) *The New Palgrave: A Dictionary of Economics*, Macmillan, London, Basingstoke, pp. 210-2.

Almekinders, G.J. and Rovers, M. (1994) 'Are Floating Exchange Rates Driven by "News"?' *Konjunkturpolitik*, 40, pp. 27-42.

Alonso, J. and Linde, L. (1993): 'Currency Markets and Foreign Exchange Crises: A Note in Connection with the Group of Ten Report of April 1993', Unpublished Manuscript, *Bank of Spain*. (A Spanish version is published in: Cuadernos de Informacion economica, Fundacion FIES, jul-ago 1993, 220-44.)

Altman, R. C. (1994) 'Why Pressure Tokyo' *Foreign Affairs* 73, May/June, pp. 2-6.

Alzola, J.L. (1991) 'La Evolucion del Tipo de Cambio de la Peseta en el Periodo 1986-90: Causas y Efectos' in FEDEA (ed.) *El Tipo de Cambio de la Peseta ante el Mercado Unico y la Union Monetaria Europea*, Ediciones Mundi-Prensa, Madrid, pp. 23-44.

Anderson, K. and Baldwin, R.E. (1981) *The Political Market for Protection in Industrial Countries: Empirical Evidence* World Bank Staff Working Papers, No. 492.

Arbeitsgemeinschaft deutscher wirtschaftswissenschaftlicher Forschungs-institute e.V. (1991) *Die Lage der Weltwirtschaft und der deutschen Wirtschaft im Frühjahr 1991*, Essen.

Auerbach, A. J. (1994) 'The U.S. Fiscal Problem: Where we are, how we got there, and where we are going' *NBER Macroeconomics Annual*, MIT Press, Cambridge, Mass. and London, pp. 141-75.

Bailey, M.J. and Tavlas G.S. (1988) 'Trade and Investment under Floating Rates: The U.S. Experience' *Cato Journal*, 8, pp. 421-42.

Balassa, B. (1964) 'Competitiveness of American Manufacturing in World Markets' in Balassa, B. (ed.) *Changing Patterns in Foreign Trade and Payments*, Norton and Company, New York, pp. 26-33.

Balassa, B. (1965) 'Trade Liberalisation and "Revealed" Comparative Advantage' *Manchester School of Economic and Social Studies*, 33, pp. 99-123.

Baldwin R.E. and Krugman, P.R. (1989) 'Persistent Trade Effects of Large Exchange Rates Shocks' *The Quarterly Journal of Economics*, CIV, pp. 635-54.

Bank deutscher Länder (1952) *Geschäftsbericht*, Frankfurt/Main.

Bank for International Settlements (BIS), Monetary and Economic Department (1993) *Central Bank Survey of Foreign Exchange Market Activity in April 1992*, Basle.

Barro, R.J. (1974) 'Are Government Bonds Net Wealth?' *Journal of Political Economy*, 8, pp. 1095-147.

Barro, R.J. (1989) 'The Ricardian Approach to Budget Deficits' *Journal of Economic Perspectives*, 3, pp.37-54.

Baumol, W.J. (1993) 'On Location of Industries Among Trading Countries: Scale Economies as Possible Offset to Comparative Disadvantage' in Otha, H. and Thisse, J.-F. (eds.) *Does Economic Space Matter? Essays in Honour of Melvin L. Greenhut*, St. Martin's Press, New York, pp. 187-206.

Bergsten, C.F. and Noland, M. (1993) *Reconcilable Differences?*, Institute for International Economics, Washington DC.

Berié, H. and Hoffmann, C.F. (1991) 'Arbeitskosten in der EG' *Bundesarbeitsblatt*, No. 10, pp. 8-13.

Bernheim, B.D. (1987) 'Ricardian Equivalence: An Evaluation of Theory and Evidence' *NBER Macroeconomics Annual*, MIT Press, Cambridge, Mass. and London, pp. 263-304.

Bhagwati, J. (1991) *The World Trading System at Risk*, Harvester Wheatsheaf, NewYork et al.

Bhagwati, J. (1994) 'Samurais No More' *Foreign Affairs* 73, May/June, pp.7-12.

Bhandari, J. and Putnam, B.H. (ed.) (1985) *Economic Interdependence and Flexible Exchange Rates*, MIT Press, Cambridge, Mass.

Blanchard, O. (1979) 'Speculative Bubbles, Crashes and Rational Expectations' *Economics Letters*, 3, pp. 387-89.

Blanchard, O. and Fischer, S. (1989) *Lectures in Macroeconomics*, MIT Press, Cambridge, Mass., London.

Blanchard, O. et al. (1985) *Employment and Growth in Europe: A Two Handed Approach'* CEPS Paper No. 21, Brussels.

Blanchard, O. et al. (1990) 'The Sustainability of Fiscal Policy: New Answers to an Old Question' *OECD Economic Studies*, No. 15, pp. 7-36.

Blecker, R.A. (1992) *Beyond the Twin Deficits: A Trade Strategy for the 1990s*, M.E. Share, Armonk, New York.

Blejer, M.I. and Cheasty, A. (ed.) (1991) *How to Measure the Fiscal Deficit: Analytical and Methodological Issues*, International Monetary Fund, Washington, D.C.

Blejer, M.I. and Frenkel, J.A. (1987) 'Monetary Approach to the Balance of Payments' in Eatwell, J., Milgate, M. and Newman, P. (eds.) *The New Palgrave: A Dictionary of Economics*, Macmillan, London, Basingstoke, pp. 497-9.

Bletschacher, G. and Klodt, H. (1992) *Strategische Industriepolitik*, Mohr, Tübingen.

Böhm-Bawerk, E. von (1914) 'Unsere passive Handelsbilanz' *Neue Freie Presse of 6/8 and 9 January 1914*, in Franz X. Weiss (ed.) *Gesammelte Schriften von Eugen von Böhm-Bawerk*, Wien 1924, Reprint Sauer & Auvermann, Frankfurt a.M. 1968, 1, pp. 499-515.

Bordo, Michael D. and Schwartz, Anna J. (1989) 'Transmissions of Real and Monetary Disturbances Under Fixed and Floating Exchange Rates' in Dorn, J.A. and Niskanen W (eds.) *Dollar, Deficits, and Trade*, Cato Institute, Dordrecht and London.

Börsenzeitung (1991) 'Kapitalimport keine Sünde', April 30, Reprint, Deutsche Bundesbank (ed.) *Auszüge aus Presseartikeln*, 32, May 4, pp. 10-1.

Boskin, M.J. (1987) *Reagan and the Economy: The Successes, Failures, and Unfinished Agenda*, ICS Press, San Francisco.

Boskin, M.J. and McLure Jr., C.E. (ed.) (1990) *World Tax Reform*, ICS Press, San Francisco.

Boss, A. (1988) *Internationaler Vergleich der Unternehmensbesteuerung*, Institut für Weltwirtschaft, Kiel.

Bossons, J. (1988) 'International Tax Competition: The Foreign Government Response in Canada and Other Countries' *National Tax Journal*, 41, pp. 347-55.

Bosworth, B.(1993) *Saving and Investment in a Global Economy*, The Brookings Institution, Washington DC.

Bosworth, B., Burtless, G. and Sabelhaus, J. (1991) 'The Decline in Saving: Evidence from Household Surveys' *Brooking Papers on Economic Activity*, Vol. 1, Washington, D.C., pp. 183-256.

Bovenberg, A.L. et al. (1990) 'Tax Incentives and International Capital Flows: The Case of the United States and Japan' in Razin, A. and Slemrod, J. (eds.) *Taxation in the Global Economy*, The University of Chicago Press, Chicago, pp. 283-324.

Bovenberg, L.A. and Tanzi, V. (1990) 'Is There a Need for Harmonizing Capital Income Taxes within EC Countries?' in H. Siebert (ed.) *Reforming Capital Income Taxation*, Mohr, Tübingen, pp. 171-97.

Bradford, D.F. (1986) *Untangling the Income Tax*, Harvard University Press, Cambridge, Mass. and London.

Bradford, D.F. and Fullerton, D. (1981) 'Pitfalls in the Construction and Use of Effective Tax Rates' in Hulten, C.R. (ed.) *Depreciation, Inflation, and the Taxation of Income from Capital*, The Urban Institute Press, Washington, D.C., pp. 251-78.

Bradford, D.F. and Stuart, C. (1986) 'Issues in the Measurement and Interpretation of Effective Taxes Rates' *National Tax Journal*, 39, pp. 307-16.

Brander, J.A. and Spencer, B.J. (1985) 'Export Subsidies and International Market Share Rivalry' *Journal of International Economics*, 18, pp.83-100.

Brandt, M., Herrmann, B. and Sabathil, M. (1991) *Förderhilfen für die neuen Bundesländer*, Bundesregierung, Bonn.

Branson, W.H. (1977) 'Asset Markets and Relative Prices in Exchange Rate Determination' *Sozialwissenschaftliche Annalen*, 1, pp. 69-89.

Branson, W.H. (1985) 'The Dynamic Interaction of Exchange Rates and Trade Flows' in Peeters, T., Praet, P. and Reding, P. (eds.) *International Trade and Exchange Rates in the Late Eighties*, Université de Bruxelles, Bruxelles, pp. 133-60.

Brennan, G. and Buchanan, J.M. (1987) 'The Logic of the Ricardian Equivalence Theorem' in Buchanan, J.M., Rowley, C.K. and Tollison, R.D. (eds.), *Deficits*, Blackwell, Oxford and New York, pp. 79-92.

Brooks, S., Cuthbertson, K. and Mayes, D.G. (1986) *The Exchange Rate Environment*, Croom Helm, London, Sydney, Wolfeboro, NH.

Brown, B. (1983) *The Forward Market in Foreign Exchange. A Study in Market-making, Arbitrage and Speculation*, Croom Helm, London, Canberra.

Bui, N. and Pippenger, J. (1990) 'Commodities Prices, Exchange Rates and Their Relative Volatility' *Journal of International Money and Finance*, 9, pp. 3-20.

Bundesanstalt für Arbeit (1991) *Amtliche Nachrichten der Bundesanstalt für Arbeit*, 39, No 4 (29 April 1991), Nürnberg.

Burda, M. and Wyplosz, C. (1993) *Macroeconomics: A European Text*, Oxford University Press, Oxford, New York and Toronto.

Canto, V.A., Joines, D.H. and Laffer, A.B. (1983) *Foundations of Supply-side Economics: Theory and Evidence*, Academic Press, New York.

Cohen, D. (1991) *Private Lending to Sovereign States: A Theoretical Autopsy*, The MIT Press, Cambridge, Mass., London.

Competitiveness Policy Council (1994) *Third Report on Promoting Long-term Prosperity from the Competitiveness Policy Council*, Hearing Before the Subcommittee on Economic Growth and Credit Formation of the Committee on Banking, Finance and Urban Affairs, House of Representatives, 103rd Congress, 2nd Session, May 12, 1994, Serial No. 103-139, Washington, D.C.

Corden, W.M. (1971) *The Theory of Protection*, Clarendon Press, Oxford.

Corden, W.M. (1974) *Trade Policy and Economic Welfare*, Oxford University Press, Oxford.

Corden, W.M. (1994) *Economic Policy, Exchange Rates and the International System*, The University of Chicago Press, Chicago.

Corden, W.M. and Neary, J.P. (1982): 'Booming Sector and De-Industrialisation in a Small Open Economy' *The Economic Journal*, 92, pp. 825-48.

Corker, R. (1989) 'External Adjustment and the Strong Yen' *IMF Staff Papers*, 36, pp. 464-93.

Côté, Agathe (1994) *Exchange Rate Volatility and Trade. A Survey*, Bank of Canada Working Paper 94-5.

Council of Economic Advisers *Economic Report of the President*, Washington, D.C., various issues.

Deardorff, A.V. (1994) 'Exploring the Limits of Comparative Advantage' *Weltwirtschaftliches Archiv*, 130, pp. 1-19.

DeGrauwe, Paul (1989) *International Money. Post-War Trends and Theories*, Clarendon Press, Oxford.

Deregulierungskommission (German Commission on Deregulation) (1991) *Marktöffnung und Wettbewerb*, Poeschel, Stuttgart.

Deutsche Bundesbank (1992) 'Öffentliche Finanztransfers für Ostdeutschland in den Jahren 1991 und 1992', *Deutsche Bundesbank* (b), März, pp. 15-22.

Deutsche Bundesbank (1994) 'Reale Wechselkurse als Indikatoren der internationalen Wettbewerbsfähigkeit' *Monatsberichte der Deutschen Bundesbank*, Mai, pp. 47-60 (the monthly reports of the Deutsche Bundesbank are also available in English).

Deutsche Bundesbank (a) *Statistische Beihefte zu den Monatsberichten der Deutschen Bundesbank*, Reihe 3, Zahlungsbilanzstatistik, various issues, Frankfurt/Main.

Deutsche Bundesbank (b) *Monatsberichte*, various issues, Frankfurt/Main.

Deutsches Institut für Wirtschaftsforschung (1992) 'Gefährdet die Lohnkostenentwicklung die Wettbewerbsfähigkeit der Bundesrepublik Deutschland?' *DIW Wochenbericht*, pp. 121-4.

Deutsches Institut für Wirtschaftsforschung and Institut für Weltwirtschaft (1991) 'Gesamtwirtschaftliche und unternehmerische Anpassungsprozesse in Ostdeutschland, zweiter Bericht', *DIW-Wochenbericht*, pp. 323-46.

Diba, B.T. and Grossman, H.I. (1988) 'The theory of rational bubbles in stock prices' *The Economic Journal*, 98, pp. 746-754.

Dicke, H. and Trapp, P. (1984) *Zinsen, Gewinne, Nettoinvestitionen: Zu den Bestimmungsfaktoren der Sachvermögensbildung westdeutscher Unternehmen*, Kiel Discussion Paper 99, Kiel.

Dixit, A. (1984) 'International Trade Policies for Oligopolistic Industries' *The Economic Journal*, Conference Papers, pp. 1-16.

Dluhosch, B. (1991) 'Privatisierung in den neuen Bundesländern: Reaktionen der Kapital- und Gütermärkte' *Wirtschaftdienst*, pp. 416-22.

Dluhosch, B. (1993) *Strategische Fiskalpolitik in offenen Volkswirtschaften*, Institut für Wirtschaftspolitik, Köln.

Dluhosch, B. (1994) 'Playing Ponzi in an Open Economy' (mimeo).

Dluhosch, B. (1995) *On the Fate of Newcomers in the EU: Lessons From the Spanish Experience*, Bank of Spain (forthcoming).

Dluhosch, B. and Krüger, M. (1991) 'Struktureller Anpassungsbedarf bei hohen Kapitalimporten und feste Wechselkursen – Der Fall Spanien –' *Zeitschrift für Wirtschaftspolitik*, 40, pp. 157-80.

Dolado, J.J. and Viñals, J. (1990) 'Macroeconomic Policy, External Targets and Constraints: The Case of Spain' in Alogoskoufis, G., Papademos, L. and Portes, R. (eds.) *External Constraints on Macroeconomic Policy: The European Experience*, Cambridge University Press, Cambridge, pp. 304-41.

Dollar, D. and Wolff, E.N. (1993) *Competitiveness, Convergence, and International Specialization*, MIT Press, Cambridge, Mass.

Donges, J.B. (1991) 'Arbeitsmarkt und Lohnpolitik in Ostdeutschland' *Wirtschaftsdienst*, 71, pp. 283-91.

Donges, J.B. and Riedel, J. (1977) 'The Expansion of Manufactured Exports in Developing Countries: An Empirical Assessment of Supply and Demand Issues' *Weltwirtschaftliches Archiv*, 113, pp. 58-87.

Dornbusch, R. (1976) 'Expectations and Exchange Rate Dynamics' *Journal of Political Economy*, 84, pp. 1161-76.

Dornbusch, R. (1988a) *Exchange Rates and Inflation*, MIT Press, Cambridge, Mass., London

Dornbusch, R. (1988b) 'Doubts About the McKinnon Standard' *Journal of Economic Perspectives*, 2, pp. 105-12.

Dornbusch, R. and Fischer, S. (1990) *Macroeconomics*, McGraw-Hill, New York.

Edwards, S. (1988) *Exchange Rate Misalignments in Developing Countries*, World Bank Occasional Papers, 2, Washington, D.C.

Eichengreen, B., Tobin, J. and Wyplosz, C. (1995) 'Two Cases for Sand in the Wheels of International Finance' *The Economic Journal*, 105, pp. 162-72.

Eisner, R. (1986) *How Real is the Federal Deficit?*, Free Press, New York and London.

Evans, P. (1985) 'Do Large Deficits Produce High Interest Rates?' *American Economic Review*, 75, pp. 68-87.

Fagerberg, J. (1988): 'International Competitiveness' *The Economic Journal*, 98, pp. 355-74.

Feldstein, M. (1986) 'The Budget Deficit and the Dollar' *NBER Macroeconomics Annual*, Cambridge, Mass, pp. 356-92.

Feldstein, M. (1994) 'Tax Policy and International Capital Flows' *Weltwirtschaftliches Archiv*, 130, pp. 675-97.

Feldstein M. and Horioka, C.Y. (1980) 'Domestic Saving and International Capital Flows' *The Economic Journal*, 90, pp.314-29.

Fellner, W. (1982) 'The Valid Core of Rational Expectations Theory and the Problem of Exchange Rate Relations' in Cooper, R.N. et al. (eds.) *The International Monetary System Under Flexible Exchange Rates*, Ballinger, Cambridge, Mass., pp. 35-49.

Fels, G. (1988a) 'Der Standort Bundesrepublik Deutschland im internationalen Standortwettbewerb' *Hamburger Jahrbuch für Wirtschafts- und Gesellschaftspolitik*, pp. 9-25.

Fels, G. (1988b) 'Zum Konzept der internationalen Wettbewerbsfähigkeit' *Jahrbuch für Sozialwissenschaft*, 39, pp. 135-44.

Fisher, I. (1930) *The Theory of Interest*, Macmillan, New York, Reprint Macmillan, Philadelphia 1977.

Flood, R.P. and Hodrick, R.J. (1990) 'On Testing for Speculative Bubbles' *Journal of Economic Perspectives*, 4, pp. 85-101.

Frankel, J.A. (1979) 'On the Mark: A Theory of Floating Exchange Rates Based on Real Interest Differentials' *American Economic Review*, 69, pp. 610-22.

Frankel, J.A. (1983) 'Monetary and Portfolio-Balance Models of Exchange Rate Determinaion' in Bhandari, J.S. and Putman, B.H. (eds.) *Economic Interdependence and Flexible Exchange Rates*, MIT Press, Cambridge, Mass, London, pp. 84-113.

Frankel, J.A. (1986) 'International Capital Mobility and Crowding Out in the U.S. Economy: Imperfect Integration of Capital markets or of Goods Markets' in Hafer R.W. (ed.) *How Open is the U.S. Economy?*, Lexington Books, Lexington and Toronto, pp. 33-67.

Frankel, J.A. (1991) 'Japanese Finance in the 1980s: A Survey' in Krugman, P. (ed.) *Trade with Japan – Has the Door Opened Wider?*, The University of Chicago Press, Chicago, pp. 225-68.

Frankel, J.A. and Froot, K.A. (1986) 'Understanding the dollar in the eighties: The expectations of chartists and fundmentalists' *The Economic Record* (special issue), pp. 24-38.

Frenkel, J.A. (1981) 'Flexible Exchange Rates and the Role of "News": Lessons from the 1970s' *Journal of Political Economy*, 89, pp. 665-705.

Frenkel, J.A. and Johnson, H.G. (eds.) (1976) *The Monetary Approach to the Balance of Payments*, The University of Toronto Press, Toronto.

Frenkel, J.A. and Mussa, M. (1985) 'Asset Markets, Exchange Rates and the Balance of Payments' in Jones, R.W. and Kenen, P.B. (eds.) *Handbook of International Economics*, II, Elsevier Science, Amsterdam, pp. 679-747.

Frenkel, J.A., Razin, A. and Sadka, E. (1991) *International Taxation in an Integrated World*, MIT Press, Cambridge, Mass.

Frenkel, J.A. and Razin, A. (1992) *Fiscal Policies and the World Economy*, (2nd ed.), MIT Press, Cambridge, Mass. and London.

Freytag, A. (1995a) *Die strategische Handels- und Industriepolitik der EG – eine politökonomische Analyse*, Institut für Wirtschaftspolitik, Köln.

Freytag, A. (1995b) 'The European Market for Protectionism: New Competitors and New Products' in Gerken, L. (ed.) *Competition Among Institutions*, Macmillan, London and Basingstoke, pp. 231-58.

Fuest, W. and Kroker, R. (1989) *Unternehmenssteuerlast: 20 oder 70 Prozent?*, Institut der deutschen Wirtschaft, Köln.

Fullerton, D. (1984) 'Which Effective Tax Rate?' *National Tax Journal*, 37, pp. 23-41.

GATT (1992) *Trade Policy Review Mechanism: Japan*, 2 Vol., Geneva.

GATT (1993) *Trade Policy Review Mechanism: European Communities*, 2 Vol., Geneva.

GATT (1994) *Trade Policy Review Mechanism: United States*, 2 Vol., Geneva.

Giebel, U.J. (1985) 'Ein investitionstheoretischer Ansatz zur Erfassung von Personalkosten bei Beschäftigungsentscheidungen' *Zeitschrift für Wirtschaftspolitik*, 34, pp. 271-92.

Giersch, H. (1986) 'Elemente einer Theorie weltwirtschaftlicher Entwicklung' in Giersch, H. (ed.) *Gegen Europessimismus, Kritische Beiträge 1977-1985*, DVA, Stuttgart, pp. 8-39.

Giersch, H., Paqué, K.-H. and Schmieding, H. (1992) *The Fading Miracle*, MIT Press, Cambridge, Mass. and London.

Giovannini, A. (1989) 'National Tax Systems Versus the European Capital Market' *Economic Policy*, 9, pp. 346-86.

Giovannini, A. (1990) 'Reforming Capital Income Taxation in the Open Economy: Theoretical Issues' in Siebert, H. (ed.) *Reforming Capital Income Taxation*, Mohr, Tübingen, pp. 3-18.

Glick, Reuven (1991) 'Japanese Capital Flows in the 1980s' *Federal Reserve Bank of San Francisco, Economic Review*, Spring, pp. 18-31.

Goodhart, Charles (1988) 'The Foreign Exchange Market: A Random Walk with a Dragging Anchor' *Economica*, 55, pp. 437-460.

Goto, F. (1991) *Is the Japanese Market Really Closed? A Critical Review of the Economic Studies*, Research Institute of International Trade and Industry, Tokyo.

Gravelle, J.G. (1994) *The Economic Effects of Taxing Capital Income*, MIT Press, Cambridge/Mass. and London.

Grossman, G.M. and Helpman, E. (1990) 'Comparative Advantage and Long-Run Growth' *American Economic Review*, 80, pp. 796-815.

Group of Thirty (1980) *The Foreign Exchange Markets Under Floating. A Study in International Finance*, New York.

Grubel, H.G. and Lloyd, P.J. (1975) *Intra-Industry Trade*, Macmillan, London and Basingstoke.

Gundlach, E. (1986) 'Gibt es genügend Lohndifferenzierung in der Bundesrepublik Deutschland?' *Die Weltwirtschaft*, pp. 74-88.

Haberler, G. (1933) *Der internationale Handel*, Julius Springer, Berlin.

Haberler, G. (1948) *Prosperität und Depression* (German edition), A. Francke, Bern.

Haberler, G. (1980) 'Notes on Rational and Irrational Expectations' in Küng, E. (ed.) *Wandlungen in Wirtschaft und Gesellschaft. Festschrift für Walter Adolf Jöhr*, Mohr, Tübingen pp. 267-281.

Hailstones, T.J. (1982) *A Guide to Supply-side Economics*, Reston Pub. Co, Reston.

Hall, R.E. and Jorgenson, D.W. (1967) 'Tax Policy and Investment Behavior' *American Economic Review*, 57, pp. 391-414.

Hayashi, F. (1986) 'Why is Japan's Saving Rate So Apparently High?' *NBER Macroeconomics Annual 1986*, Cambridge, Mass., pp. 144-233.

Haynes, S.E., Hutchison, M.M. and Mikesell, R.F. (1986) *Japanese Financial Policies and the U.S. Trade Deficit*, Essays in International Finance, 162, Princeton University.

Heitger, B. (1983) *Strukturwandel und realer Wechselkurs*, Mohr, Tübingen.

Heitger, B. and Stehn, J. (1988) 'Protektion in Japan – Interessendruck oder gezielte Intervention?' *Die Weltwirtschaft*, pp. 123-37.

Helpman, E. and Razin, A. (1982) 'Dynamics of a Floating Exchange Rate Regime' *Journal of Political Economy*, 90, pp. 728-54.

Hemmer, E. (1991) 'Personalzusatzkosten im Produzierenden Gewerbe und im Dienstleistungsbereich' *iw-trends*, 18. Jahrgang, 1, D1-D8.

Heyne, P. (1989) 'Do Trade Deficits Matter?' in Dorn, J.A. and Niskanen, W. (eds.) *Dollars, Deficits, and Trade*, Cato Institute, Dordrecht and London, pp. 351-62.

Hilke, J.C. and Nelson, P.B. (1987) *International Competitiveness and the Trade Deficit*, Federal Trade Commission, Washington, D.C.

Hilke, J.C. and Nelson, P.B. (1988) *U.S. International Competitiveness: Evolution or Revolution?*, Praeger, New York.

Hirsch, S. (1974) 'Hypotheses Regarding Trade Between Developing and Industrial Countries' in Giersch, H (ed.) *The International Division of Labour Problems and Perspectives*, Mohr, Tübingen, pp.65-82.

Hirschman, A.O. (1970) *Exit, Voice, and Loyalty*, Harvard University Press, Cambridge, Mass.

Hirshleifer, J. (1970) *Investment, Interest and Capital,* Prentice Hall, Englewood Cliffs.

Hoffmann, J. (1989) *Sparen im Dienst der Altersvorsorge als volkswirtschaftliches Problem*, Institut für Wirtschaftspolitik, Köln.

Hoffmann, J. and Homburg, S. (1990) 'Explaining the Rise and Decline of the Dollar' *Kyklos*, 43, pp. 53-68.

Holzmann, R. (1990) 'Internationaler Vergleich von Alterssicherungssystemen: Konzepte, Strukturen und ökonomische Effekte' in Gahlen, B. et al. (eds.) *Theorie und Politik der Sozialversicherung*, Mohr, Tübingen, pp. 141-67.

Homburg, S. (1988) *Theorie der Alterssicherung*, Springer, Berlin, Heidelberg, New York.

Homburg, S. (1989) 'Some Notes on Overshooting' *Zeitschrift für Wirtschafts- und Sozialwissenschaften*, 109, pp. 443-7.

Horioka, C.Y. (1986) 'Why is Japan's Private Savings Rate so High?' *Finance & Development*, 23, No. 4, December.

Horioka, C.Y (1994) 'Japan's Consumption and Saving in International Perspective' *Economic Development and Cultural Change*, 42, pp. 293-316.

Ihori, T. (1991) 'Capital Income Taxation in a World Economy: A Territorial System Versus a Residence System' *The Economic Journal*, 101, pp. 958-65.

Institut der deutschen Wirtschaft (1991) 'Konjunkturtendenz: Der Außenhandel' *iwd*, No. 21 from May 23, p. 3.

Institut der deutschen Wirtschaft (1992a) 'Arbeitskosten der Industrie: 40 Mark überschritten' *iwd*, 13, from March 20, p. 3.

Institut der deutschen Wirtschaft (1992b) 'Unternehmenssteuern: Wie Hase und Igel' *iwd*, 18. Jahrgang, 16 from April 16, pp. 4-5.

Institute for Fiscal Studies (1978) *The Structure and Reform of Direct Taxation (Report of the Meade Committee)*, George Allen and Unwin, London and Boston.

International Monetary Fund (IMF) (a) *International Financial Statistics*, various issues and Database, Washington, D.C.

International Monetary Fund (IMF) (b) *International Financial Statistics*. Yearbook, various issues, Washington, D.C.

International Monetary Fund (IMF) (1984) *Exchange Rate Volatility and World Trade*, Occasional Paper 28, Washington, D.C.

International Monetary Fund (IMF) (1985) *Foreign Private Investment in Developing Countries*, Occasional Paper 33, Washington, D.C.

Isard, P. (1977) 'How Far Can We Push the "Law of One Price"?' *American Economic Review*, 67, pp. 942-8.

Issing, O. and Masuch, V. (1989) 'Zur Frage der normativen Interpretation von Leistungsbilanzsalden' *Kredit und Kapital*, pp. 1-17.

Johnson, H.G. (1969) 'The Case for Flexible Exchange Rates 1969' in Johnson, H.G. and Nash, J.E. (eds.) *U.K. and Floating Exchanges: A Debate on the Theoretical and Practical Implications*, Institute of Economic Affairs, London, pp. 9-37.

Jorgenson, D.W. and Landau, R. (eds.) (1993) *Tax Reform and the Cost of Capital: An International Comparison*, Brookings Institution, Washington, D.C.

Jorgenson, D.W. and Yun, K.-Y. (1991) *Tax Reform and the Cost of Capital*, Oxford.

Kenen, P.B. (1985) 'Macroeconomic Theory and Policy: How the Closed Economy was Opened' in Jones, R.W. and Kenen, P.B. (eds.) *Handbook of International Economics*, II, Elsevier Science, Amsterdam, pp. 625-77.

Kenen, P.B. (1994) *The International Economy*, Cambridge University Press, Cambridge, New York, Melbourne.

Keynes, J.M. (1929/50) 'The German Transfer Problem' *The Economic Journal*, 39, March 1929, pp. 1-7, reprinted in Ellis, H.S. and Metzler,

L.A. (1950) *Readings in the Theory of International Trade*, George Allen and Unwin, London, pp. 161-69.

Keynes, J.M.(1936/64) *The General Theory of Employment, Interest, and Money*, Harcourt Brace Janovich, San Diego, New York, London.

Kindleberger, C.P. (1989) *Manias, Panics, and Crashes: A History of Financial Crisis*, Basic Books, New York.

King, M.A. and Fullerton, D. (1984) *The Taxation of Income From Capital: A Comparative Study of the United States, United Kingdom, Sweden and West Germany*, The University of Chicago Press, Chicago.

Klodt, H. (1992) 'Staatsverschuldung hat die Belastung der Privatwirtschaft nur aufgeschoben' *Handelsblatt* No. 77 from April 21,1992, p. 8.

Klodt, H., Schmidt, K.-D. et al. (1989) *Weltwirtschaftlicher Strukturwandel und Standortwettbewerb – Die deutsche Wirtschaft auf dem Prüfstand*, Mohr, Tübingen.

Koromzay, V., Llewellyn, J. and Potter, S. (1987) 'The Rise and Fall of the Dollar: Explanations, Consequences and Lessons' *The Economic Journal*, 97, pp. 23-43.

Kotlikoff, L. (1992) *Generational Accounting*, Free Press, New York.

Kouri, P.J.K. (1976) 'The Exchange Rate and the Balance of Payments in the Short Run and in the Long Run: A Monetary Approach' *Scandinavian Journal of Economics*, 78, pp. 280-304.

Kroker, R. (1990) 'Lohnstückkosten im Verarbeitenden Gewerbe. Ein internationaler Vergleich' *iw-trends*, 17, Heft 1, D1-D12.

Krueger, A.O. (1974) 'The Political Economy of the Rent-Seeking Society' *American Economic Review*, 64, pp. 291-303.

Krueger, A.O. (1983) *Exchange-Rate Determination*, Cambridge University Press, Cambridge etc.

Krueger, A.O. (1984) 'Trade Policies in Developing Countries' in Jones, R.W. and Kenen, P.B. (eds.) *Handbook of International Economics*, I, Elsevier Science, Amsterdam, pp.520-69.

Krüger, M. (1992) Was dem EWS geschehen ist' *Wirtschaftsdienst*, pp. 516-19.

Krüger, M. (1994) *Finanzmarktungleichgewichte und Wechselkursvolatilität. Zur Bedeutung der internationalen Finanzmärkte für die Entwicklung der Wechselkurse*, Institut für Wirtschaftspolitik, Köln.

Krüger, M. (1995) *Speculation, Hedging and Arbitrage in the Foreign Exchange Market*, Bank of Spain (forthcoming).

Krugman, P.R. (1984) 'Import Protection as Export Promotion: International Competition in the Presence of Oligopoly and Economies of Scale' in Kierzkowski, H. (ed.) *Monopolistic Competition and International Trade*, Clarendon Press, Oxford, pp. 180-93.

Krugman, P.R. (1987) 'Is Free Trade Passé?' *Journal of Economic Perspectives*, 1, pp. 131-44.

Krugman, P.R. (1989) 'The Case for Stabilizing Exchange Rates' *Oxford Review of Economic Policy*, 5, pp. 61-72.

Krugman, P.R. (1993) 'The J-Curve, the Fire Sale, and the Hard Landing' in Krugman, P.R., *Currencies and Crises*, MIT Press, Camb./Mass. and London, pp. 33-9.

Krugman, P.R. (1994) 'Competitiveness: A Dangerous Obsession' *Foreign Affairs*, March/April, pp. 29-44.

Krugman, P.R. and Lawrence, R. (1993) *Trade, Jobs, and Wages*, NBER Working Paper 4478, Cambridge, Mass.

Krugman, P.R. and Obstfeld, M. (1994) *International Economics*, Harper Collins, New York.

Laidler, D. (1993) *The Demand for Money. Theory, Evidence and Problems*, Harper Collins College Publishers, New York.

Lawrence, R.Z. (1987) 'Imports in Japan: Closed Markets or Minds?' *Brookings Papers on Economic Activity*, Washington, D.C., pp. 517-54.

Lawrence, R.Z. (1990) 'U.S. Current Account Adjustment: An Appraisal' *Brookings Papers on Economic Activity*, Washington, D.C., pp. 343-92.

Lawrence, R.Z. (1991) 'Efficient or Exclusionist? The Import Behavior of Japanese Corporate Groups', *Brookings Papers on Economic Activity*, Washington, D.C., pp. 311-41.

Lawrence, R.Z. (1993) 'Japan's Different Trade Regime: An Analysis with Particular Reference to Keiretsu' *The Journal of Economic Perspectives*, 7, No. 3, pp. 3-19.

Lazear, E. (1990) 'Job Security Provisions and Employment' *The Quarterly Journal of Economics*, CV, pp. 701-26.

Leamer, E.E. and Stern R.M. (1970) *Quantitative International Economics*, Aldine Publishing Company, Chicago.

Leibfritz, W. (1986) *Steuerliche Belastung und staatliche Förderung der Kapitalbildung in der Bundesrepublik Deutschland*, ifo Studien zur Finanzpolitik, 36, München.

Lenz, A.J. (1991) *Beyond Blue Economic Horizons: U.S. Trade Performance and International Competitiveness in the 1990s*, Praeger, New York.

Levich, R.M. (1985) 'Empirical Studies of Exchange Rates: Price Behavior, Rate Determination and Market Efficiency' in Jones, R.W. and Kenen, P.B. (eds.) *Handbook of International Economics*, II, Elsevier Science, Amsterdam, pp. 979-1040.

Lincoln, E.J. (1990) *Japan's Unequal Trade*, The Brookings Institution, Washington, D.C.

Lipschitz, L. and McDonald, D. (1992) 'Real Exchange Rates and Competitiveness' *Empirica-Austrian Economic Papers*, 19, No. 1, pp. 37-69.

Lucas, R.E. (1990) 'Supply-side Economics: An Analytical Review' *Oxford Economic Papers*, 42, pp. 293-316.

Lüdiger, M. (1989) 'Wechselkursovershooting contra effiziente Devisenmärkte' *Kredit und Kapital*, 22, pp. 173-95.

MacDonald, R. and Taylor, M.P. (1992) 'Exchange Rate Economics: A Survey' *IMF Staff Papers*, 39, pp. 1-57.

Machlup, F. (1939/40) 'The Theory of Foreign Exchange Rates' *Economica* VI (N.S.), Nov. 1939, pp. 375-397 and Febr. 1940, pp. 23-49.

Machlup, F. (1950) 'Elasticity Pessimism in International Trade' *Economia Internazionale*, 3, pp. 118-41.

Machlup, F. (1964) 'Equilibrium and Disequilibrium: Misplaced Concretness and Disguised Politics' in Machlup, F. *International Monetary Economics*, George Allen & Unwin, London, pp. 110-35.

Machlup, F. (1980) 'Explaining Changes in Balances of Payments and Foreign Exchange Rates: A Polemic Without Graphs, Algebra, and Citations' in Chipman, J S. and Kindleberger, C.P. (eds.) *Flexible Exchange Rates and the Balance of Payments. Essays in Honour of Egon Sohmen*, North Holland, Amsterdam, New York, pp. 99-109.

Magaziner, I.C. and Reich, R.B. (1982) *Minding America's Business: The Decline and Rise of the American Economy*, Harcourt Brace Janovich, New York.

Markusen, J.R. et al. (1995) *International Trade: Theory and Evidence*, McGraw-Hill, New York.

Marris, S. (1985) *Deficits and the Dollar: The World Economy at Risk*, Institute for International Economics, Washington, D.C.

Marsh, I.W. and Tokarick, S.P. (1994) *Competitiveness Indicators: A Theoretical and Empirical Assessment*, IMF Working Paper, WP/94/29, Washington, D.C.

Marshall, A. (1920/61) *Principles of Economics* (6th ed.), Macmillan, London.

Marshall, A. (1922) *Money, Credit and Commerce*, Macmillan, London.

Mastroberardino, M.G. (1994) *Kapitalflucht: Die Erfahrungen Argentiniens 1976-92*, Institut für Wirtschaftspolitik, Köln.

Mayer, Helmut W. (1985) *Interaction Between the Euro-Currency Markets and the Exchange Markets*, BIS Economic Papers, 15, Basle.

McKee, M.J., Visser, J.J.C. and Saunders, P.G. (1986) 'Marginal Tax Rates on the Use of Labour and Capital in OECD Countries' *OECD Economic Studies*, No. 7, pp. 45-101.

McKinnon, R.I. (1986) 'Foreign Exchange Dealers, the Domestic Money Market and Stabilising Speculation' in Cohen, J.S. (ed.) *International Monetary Problems and Supply Side Economics*, Macmillan, Houndsmills, Basingstoke and London, pp. 28-55.

McKinnon, R.I. (1988) 'Monetary and Exchange Rate Policies for International Stability: A Proposal' *Journal of Economic Perspectives*, 2, pp. 83-103.

Meade (1951) *The Balance of Payments* (The Theory of International Economic Policy, Vol.1), Oxford University Press, London, New York, Toronto.

Meese, Richard A. (1986) 'Testing for bubbles in exchange markets: a case of sparking rates?' *Journal of Political Economy*, 94, pp. 345-73.

Meese, Richard A. and Rogoff, Kenneth (1983) 'Empirical Exchange Rate Models of the Seventies: Do They Fit Out of Sample?' *Journal of International Economics*, 14, pp. 3-24.

Menger, Carl (1892) 'On the Origin of Money' *The Economic Journal*, 2, pp. 239-55.

Meyer, F.W. (1938) *Der Ausgleich der Zahlungsbilanz*, G. Fischer, Jena.

Meyer, F.W. and Willgerodt, H. (1956) *Internationale Lohngefälle. Teil I: Der wirtschaftspolitische Aussagewert internationaler Lohnvergleiche*, Bonn.

Modigliani, F. (1986) 'Life Cycle, Individual Thrift, and the Wealth of Nations' *American Economic Review*, 76, pp. 297-313.

Mundell, R.A. (1968) 'Capital Mobility and Stabilization Policy under Fixed and Flexible Exchange Rates' in Mundell, R.A. *International Economics*, New York and London, pp. 250-71.

Musgrave, P.B. (1991) 'Fiscal Coordination and Competition in an International Setting' in Eden, L. (ed.) *Retrospectives on Public Finance*, Duke University Press, Durham and London, pp. 276-305.

Mussa, M. (1984) 'The Theory of Exchange Rate Determination' in Bilson, J.F.O. and Marston, R.C. (eds.) *Exchange Rate Theory and Practice*, University of Chicago Press, Chicago, London, pp. 13-78.

Nelson, R.R. and Wright, G. (1992) 'American Technological Leadership: The Postwar Area in Historical Perspective' *Journal of Economic Literature*, 30, pp. 1931-64.

Neumann, M.J.M. and Klein, M. (1982) 'Probleme der Theorie effizienter Märkte und ihrer empirischen Überprüfung' *Kredit und Kapital*, 15, pp. 165-85.

Niehans, J. (1985) 'International Debt with Unenforcable Claims' *Federal Reserve Bank of San Francisco Economic Review*, pp. 64-79.

Niehans, J. (1994): 'Arbitrage Equilibrium with Transaction Costs' *Journal of Money, Credit, and Banking*, 26, pp. 249-70.

Niskanen, W.A. (1971) *Bureaucracy and Representative Government*, Aldine Atherton, Chicago.

O'Connell, S.A. and Zeldes, S.P. (1988) 'Rational Ponzi Games' *International Economic Review*, 29, pp. 431-50.

Obstfeld, M. (1985) 'Floating Exchange Rates: Experience and Prospects' *Brookings Papers on Economic Activity*, Washington, D.C., pp. 369-450.

Obstfeld, M. (1992) 'Comment on Alesina et al.: Default Risk on Government Debt in OECD Countries' *Economic Policy*, 15, pp. 451-5.

Obstfeld, M. and Stockman, A.C. (1985) 'Exchange-Rate Dynamics', in Jones, R.W. and Kenen, P.B. (eds.) *Handbook of International Economics*, II, Elsevier Science, Amsterdam, pp. 917-77.

Obstfeld, Maurice and Rogoff, Kenneth (1994) *The Intertemporal Approach to the Current Account*, NBER Working Paper No. 4893.

OECD (1988) *OECD Economic Surveys: Spain*, Paris.

OECD (1989/90) *OECD Economic Surveys: Japan*, Paris.

OECD (1991a) *National Accounts, Main Aggregates*, I, 1960-1989, Paris.

OECD (1991b) *Taxing Profits in a Global Economy: Domestic and International Issues*, Paris.

OECD (1993) *OECD Economic Surveys: Germany*, Paris.

OECD (1994a) *OECD Economic Surveys: Japan*, Paris.

OECD (1994b) *OECD Economic Surveys: United States*, Paris.

OECD (1994c) *Economic Outlook 56* (December 1994), Paris.

OECD (1994d) *Taxation and Household Saving*, Paris.

OECD (a) *Trade by Commodities*, various issues, Paris.

Ohlin, Bertil (1929/50) 'The Reparation Problem: A Discussion' *The Economic Journal*, 39, June 1929, pp. 172-3, reprinted in Ellis, H.S. and Metzler, L.A. (1950) *Readings in the Theory of International Trade*, George Allen and Unwin, London, pp. 170-8.

Ohmae, K. (1990) *Fact and Friction*, The Japan Times, Tokyo.

Ohr, R. (1985) 'Wechselkurserwartungen und Stabilität des Devisenmarktes' *Jahrbuch für Nationalökonomie und Statistik*, pp. 298-309.

Ohr. R. (1991) 'Finanzpolitik, Leistungsbilanz und realer Wechselkurs' in Siebke, J. (ed.) *Monetäre Konfliktfelder der Weltwirtschaft*, Duncker & Humblot, Berlin, pp. 99-112.

Orlowski, D. (1982) *Die internationale Wettbewerbsfähigkeit einer Volkswirtschaft*, Vandenhoeck und Ruprecht, Göttingen.

Ortega, E., Salaverría, J. and Viñals, J. (1990) 'Spain's Current and Capital Account Balances within the EEC' in Bank for International Settlements, Monetary and Economic Department (ed.) *International Capital Flows, Exchange Rate Determination and Persistent Current-Account Balances*, Basle, 190-219.

Paqué, K.-H. (1991) *Structural Wage Rigidity in West Germany 1950-1989: Some New Econometric Evidence*, Kiel Working Paper 489, Kiel.

Patrick, H. (1994) 'The Relevance of Japanese Finance and its Main Bank System' in Aoki, M. and Patrick, H. (eds.) *The Japanese Main Bank System*, Oxford University Press, Oxford, pp.353-408.

Pechman, J. (ed.) (1988) *World Tax Reform: A Progress Report*, Brookings Institution, Washington, D.C.

Penner, R.G. (1987) 'Government Deficits: The Case of the United States', in Boskin, M.J., Fleming, J.S. and Gorini, S. (eds.) *Private Saving and Public Debt*, Oxford and N.Y., pp. 105-25.

Petri, P.A. (1991) 'Market Structure, Comparative Advantage, and Japanese Trade under the Strong Yen' in Krugman, P.R. (ed.), *Trade with Japan – Has the Door Opened Wider?*, The University of Chicago Press, Chicago, pp. 51-82.

Poterba, J.M. (1991) 'Comparing the Cost of Capital in the United States and Japan: A Survey of Methods' *Federal Reserve Bank of New York Quarterly Review*, 15, No. 3-4, pp. 20-32.

Presse- und Informationsamt der Bundesregierung (ed.) (1991) 'Gemeinschaftswerk Aufschwung Ost' *Bulletin* No. 25, March 12, pp. 177-82, Bonn.

Ragnitz, J. (1989) *Der internationale Zinszusammenhang*, Institut für Wirtschaftspolitik, Köln.

Ricardo, D. (1819) *On the Principle of Political Economy and Taxation*, Joseph Milligan, Georgetown D.C.

Robinson, J. (1949) 'The Foreign Exchanges' in Ellis, H.S. and Metzler, L.A. (eds.) *Readings in the Theory of International Trade*, Philadelphia and Toronto, pp. 83-103.

Romer, P.M. (1990) 'Endogenous Technical Change' *Journal of Political Economy*, 98, pp. 71-101.

Rowley, C.K. (1987) 'Classical Political Economy and the Debt Issue' in Rowley, C.K and Tollison, R.D. (eds.) *Deficits*, Blackwell, Oxford and New York.

Sachs, J.D. (1981) 'The Current Account and Macroeconomic Adjustment in the 1970s' *Brookings Papers on Economic Activity*, Washington, D.C., pp. 202-68.

Sachs, J.D. (1982) 'The Current Account in the Macroeconomic Adjustment Process' *Scandinavian Journal of Economics*, 84, pp. 147-59.

Sachverständigenrat zur Begutachtung der gesamtwirtschaftlichen Entwicklung (Sachverständigenrat; German Council of Economic Experts) *Jahresgutachten*, Klett, Stuttgart, various issues.

Salin, P. (1990) 'Comment on Vito Tanzi and A. Lans Bovenberg: Is There a Need for Harmonizing Capital Income Taxes within the EC Countries?' in Siebert, H. (ed.) *Reforming Capital Income Taxation*, Tübingen: Mohr, pp. 198-205.

Salowsky, H. (1991) 'Industrielle Arbeitskosten im internationalen Vergleich 1970-1990' *iw-trends*, pp. D1-D20.

Salter, W.E.G. (1959) 'Internal and External Balance: The Role of Price and Expenditure Effects' *Economic Record*, 35, pp. 226-38.

Samuelson, Paul A. (1952) 'The Transfer Problem and Transport Costs: The Terms of Trade when Impediments are Absent' *The Economic Journal*, 62, pp. 278-304.

Samuelson, P.A. (1964) 'Tax Deductability and Economic Depreciation to Insure Invariant Valuations' *Journal of Political Economy*, 72, pp. 604-6.

Samuelson, P.A. (1980) 'A Corrected Version of Hume's Equilibrating Mechanisms for International Trade' in Chipman, J.S. and Kindleberger, C.P. (eds.) *Flexible Exchange Rates and the Balance of Payments*, North Holland, Amsterdam, pp. 141-58.

Saxonhouse, G.R. (1993) 'What Does Japanese Trade Structure Tell Us About Japanese Trade Policy?' *The Journal of Economic Perspectives*, 7, pp. 21-43.

Sazanami, Y., Urata, S. and Kawai, H (1994) *Measuring the Costs of Protection in Japan*, Institute for International Economics, Washington, D.C.

Schadler, S. (1993) *Recent Experiences with Surges in Capital Inflows*, IMF Occasional Paper, 108, Washington, D.C.

Scheid, H.-J. (1987) *Weltwirtschaftliche Auswirkungen der amerikanischen Haushalts- und Leistungsbilanzdefizite*, Institut für Wirtschaftspolitik, Köln.

Seitz, K. (1991) *Die japanisch-amerikanische Herausforderung: Deutschlands Hochtechnologie-Industrien kämpfen ums Überleben*, Bonn Aktuell, München.

Servant-Schreiber, J.-J. (1967) *Le défi americain*, Denoël, Paris.

Shiller, Robert (1990) *Market Volatility*, MIT Press, Cambridge, Mass., London.

Shleifer, Andrei and Summers, Lawrence H. (1990) 'The Noise Trader Approach to Finance' *Journal of Economic Perspectives*, 4, pp. 19-33.

Siebert, H. (1987) 'Foreign Debt and Capital Accumulation' *Weltwirtschaftliches Archiv*, 123, pp.618-30.

Siebert, H. (1989) 'The Half and the Full Debt Cycle' *Weltwirtschaftliches Archiv* 125, pp. 217-29.

Siebert, H. (1991) *Außenwirtschaft*, 5. Auflage, UTB, Stuttgart.

Siegel, J.J. (1979) 'Inflation Induced Distortions in Government and Private Saving Statistics' *Review of Economics and Statistics*, 61, pp. 83-90.

Sievert, O. (1986) 'Gibt es eine Alternative zu flexiblen Wechselkursen?' *Wirtschaftsdienst*, 66, pp. 335-44.

Sievert, O. et. al. (1989) *Steuern und Investitionen*, 2 Volumes, Lang, Frankfurt/Main.

Sinn, H.-W. (1984) 'Die Bedeutung des Accelerated Cost Recovery System für den International Kapitalverkehr' *Kyklos*, 37, pp. 542-576.

Sinn, H.-W. (1987) *Capital Income Taxation and Resource Allocation*, North Holland, Amsterdam.

Sinn, G. and Sinn, H.-W. (1991) *Kaltstart: Volkswirtschaftliche Aspekte der deutschen Vereinigung*, Mohr, Tübingen.

Sinn, S. (1990) *Net External Positions of 145 Countries. Estimation and Interpretation*, Mohr, Tübingen.

Slemrod, J. (1988) 'Effect of Taxation with International Capital Mobility' in Aaron, H.J., Galper, H. and Pechman, J. (eds.) *Uneasy Compromise: Problems of a Hybrid Income-Consumption Tax*, Brookings Institution, Washington, D.C., pp. 115-55.

Sohmen, Egon (1969) *Flexible Exchange Rates*, University of Chicago Press, Chicago, London.

Sowell, Thomas (1974) *Classical Economics Reconsidered*, Princeton University Press, Princeton.

Spahn, P.B. and Kaiser, H. (1991) 'Tax Harmonization and Tax Competition as Means to Integrate Western Europe' *Konjunkturpolitik*, 37, pp. 1-44.

Statistisches Bundesamt (a) *Statistisches Jahrbuch für die Bundesrepublik Deutschland*, various issues, Wiesbaden.

Statistisches Bundesamt (b) *Länderbericht, verschiedene Länder*, various issues, Wiesbaden.

Statistisches Bundesamt (c) *Volkswirtschaftliche Gesamtrechnungen*, Fachserie 18, Reihe 1.3: Konten und Standardtabellen, Hauptbericht, various issues, Wiesbaden.

Statistisches Bundesamt (d) Fachserie 16, Reihe 5, *Löhne und Gehälter im Ausland*, various issues, Wiesbaden.

Statistisches Bundesamt (e) Außenhandel, Fachserie 7, Reihe 8, *Außenhandel nach dem Internationalen Warenverzeichnis (SITC-Rev. 3) und Ländern (Spezialhandel)*, various issues, Wiesbaden.

Stehn, J. (1991) *Direktinvestitionen in Industrieländern: Theoretische Erklärungsansätze und empirische Evidenz*, Moh, Tübingen.

Stern, R.M., Francis, J. and Schumacher, B. (1976) *Price Elasticities in International Trade – An Annoted Bibliography*, Macmillan, Basingstoke and London.

Stiglitz J.E. and Weiss, A. (1981) 'Credit Rationing in Markets with Imperfect Information' *American Economic Review*, 71, pp. 393-410.

Stockman, A.C. (1980) 'A Theory of Exchange Rate Determination' *Journal of Political Economy*, 88, pp. 673-98.

Stützel, W. (1978) *Volkswirtschaftliche Saldenmechanik*, Mohr, Tübingen.

Tanzi, V., Blejer, M.I. and Teijeiro, M.O. (1987) 'Inflation and the Measurement of Fiscal Deficits' *IMF Staff Papers*, 34, pp.711-38.

Tavlas, G.S. and Ozeki, Y. (1992) *The Internationalization of Currencies: An Appraisal of the Japanese Yen*, IMF Occasional Paper, 90, Washington, D.C.

The Economist (1990) 'Spanish Lessons for EMS Entry', June 16, p. 73.

The Economist (1995) 'Germany's Embattled Banks', January 21, p. 77.

Thurow, L. (1992) *Head to Head: The Coming Economic Battle among Japan, Europe, and America*, Morrow, New York.

Tirole, J. (1982) 'On the Possibility of Speculation under Rational Expectations' *Econometrica*, 50, pp. 1163-81.

Tirole, J. (1985) 'Asset Bubbles and Overlapping Generations' *Econometrica*, 53, pp. 1071-100.

Tobin, J. (1982a) 'A Proposal for International Monetary Reform', in Tobin, J. *Essays in Economics. Theory and Policy*, MIT Press, Cambridge, Mass. and London, pp. 488-94.

Tobin, James (1982b) 'Money and Finance in the Macroeconomic Process' *Journal of Money, Credit, and Banking*, 14, pp. 171-204.

Tsiang, S.C. (1989) *Finance Constraints and the Theory of Money* Selected Papers of S.C. Tsiang, ed. by Meir Kohn, Harcourt Brace Janovich, Boston etc.

Turner, P. (1991) *Capital Flows in the 19802: A Survey of Major Trends*, BIS Economic Papers, 30, Basle.

Turner, P. and Van't dack, J. (1993) *Measuring International Prize and Cost Competitiveness*, BIS Economic Papers, 39, Basle.

Tyson, L.D'A. (1992) *Who's Bashing Whom: Trade Conflict in High-Technology Industries,* Institute for International Economics, Washington, D.C.

United Nations (1993) *International Trade Statistics Yearbook*, 2 Volumes, New York.

United Nations (1994) *Monthly Bulletin of Statistics*, XLVIII, No. 11 (Nov.), New York.

van Suntum, U. (1986) 'Internationale Wettbewerbsfähigkeit einer Volkswirtschaft. Ein sinnvolles politisches Ziel?' *Zeitschrift für Wirtschafts- und Sozialwissenschaften*, 106, pp. 495-507.

Vehrkamp, R. (1992) 'Der Dollar schlägt trotz massiver Eingriffe am Devisenmarkt weiterhin Kapriolen' *Handelsblatt,* February 20.

Vernon, R. (1966) 'International Investment and International Trade in the Product Cycle' *Quarterly Journal of Economics*, 80, pp. 190-207.

Vernon, R. (1979) 'The Product Cycle Hypothesis in a New International Environment' *Oxford Bulletin of Economics and Statistics*, pp. 255-67.

Viñals, J. (1986) 'Fiscal Policy and the Current Account' *Economic Policy*, pp. 712-31.

Viñals, J. (1990) *The EMS, Spain and Macroeconomic Policy*, CEPR Discussion Paper 389, London.

Viñals, J. (1992) 'La Economía Española ante el Mercado Unico' in Viñals, J. (ed.) *La Economía Española ante el Mercado Unico Europeo*, Alianza Editorial, Madrid, pp. 15-116.

Walter, N. (1991) 'German External Adjustment Since 1985' in Bergsten, C.F. (ed.) *International Adjustment and Financing*, Institute for International Economics, Washington, D.C., pp. 155-77.

Wärneryhd, Karl (1989) 'Legal Restrictions and the Evolution of Media of Exchange' *Journal of Institutional and Theoretical Economics (JITE)*, 145, pp. 613-626.

Watrin, C. and Krüger, M. (1995) *The Shift from Net Capital Exporter to Net Capital Importer – The Case of Germany*, forthcoming.

Weizsäcker, C.C. von (1979) 'Das eherne Zinsgesetz' *Kyklos*, 32, pp. 270-82.

Weizsäcker, C.C. von (1984) 'Was leistet die Property Rights Theorie für aktuelle wirtschaftspolitische Fragen?' in Neumann, M. (ed.) *Ansprüche, Eigentums- und Verfügungsrechte*, Duncker und Humblot, Berlin, pp. 123-52.

Whalley, J. (1990) 'Foreign Responses to U.S. Tax Reform' in Slemrod, J. (ed.) *Do Taxes Matter?*, MIT Press, Cambridge, Mass. and London, pp. 286-314.

White, M. and White, A. (1981) Tax Neutrality of Instantaneous Versus Economic Depreciation' in Hulten, C.R. (ed.) *Depreciation, Inflation and the Taxation of Income from Capital*, The Urban Institute Press, Washington, D.C., pp. 105-16.

Willgerodt, H. (1961) 'Kapitalbilanz und Devisenströme' in Greiß, F. and Meyer, F.W. (eds.), *Wirtschaft, Gesellschaft und Kultur*, Duncker und Humblot, Berlin, pp. 459-70.

Willgerodt, H. (1964) *Die importierte Inflation und das Beispiel der Schweiz*, Institut für Wirtschaftspolitik, Köln.

Willgerodt, H. (1978) 'Die "motivierte Zahlungsbilanztheorie" – Vom "schicksalhaften Zahlungsbilanzdefizit" und der Unsterblichkeit falscher Inflationslehren' in Gröner, H. and Schüller, A. (eds.) *Internationale Wirtschaftsordnung*, G. Fischer, Stuttgart and New York, pp. 215-38.

Willgerodt, H. (1981) 'Unsere passive Leistungsbilanz' *Zeitschrift für Wirtschaftspolitik*, 30, pp.189-205.

Willgerodt, H. (1991) 'Die deutsche Wirtschaft zwischen Kapitalbildung und Kapitalvergeudung' *Finanzierung, Leasing, Factoring*, 5, pp. 186-90.

Williamson, J. (1985) *The Exchange Rate System*, Institute for International Economics, Washington, D.C.

Williamson, J. (1987) 'Exchange Rate Management: The Role of Target Zones' *American Economic Review, Papers and Proceedings*, 77, pp. 200-4.

Wissenschaftlicher Beirat beim Bundesministerium für Wirtschaft (1990) 'Außenwirtschaftspolitische Herausforderung der Europäischen Gemeinschaft an der Schwelle zum Binnenmarkt' *Bundesanzeiger*, No. 140 from July 31, pp. 1-11.

Wissenschaftlicher Beirat beim Bundesministerium für Wirtschaft (1991) *Lohn- und Arbeitsmarktprobleme in den neuen Bundesländern*, Bonn.

Wohltmann, H.-W. (1991) 'Die internationalen Auswirkungen nationaler geldpolitischer Maßnahmen' *Weltwirtschaftliches Archiv*, 127, pp. 223-45.

World Bank (1983) *World Development Report*, Washington, D.C.

World Economic Forum (1993) *The World Competitiveness Report 1993*, June, Lausanne and Geneva.

Subject Index